Addressing Systems Safety Challe

Chris Dale • Tom Anderson
Editors

Addressing Systems Safety Challenges

Proceedings of the Twenty-second
Safety-critical Systems Symposium,
Brighton, UK, 4-6th February 2014

Safety-Critical
Systems Club

The publication of these proceedings is
sponsored by BAE Systems plc

BAE SYSTEMS

Editors
Chris Dale
Dale Research Ltd
2 Reppersfield Row
Breage
Helston TR13 9PG
United Kingdom

Tom Anderson
Centre for Software Reliability
Newcastle University
Newcastle upon Tyne NE1 7RU
United Kingdom

ISBN 978-1491263648

Preface

This volume contains papers presented at the twenty-second Safety-critical Systems Symposium (SSS 2014). This year's authors have, as usual, delivered informative material touching on many topics that are of current concern to the safety-critical systems community; we are grateful to them for their contributions.

The opening keynote, by John Knight, proposes a new approach to safety standards. Sticking with the standards theme, two papers discuss recent developments in civil aviation and defence, two papers present standards-related material in new areas, and the final paper tackles the problem of combining safety standards.

Business-strategic implications of safety are addressed by a paper from the automotive industry. Next are two papers looking at different aspects of railway safety.

Harold Thimbleby's keynote paper considers the interplay between safety and security in healthcare IT. This is followed by a paper viewing safety and human factors as two sides of the same coin, and one proposing a safety maturity model.

The keynote paper from Pippa Moore discusses aircraft system safety assessment, and in particular the challenge for future design and certification. The next paper reports on the development and certification of a safety-critical touch screen avionics display. This is followed by a paper on the safety of software-based systems in the nuclear industry, by one on common cause failures, and by one proposing an assessment framework for data-centric systems.

The final keynote address, by Tim Kelly, looks at establishing confidence in software certification. Next is a paper on safety acceptance decision making processes in the UK Ministry of Defence, and the final paper questions whether we should be validating compilers or compilations.

We are grateful to our sponsors for their valuable support and to the exhibitors at the Symposium's tools and services fair for their participation. And we thank Joan Atkinson and her team for laying the event's foundation through their exemplary planning and organisation.

CD & TA
December 2013

A message from the sponsors

BAE Systems is pleased to support the publication of these proceedings. We recognise the benefit of the Safety-Critical Systems Club in promoting safety engineering in the UK and value the opportunities provided for continued professional development and the recognition and sharing of good practice. The safety of our employees, those using our products and the general public is critical to our business and is recognised as an important social responsibility.

The Safety-Critical Systems Club

organiser of the

Safety-critical Systems Symposium

Safety-critical systems and the accidents that don't happen

When a plane crashes, it makes headlines. That hundreds of thousands of flights each week do not crash is accepted as routine. Airliners, air traffic control systems, railway signalling, car braking systems, defence systems, nuclear power stations and medical equipment (increasingly including home medical electronics) are some of the complex, normally digital, systems in use, on which life and property depend. That these safety-critical systems do work well is because of the expertise and diligence of professional systems safety engineers, regulators and other practitioners who work to minimise both the likelihood that accidents will occur, and the consequences of those that do. Their efforts prevent untold deaths every year. The Safety-Critical Systems Club (SCSC) has been actively engaged for more than twenty years to help to ensure that this continues to be the case.

What is the Safety-Critical Systems Club?

The SCSC is the UK's professional network for sharing knowledge about safety-critical systems. It brings together engineers and specialists from a range of disciplines working on safety-critical systems in a wide variety of industries, academics researching the arena of safety-critical systems, providers of the tools and services that are needed to develop the systems, and the regulators who oversee safety. It provides, through publications, seminars, workshops, tutorials, a web site and, most importantly, at the annual Safety-critical Systems Symposium, opportunities for them to network and benefit from each other's experience in working hard at the accidents that don't happen. It focuses on current and emerging practices in safety engineering, software engineering, and product and process safety standards.

What does the SCSC do?

The SCSC maintains a website (scsc.org.uk), which includes directories of tools and services that assist in the development of safety-critical systems. It publishes a regular newsletter, Safety Systems, three times a year. It organises seminars, workshops and training on general matters or specific subjects of current concern, which are prepared and led by world experts. Since 1993 it has organised the annual Safety-critical Systems Symposium (SSS) where leaders in different aspects of safety, from different industries, including regulators and academics, meet to exchange information and experience, with the papers published in a proceedings volume. From time to time, the SCSC supports relevant initiatives, such as the current Data Safety Initiative that is addressing concerns raised about data in safety-related systems. The SCSC carries out all these activities to support its mission:

> ... to raise awareness and facilitate technology transfer in the field of safety-critical systems ...

History

The SCSC began its work in 1991, supported by the Department of Trade and Industry and the Engineering and Physical Sciences Research Council. The Club has been self-sufficient since 1994, but enjoys the active support of the Health and Safety Executive, the Institution of Engineering and Technology, and BCS, The Chartered Institute for IT; all are represented on the SCSC Steering Group.

Membership

Membership may be either corporate or individual. Individual membership, which costs £95 a year, entitles the member to Safety Systems three times a year, other mailings, and discounted entry to seminars, workshops and the annual Symposium. Frequently individual membership is paid by the employer.

Corporate membership is for organisations that would like several employees to take advantage of the benefits of SCSC programmes. The amount charged is tailored to the needs of the organisation.

For more information about membership, or to join, please call Joan Atkinson on +44 191 221 2222 or email Joan.Atkinson@ncl.ac.uk.

Contents

Safety Standards – a New Approach

John Knight

University of Virginia

Charlottesville, VA USA

Abstract Safety standards provide great value, but despite their benefits, standards and the culture that goes with them have a variety of weaknesses. In this paper, I review these various weaknesses and propose a new approach that defines a technical structure for standards based on desired properties of conformant artifacts, a development and maintenance process designed to ensure technical quality, and a funding model designed to make standards both freely available and revenue generators for their developers.

1 Introduction

Underlying much of safety engineering is a collection of standards. Standards provide immense value. There is no question that the various standards that are used in the safety-engineering field have provided the safety community, and thereby the public at large, with safer systems at lower cost.

Despite their demonstrated value, standards have weaknesses, for example they tend to trail behind the technical state of the art. They can also do harm, for example in some cases, standards imply a level of quality in conforming artifacts that is not necessarily present, and standards can lead to excessive resource consumption in achieving conformance.

A careful examination of standards themselves, their development, and their uses reveals a number of technical and procedural issues, and I claim that the time has come for standards to be held to a higher standard, a much higher standard. In this paper, I argue that a new approach is needed to all aspects of the preparation, content, availability and maintenance of standards. I refer to this new approach as the Standard for Standards, or SfS.

The new approach to standards is centred on the need to structure standards so that they establish properties of the subject artifact. In this paper, I introduce the SfS and base many of the ideas on earlier work that developed the filter model of critical system certification (Steele and Knight 2014). Along with the core focus on artifact properties, I introduce a revised development process and a new financial model for standards. The SfS maintains the established benefits that standards bring, adds additional benefits, and eliminates many of the difficulties that standards present.

2 The roles of standards

Standards play a special role in engineering, because standards are not themselves an engineering technology. In various ways, standards define the techniques and technologies that are used in safety engineering by pointing engineers in specific directions. Whether a standard is prescriptive, i.e., demands the use of certain techniques, is goal oriented, i.e., establishes goals that safety engineering has to meet, or is somewhere in between, the standard sets a direction that has to be followed if conformance is to be claimed.

Looking more closely at existing standards, we see that standards tend to play roles in three major areas of safety engineering:

Development. In many aspects of safety engineering, standards are written with the goal of ensuring that certain technical methods are used. By including expected technical methods, various properties are assumed in conforming system artifacts, at least implicitly.

Certification. By definition, if certification includes conformance with one or more standards, the associated standards help to define the certifying organization's meaning of the term certification and thereby the expectations of the organization.

Education. Standards educate those subject to the standard. Because a standard embodies the experience and opinions of its authors and, in some cases, its users, a standard plays a major role in education. Successful conformance with a standard requires an understanding of the technology, goals, and intent of the standard. Such depth and breadth are unlikely to be in the experience of all involved in safety-critical systems development, and standards itemize the many applicable techniques and technologies.

3 Issues with standards

Despite their immense value, there are issues with standards that need to be addressed. The issues are in the areas of preparation, content, meaning, maintenance and availability. Each of these areas is examined in the following subsections.

3.1 Preparation of standards

Clearly, standards influence device safety. Thus, their preparation has to be undertaken with great care. Presently, most standards-development processes strive to achieve the necessary levels of care by making public the discussions surrounding the creation of the standard. In essence, participation is voluntary and open to all.

This volunteer/open-to-all approach is attractive, but the approach is flawed in several ways:

- There is no guarantee than the group creating a safety standard will have the necessary technical skills. Safety expertise is highly specialized, diverse, and, in some essential areas, held by relatively few. Standards bodies could seek out specialists, but there is neither a requirement to do so nor any substantial evidence that they do.
- Participation is restricted to those who can volunteer where 'volunteer' actually means that a participant has the time and resources to participate. Inevitably, the effect is that industry representatives dominate many standards development groups. Since, by definition, an industry representative represents his or her employer, that representative is likely to be influenced by the interests of his or her employer.
- Standards are prepared by discussion and inspection but not assessed through practical application before being published. With a document as complex as a safety standard that is stated in natural language, what are the chances that there will be elements that are incomplete, ambiguous, inconsistent or otherwise inadequate? The problem is amply illustrated by the explanatory documents that have evolved for many standards.

These flaws can easily detract from the value of a standard. Some standards are presented to the community in draft form in order to elicit comment from a wide audience. The generality of the elicitation inevitably means that the comment process is not necessarily complete and is certainly ad hoc.

3.2 Content of standards

There is an expectation by the community that standards will embody the best available technology and that their presentation will allow determination of conformance to be fairly straightforward. A criticism that is seldom heard is that some standards are, in fact, technically flawed and poorly presented. Here are some examples of the problem:

> **From IEC 61508:** 'This International Standard sets requirements for the avoidance and control of systematic faults, which are based on experience and judgment from practical experience gained in industry. Even though the probability of occurrence of systematic failures cannot in general be quantified the standard does, however, allow a claim to be

made, for a specified safety function, that the target failure measure associated with the safety function can be considered to be achieved if all the requirements in the standard have been met.' (IEC 2010)

This statement says that required probabilities of failure, even in the ultra-dependable range (for example the region of 10^{-9} failures per hour of operation) in the presence of systematic (design) faults can be assumed provided the procedural elements of the standard are followed. There is no scientific basis for this assumption.

> **From IEC 61508:** 'The appropriateness of competence shall be considered in relation to the particular application, taking into account all relevant factors including safety engineering knowledge appropriate to the technology." (IEC 2010)

This statement appears in the part of the standard addressing the competence of personnel. There is no definition of 'appropriate', and so the meaning of 'appropriate' (and hence conformance with the standard in this area) is left to chance.

> **From RTCA DO-178B:** 'The basic principle is to choose requirements development and design methods, tools, and programming languages that limit the opportunity for introducing errors, and verification methods that ensure that errors introduced are detected.' (RTCA 1992)

This statement appears in the section of the standard that relates to software life-cycle planning. DO-178B is a software assurance standard not a safety standard, and so the focus of the standard is on software technology. The intent of the quoted statement is quite clear and seems to dictate the use of programming languages that can support the best possible software fault detection. The implication is that languages with weak type systems and confusing syntax, such as C, would be rejected in favour of languages more capable of supporting software assurance, such as Ada. In practice, the quoted statement is rarely followed in the development of systems with the result that safety-critical systems judged to be in conformance with DO-178B are often written in C.

> **From Defence Standard 00-56:** 'The Safety Case shall consist of a structured argument, supported by a body of evidence, that provides a compelling, comprehensible and valid case that a system is safe for a given application in a given environment." (MoD 2007)

This statement is at the core of the standard and defines the expected material for submission of an application for conformance. Surprisingly, the standard does not define the terms 'compelling', 'comprehensible' and 'valid'. Thus, conformance is subject to local definitions of these terms, and, as a result, determination of conformance is likely to be inconsistent. An attempt to define these terms can be found in the work of Graydon et al. (Graydon et al. 2010).

3.3 The meaning of conformance to standards

At the heart of the technical difficulties with standards is the following question:

> If an entity is determined to be in conformance with a standard, what can be said about properties that the entity possesses as a result of conformance?

Answering this question is problematic, because standards, including safety standards, usually do not address the goal of establishing precise, rigorous properties of the subject artifact directly. Rather, standards require various process, procedure, or process goal activities that tend only to imply properties of the subject artifact.

As an example of the problem, consider the following example from RTCA DO-178B (RTCA 1992). Objective 2 in Table A3 of Annex A is defined as: 'High-level requirements are accurate and consistent'. The objective references the following from the body of the standard:

> '6.3.1b. Accuracy and consistency: The objective is to ensure that each high-level requirement is accurate, unambiguous and sufficiently detailed and that the requirements do not conflict with each other.'

Nothing further is presented about exactly what can be expected from conformance with this objective. In practice, experts with experience using the standard, both developers and experts licensed by the FAA, provide a great deal of interpretation of such statements.

A significant consequence of the issues raised by the question above arises with safety cases. The reason that safety cases have to distinguish between direct and indirect evidence is precisely because of this issue. Direct evidence is evidence about the artifact itself. Indirect evidence is evidence about the development process (likely in conformance with one or more standards). Indirect evidence provides less confidence in claims based on that evidence because the evidence is not directly about the artifact.

3.4 Maintenance of standards

A common criticism is that standards limit innovation. To the extent that standards reflect the state of the art when written, they actually encourage innovation. In addition, their role in educating the community that has access to them likely introduces newer technology.

But standards are expensive to produce, and standards development organizations, such as RTCA, the IEC, and the IEEE, are understandably reluctant to change them. Once in place, standards tend to be static and so tend to drop behind the state of the art. For example, RTCA DO-178B was published in 1992, and it was in effect for 20 years before DO-178C replaced it in 2012. Although standards like DO-178B try to include provision for the introduction of new technology as time passes, the community tends to reject innovation because of the likelihood of certification difficulty.

3.5 Availability of standards

In principle, standards are freely available. In practice, the cost of obtaining a copy of many standards limits their availability substantially. Some standards documents are available for download for no charge (e.g., U.K. Defence Standard 00-56 (MoD 2007) and U.S. Department of Defense Standard 882E (DoD 2013)), but the majority of standards are available for download only after a purchase price has been paid. IEC 61508 Edition 2, for example, costs $2,743 from the International Electrotechnical Commission. A hardcopy of DO-178C costs $290 from RTCA Inc. Charging for copies of standards is a major source of revenue for standards organizations.

As has been noted by others (Jelliffe 2013), prices such as that for IEC 61508 Edition 2 limit access considerably. In practice, standards though nominally available are basically unavailable to many, e.g., educational institutions and those not required to use the standard. The price might even preclude consideration of use of the standard by development organizations that are not required to use the standard even though the developers expected to realize value from use of the standard.

The lack of availability of standards to educational institutions severely hampers the technical value of standards. Students are unlikely to be able to gain exposure to the whole field of development using safety standards under present circumstances.

Charging for individual copies of standards also has the effect of promoting the creation of pirate copies and of organizations restricting the number of copies available to their staff in order to keep the cost down.

4 A new approach

With the issues outlined in the previous section as a starting point, I propose a Standard for Standards (SfS), i.e., a new approach to all the different aspects of safety standards.

The SfS that I propose has three parts:

- a technical structure based on desired properties of conformant artifacts
- a development and maintenance process designed to ensure technical quality
- a funding model that generates revenue for standards-development organizations from those who gain significant value from standards.

Each of these parts is explored in detail in the following three subsections.

4.1 Technical structure of standards

4.1.1 Certification and standards

The role of certification is to protect the public interest. The challenge faced by any regulating agency is to discriminate between entities submitted for certification that would expose the public to an unacceptable level of risk from those that do not. This discrimination has to be as accurate as possible. The worst possible outcome would be a false positive, i.e., a decision to certify an entity that, in fact, would expose the public to an unacceptable level of risk.

The primary use of standards is within certification processes. Certifying agencies frequently require the use of standards, and establishing conformance is the most significant aspect of the certification process. Understanding the role of standards in certification is an important first step in understanding standards, and how best to develop and use them.

4.1.2 The filter model of certification

The filter model (Steele and Knight 2014) is a framework for certification that provides a structure for modelling and analysis of certification. The thesis of the filter model is that certification is fundamentally a mechanism for filtering the stream of applications received by the agency, i.e., for stopping deployment of entities that are unacceptable.

The notion of filtering leads to the question: 'What would cause an application to be filtered out?' Or, to put the question another way: 'What is going to get trapped in the filter?' The statement in the paragraph above -- *stopping deployment of entities that are unacceptable* -- is intuitively reasonable but not a statement upon which one could reasonably act.

The answer to these questions is that the filter has to trap applications with defects that would make the entity unacceptable. In the case of safety-critical software, for example, a filter needs to detect faults in the software that could lead to service failures at a rate or of a severity that is unacceptable.

In principle, this filtering could be effected by the regulating agency entirely internally. The agency could construct a filtering infrastructure that examines the entities for which certification is sought and makes an informed decision. Although possible, this approach is quite impractical for any entity of reasonable complexity. For example, a suitable filter for safety-critical software would entail comprehensive analysis of the software and all the development artifacts to establish a suitable level of freedom from faults. The resources required alone make the notion of filtering within the certifying agency quite untenable. Also significant is the fact that what the agency would be doing within its filtering infrastructure would duplicate much of what the developers did. The duplication would not be complete, but there would likely be extensive overlap.

4.1.3 Standards as filters

In practice, standards deployed throughout development organizations *are* the filter needed by certifying agencies. The filter is manifested as one or more standards and the filter, i.e., the standards, is located in the development organizations. The purpose of standards in this context is twofold:

- to shift the burden and therefore the cost of undertaking the filtering process to the development organization
- to align the filter concept desired by the certifying agency with the practices undertaken by the developers thereby ensuring that development activities match the necessary filter structure.

Standards define combinations of processes, procedures, techniques, technologies and goals. Each element of a standard is present to help filter defects that otherwise might be present in a safety-critical entity. By combining elements in various ways, standards endeavour to provide a series of filter planes, each of which filters one or more types of defect. A standard defines a filter designed to 'catch' entities that do not have the properties desired for the entities of interest.

Separately, the results of conformance assessments are the decision processes that certifying agencies require about an artifact that is submitted for certification. The existence of a standard does not ensure that the filter provided by the standard has been used properly. If the filter has been used properly as determined by an assessment of conformance, then the effects of the filter in detecting defects and thereby potentially identifying defective applications can be assumed.

An immediate consequence of the filter model is that it provides a structure for modelling and analysis of standards. Since a standard is the manifestation of at least a major part of the filter required by a certifying agency, the goals of a certification filter can be used to create the associated standard.

4.1.4 Requirements for conformance to standards

Existing standards are influenced by the filtering concept. That is why safety standards, for example, attempt to encompass best practices. The associated practices are 'best' because their application tends to limit defects. But the content of most standards is developed in what amounts to an ad hoc and informal manner with no explicit, testable technical goal. The result is that there is no assurance of completeness of the resulting filter.

By contrast, a critical part of the SfS is to define precisely the properties required for entities conforming to a standard. For the most part a property will be the absence of a class of defects. The properties will be organized as hierarchies of abstraction to facilitate analysis.

With the properties defined, the filter elements within the standard that will be used to detect instances of the defects within the properties can be elaborated. The exact form of the filter will depend on the degree of assurance that is required for the various properties. So, for example in a software standard, a property that requires absence of real-time frame overruns might use a filter element based on testing if the software is not safety critical or a filter based on detailed worst-case-execution-time analysis combined with proof of the scheduling algorithm for safety-critical software.

As an example of this concept, again consider a standard for safety-critical software. Rather than dictate procedures or processes, the standard might include the need to establish properties of a conformant entity such as the following:

Absence of faults in the software requirements. This high level of abstraction might be refined to a list of fault classes that are known to occur in the determination of software requirements. This property might be shown by a rigorous assurance argument that the software requirements are complete, consistent and unambiguous.

Absence of faults in the software specification. This property might be shown by a proof or rigorous assurance argument that the software specification is a solution to the stated requirements.

Absence of faults in the implementation of safety requirements. This property might be shown by a proof of compliance with formally stated safety requirements.

Absence of faults that raise exceptions during execution. This high level of abstraction might be refined to a list of types of exception that are known to be possible. This property might be shown by proofs of freedom from execution-time exceptions for each of the types of exceptions listed.

The union of a set of properties such as these provides a clear statement of what can be expected of an entity that conforms to the associated standard. The filter elements designed to ensure that the entity possesses the properties are clear and the degrees of confidence warranted in the filter elements are also clear.

4.1.5 Filters as safety-critical systems

A false positive in certification, i.e., a failure of the filter, is a serious outcome. The potential severity of a filter failure leads to the idea of treating the certification process itself as a safety-critical system, i.e., the activities associated with reaching a decision about certification are treated as a safety-critical activity. With this view, incorrectly certifying a system that might subject the public to an unacceptable level of risk is an accident, i.e., a certification accident.

With that view, certification itself can be analyzed with all of the technology of safety engineering. In particular, techniques such as fault-tree analysis and FMECA can be applied directly and immediately to certification and used to reveal deficiencies in the filter. Fault-tree analysis, for example, can be applied by treating a certification false positive as a hazard and developing the associated fault tree. The faults identified in that process are actually weaknesses in the certification process.

Since standards are the realization of certification filters, the analysis of certification as a safety-critical activity can be applied to standards. This process leads to an assessment approach for standards. Fault-tree analysis applied to a standard, for example, provides an assessment not possible by any other means.

4.2 Development of standards

Irrespective of the technical structure of standards, the key requirements in the development of standards are to achieve technical excellence and to maintain technical excellence. To meet these requirements, the SfS includes the following three elements:

- Prior to coming into effect, a standard will be subjected to review by a panel of experts acting anonymously who were not involved in the development of the standard and whose participation in the panel is funded. The role of the panel is to comment on the completeness, accuracy, presentation, and appropriateness of the standard. Clearly, the deficiencies identified by the panel should be corrected before the standard is published.
- Prior to coming into effect, a standard will be subjected to an empirical study where the standard is used in the development of a typical system and the use of the standard is monitored. This empirical study could be based on a commercial development that would produce a product that would ultimately be considered conformant with the new standard. Again, the deficiencies identified by the empirical study should be corrected before the standard is published.
- After coming into effect, a standard will be subject to review and update after a specified interval. A typical interval might be five years. Some existing standards are subject to periodic review but by no means all. A standard might not need review after several years of use, but the most likely circumstances are that: (a) technological advances will necessitate change, and (b) experience with the standard will lead to insights that could improve the standard substantially.

4.3 Financing standards

To finance development, distribution, and maintenance of standards, the SfS includes a new funding model. This funding model would apply to any standard that is: (a) produced by volunteer group for public use; and (b) integral to a certification process that protects the public interest. The funding model is:

- The standard will be made available for the cost of reproduction no matter whom the publisher and purchaser are. For paper copies of standards that are delivered by regular mail, the cost would be the printing and mailing costs only. For electronic copies that are delivered via the Internet, the cost would be zero.
- A fee would be paid to the organization that developed the standard by any organization, public or private, making a claim of conformance with the standard for any artifact. Such a claim would arise with an application for certification or when offering an artifact for sale. Certifying authorities would not accept an application that claimed conformance with the standard without documented evidence that the requisite fee had been paid. The fee would be made up of two parts: (a) an initial fixed fee that gave the right to claim conformance; and (b) a fee for each instance of an artifact deployed that was established as a result of the claim of conformance.

The funding model is perhaps the most important and certainly the most radical aspect of the SfS. Nevertheless, the concept is quite simple – the value returned to the publisher of the standard is directly related to the commercial value of the standard to the users of the standard.

An electronic copy of a safety standard downloaded from a publisher's web site has a value that lies mainly in the reduction in risk that the copy yields. In many cases this is zero, because the person using the standard is not directly involved in system development. Despite the fact that the value is highly variable, difficult (actually impossible) to ascertain, and often zero, at present an electronic copy of almost all standards has a fixed cost that has to be paid to the publisher.

However, if a device is created using one or more standards, then part of that device's value results directly from being able to claim conformance with those standards. The value of a standard to the developer and to the community at large in that case is explicit and clear. Charging for claiming conformance as proposed in the SfS is a rational way to associate value with a standard where the value of the standard is realized when the standard supports a commercial activity.

To see the merit of this funding model, one only has to consider the 'value' of a copy of a standard that is never actually used to develop safety-critical systems, such as in an educational context. Charging for copies of the standard would be the normal practice despite the fact that the standard actually has value mostly in areas that are not immediately commercial, such as training.

5 Conclusion

Standards in the field of safety engineering are both essential and valuable. But the present approach to their creation and management leaves a lot to be desired.

I have proposed a new approach to the preparation, content, meaning, maintenance and availability of standards designed to enhance the value of standards and to make their value explicit. Finally, I repeat the claim that the time has come for standards to be held to a higher standard, and I propose the SfS as a way to achieve that.

References

Graydon P, Knight J, Green M (2010) Certification and safety cases. International System Safety Conference, Minneapolis, MN

IEC (2010) IEC 61508 Functional safety of electrical/electronic/programmable electronic safety-related systems. International Electrotechnical Commission

Jelliffe R (2007) Where to get ISO standards on the internet free. http://www.oreillynet.com/xml/blog/2007/08/where_to_get_iso_standards_on.html. Accessed 24 October 2013

RTCA (1992) RTCA/DO-178B/ED-12B Software considerations in airborne systems and equipment. Federal Aviation Administration software standard, RTCA Inc.

Steele P, Knight J (2014) Analysis of critical system certification. HASE 2014: 15th IEEE International Symposium on High Assurance Systems Engineering, Miami FL

DoD (2013) MIL STD-882E Standard practice, system safety. U.S. Department of Defense

MoD (2007) Defence Standard 00-56 Safety management requirements for defence systems. U.K. Ministry of Defence

DO-178C – a Perspective

Nick Tudor, Dewi Daniels and Ross Hannan[1]

Aeronautique Associates Ltd

Trowbridge, UK

Abstract   This paper gives a perspective on the suite of documents that has replaced DO-178B. It covers the rationale behind DO-178C, why it was needed and what publications have been produced as a result of the six years of effort in WG-71 and SC-205. It also highlights the follow on activity in the Forum on Aeronautical Software.

1 Introduction

The document widely known as DO-178B and also as ED-12B (RTCA 1992) has been updated. RTCA and EUROCAE, the bodies that publish these documents, agreed to the reconstitution of the panels that develop them (EUROCAE Working Group 71 and RTCA Special Committee 205). The terms of reference were written to encompass various remits, which included the examination of the possibility of 'technology specific supplements'. The overall aim for DO-178C/ED-12C[2] (RTCA 2012a) was, as far as possible, to incorporate errata and other guidance where available and to produce a rationale. A general principle was that raising the bar was not necessary, lowering it was not to happen and therefore the document should enable an applicant to be at least as safe as DO-178B.

2 Rationale for DO-178B/ED-12B development

The first version of DO-178/ED-12 had been produced in the early 1980s to provide guidance for the growing number of equipment suppliers who were introducing software on commercial aircraft. Familiarity in the application of the docu-

---

[1] The opinions where expressed in this paper are those of the authors and do not represent those of RTCA, EUROCAE or any other agency, company or body.

[2] For ease of reading, this first reference to the document number includes both RTCA and EUROCAE references, hereafter just the RTCA reference.

ment led to a revision (DO-178A/ED-12A) being commissioned in 1983 to reflect experience that had been gained by both the certification authorities and applicants in the application of the original document.

By 1988, the rapid advances in software technology and complexity, which were never envisioned by the earlier committees, led to RTCA Inc. (or the Radio Technical Commission for Aeronautics as it was at the time) and EUROCAE to consider, and subsequently endorse, the creation of a joint special committee/ working group to further revise the document. In early 1989, RTCA Special Committee SC-167 and EUROCAE Working Group WG-12 were convened for the first of what were to be numerous meetings.

SC-167/WG-12 was tasked to provide the aviation community with guidance for determining, in a consistent manner and with an acceptable level of confidence, that the software in airborne systems complies with airworthiness requirements and performs its intended function.

It became clear very early in the revision process that the level of complexity of software now being put on aircraft greatly increased the probability for development errors (requirements determination and design errors) and undesirable, unintended effects being resident in the certified product. Additionally, at that time it was realized that it would not be practical (or potentially not even be possible) to develop a finite verification suite for software which conclusively demonstrated that there were no residual development errors. Since such errors are generally not determinable and suitable numerical methods for characterizing them are not available, other qualitative means would need to be used to establish that the software can satisfy safety objectives.

The joint committee realized that it would be necessary to write an entirely new document taking a completely different approach than had previously been in effect. Until DO-178B/ED-12B was developed, the document had very much laid down a prescriptive life cycle – in a similar way to the military standards for software. However, the joint committee decided to make the revised document objective based – effectively informing applicants what they needed to achieve in supporting their application, rather than telling them how to develop the software. This new approach would be supported by assurance activities as a qualitative means to establish that the system can satisfy safety objectives. This, therefore, would provide confidence that the software has been developed and verified in a sufficiently disciplined manner to limit the likelihood of development errors that could impact aircraft safety remaining in the equipment when certified.

3 The working group

The working group was a joint committee between EUROCAE and RTCA. The executive committee was as follows:

- SC205 chair – Jim Krodel (Pratt & Whitney)

- WG-71 chair – Gérard Ladier (Airbus/Aerospace Valley)
- SC205 secretary –Leslie A Alford (Boeing)
- WG-71 secretary – Ross Hannan (Sigma Associates (Aerospace))
- FAA representative/CAST chair– Barbara Lingberg (FAA)
- EASA representative – Jean-Luc Delamaide (EASA)
- website liaison – Matt Jaffe (Embry-Riddle Aeronautical   University)
- collaborative technology software liaison – Todd White (L-3 Communications/Qualtech)
- subgroup liaison – John Coleman (Dawson Consulting).

This working group was split into seven subgroups to deal with specific groups of subjects or specific supplements. Each had a EUROCAE chair and RTCA chair – i.e. a European representative and a US representative. These groups were as follows:

- SG1: Document integration – Marty Gasiorowski (Worldwide Certification Services) and Ron Ashpole (Silver Atena)
- SG2: Issues and rationale – Fred Moyer (Rockwell Collins) and Ross Hannan (Sigma Associates (Aerospace))
- SG3: Tool qualification – Leanna Rierson (Digital Safety Consulting) and Frédéric Pothon (ACG Solutions)
- SG4: Model based design – Mark Lillis (Goodrich GPECS) and Pierre Lionne (EADS APSYS)
- SG5: Object oriented technologies – Greg Millican (Honeywell) and Jan-Hendrik Boelens (Eurocopter)
- SG6: Formal methods – Kelly Hayhurst (NASA) and Duncan Brown (Rolls Royce)
- SG7: Special considerations and CNS/ATM – Don Heck (Boeing) and Jim Stewart (NATS).

Finally, there was an editorial committee, comprising:

- Leanna Rierson (Digital Safety Consulting)
- Ron Ashpole (Silver Atena)
- Alex Ayzenberg (Boeing Company)
- Patty (Bartels) Bath (Esterline AVISTA)
- Dewi Daniels (Verocel)
- Hervé Delseny (Airbus)
- Andrew Elliott (Design Assurance)
- Kelly Hayhurst (NASA)
- Barbara Lingberg (FAA)
- Steven C. Martz (Garmin)
- Steve Morton (TBV Associates)
- Marge Sonnek (Honeywell).

The outcome was a suite of documents (RTCA 2012a-g).

4 What are the differences between DO-178B and DO-178C?

The differences can be categorised in ten different groups. The issues relating to each were given to each of the seven subgroups.

4.1 Errors and inconsistencies

DO-178C addresses DO-178B's known errors and inconsistencies. For example, DO-178C has addressed the errata of DO-178B and has removed inconsistencies between the different tables of DO-178B Annex A.

4.2 Consistent terminology

DO-178C addresses issues regarding the use of specific terms such as 'guidance', 'guidelines', 'purpose', 'goal', 'objective' and 'activity' by changing the text so that the use of those terms was consistent throughout the document.

4.3 Wording improvements

DO-178C made wording improvements throughout the document. All such changes were made simply to make the document more precise; they were not meant to change the original intent of DO-178B.

4.4 Objectives and activities

DO-178C reinforces the point that, in order to fully understand the recommendations, the full body of this document should be considered. For example, Annex A now includes references to each activity as well as to each objective; and section 1.4, entitled 'How to use this document', reinforces the point that activities are a major part of the overall guidance.

4.5 Supplements

DO-178C recognizes that new software development methods and techniques may result in new issues. Rather than expanding text to account for all the current software development methods and techniques (and being revised yet again to account for future methods and techniques), DO-178C acknowledges that one or more supplements may be used in conjunction with DO-178C to modify the guidance for specific methods and techniques. These are:

- tool qualification
- model-based development and verification
- Object Oriented Technology (OOT)
- formal methods.

4.6 Tool qualification

DO-178C replaces the terms 'development tool' and 'verification tool' with three tool qualification criteria that determine the applicable tool qualification level based upon the software level. The guidance to qualify a tool is moved from DO-178C to DO-330, the new 'Tool qualification' document.

4.7 Coordinated system/software aspects

DO-178C updates Section 2, which provides system aspects relating to software development, to reflect current system practices and coordinates the information flow between the system process and the software process. The latter updates were coordinated with SAE S-18 and WG-63 when they were updating ARP4754A/ED-79A. The software level will now be provided to the software process by the system process.

4.8 DO-178B 'hidden' objectives

DO-178C added the so-called 'hidden objectives' to Annex A:
- A means for detecting additional code that is not directly traceable to the source code and a means to ensure its verification coverage are defined (see Table A-7, Objective 9).
- Assurance is obtained that software plans and standards are developed and reviewed for consistency (see Table A-9, Objective 1).

4.9 General topics

DO-178C addressed some general topics that resulted in changes to several sections of the document. The topics included a variety of subjects such as applicant's oversight of suppliers, parameter data items and traceability. In addressing these topics, two additional objectives were added to Annex A:

- Parameter data item file is correct and complete (see Table A-5, Objective 8).
- Verification of parameter data item file is achieved (see Table A-5, Objective 9).

Also, trace data was identified as software life cycle data (see Section 11.21, Table A-2 and Table A-6).

4.10 DO-178B gaps and clarifications

DO-178C addressed several specific issues that resulted in change to only one or two paragraphs. Each such change may have an impact upon the applicant as the changes either addressed clear gaps in DO-178B or clarified guidance that was subject to differing interpretations. Examples of gaps addressed include:

- The Modified Condition/Decision Coverage (MC/DC) definition changed. Masking MC/DC and short circuit MC/DC, as well as DO-178B's definition of MC/DC (often termed unique-cause MC/DC), are now allowed.
- Derived requirements should now be provided to the system processes, including the system safety assessment process, rather than just provided to the system safety assessment process (see Sections 5.1.1b and 5.2.1b).

Examples of clarifications include:

- The structural coverage analysis of data and control coupling between code components should be achieved by assessing the results of the requirements-based tests (see Section 6.4.4.2c).
- All tests added to achieve structural coverage are based on requirements (see Section 6.4.4.2d).

4.11 Annex A

There are a number of changes to Annex A, not least of which is the change to reference the activities as well as the objectives. For clarification, if there were any 'mandatory' aspects to DO-178C, then the objectives would be the most obvious choice. Activities therefore are merely advisory. This might be a convoluted way of saying that 'nothing is mandatory' but the whole document is not a 'standard' as such and hence cannot be deemed 'mandatory'. DO-178C and associated documents are acceptable means of compliance. There are a number of clarifications to the Annex A tables and the addition of a few objectives, notably the inclusion of parameter data item objectives and the previously 'hidden objective'. There was also some tidying up of certain objectives relating to Level D, as, for example, there is no certification credit for low-level requirements, so any objectives relating to them at Level D were therefore removed.

5 What are the differences between DO-278 and DO-278A?

There is one large difference that the introduction of DO-278A makes. This is that it is now a stand-alone document so it is no longer necessary to use two documents to get a total picture. The documents were developed in parallel and hence there is a lot of common language between the two. There are, however, a number of notable differences.

5.1 Certification (DO-178C) versus approval (DO-278A)

For DO-178C, an applicant works with an organization or person responsible within the state, country or other relevant body, concerned with the certification or approval of a product in accordance with requirements. For DO-278A, an applicant works with the relevant body responsible for the approval in accordance with applicable approval requirements.

5.2 Parameter data item (DO-178C) versus adaptation data (DO-278A)

For DO-178C, a Parameter Data Item (PDI) is a set of data that influence the behaviour of the software without modifying the Executable Object Code (EOC)and that is managed as a separate configuration item. Examples include databases and configuration tables. For DO-278A, adaptation data is data used to customize elements of the air traffic system for its designated purpose and is a set of data that influence the behaviour of the software without modifying the EOC and that is managed as a separate configuration item. Examples include databases and configuration tables.

5.3 Commercial Off-The-Shelf (COTS) software

DO-178C is relatively unchanged as the plenary was about equally divided on the type of additional information to be included in the document. The CNS/ATM community uses a wide variety of COTS software for their equipment. DO-278A was updated with 28 pages that provide additional information, methods and improved annex tables to assist software approvals. These updates were generated from accepted techniques and methods from international experts on past approved projects

5.4 Product service history (DO-178C) versus service experience (DO-278A)

Service data has different characteristics in airborne to that found in the ground environment:

- DO-178C: typically collected only during operating flight hours
- DO-278A: accumulated during in-service hours, or during test or evaluation of the system.

Software configuration similarly has a difference between the two environments:

- DO-178C: Installed software is running the same input data sets.
- DO-278A: Installed software may be running different input data sets. For example, air traffic control software contains the adaptation data for its local geographic installation (New York versus London versus Chicago versus Paris, etc.).

6 Supplements

The technology specific supplements were written to be applicable to both DO-178C and DO-278A equally and probably represent the biggest change to the previous regime. The need for the three supplements was the first question to be answered by each of the technology specific subgroups. There were various issues raised regarding technologies since the issue of DO-178B and these were increasing as technology developed. Consequently, the issues were grouped and distributed to the relevant subgroup to address. It was then decided that there was a need for technology specific guidance for OOT, model based design and formal methods.

The format of the supplements was effectively set by the formal methods subgroup. The approach was to define the certification credit that could be gained through demonstration of existing objectives using formal methods. As such, where there was no need to change existing text, a statement to that effect was made. Where it was felt necessary for context that DO-178C text was required, this was inserted in italics and the formal aspects written in normal text. The section and paragraph numbers were mirrored so the structure is the same as DO-178C and hence a mapping can be easily made. The Annex A tables then were repeated (as necessary) with the new paragraph references or, where necessary, references to DO-178C paragraphs. Additional objectives were also added and in some cases removed or overridden by technology specific objectives. As the supplements also relate to DO-278A/ED109A, there is a similar table at Annex C.

6.1 Model based design and verification DO-331/ED218

The subgroup responsible for the production of this document had the most interest. The document focuses on simulation and process evidence. There were concerns over the role of the person undertaking development and hence there is some introduced terminology and concepts. Table 1 is guidance from EASA in the Certification Memo-002 and is included in DO-331.

Table 1. Model usage examples

Process that generates the life-cycle data	MB example 1	MB example 2	MB example 3	MB example 4	MB example 5
System requirement and system design processes	Requirements allocated to software	Requirements from which the model is developed	Requirements from which the model is developed	Requirements from which the model is developed	Requirements from which the model is developed
Software requirement and software design processes	Requirements from which the model is developed	Specification model	Specification model	Design model	Design model
	Design model	Design model	Textual description		
Software coding process	Source code	Source code	Source code	Source code	Source code

The interpretation of Table 1 and its terminology is covered in guidance within the document. The documents structure largely mirrors the structure of DO-178C, but also has a large Frequently Asked Questions section.

The approach to deriving adequate verification credit for simulation is very detailed. The supplement defines the circumstances under which simulation credit may be considered and against which artefacts. For instance, there is a very detailed explanation of the requirements for the use of simulation for partially meeting the objectives for executable object code.

6.2 Object oriented technologies DO-332/ED217

The subgroup that was responsible for developing DO-332 based guidance on the NASA-led project Object Oriented Technology in Aerospace (OOTiA). There are various concerns over many aspects of OOT with respect to certification. The major concerns are over class hierarchies (inheritance) and dynamic memory management and there are new objectives to be met, which are in addition to those in DO-178C. There is a very good overview of the issues related to OOT in both the introduction and, in a departure from the template for supplements, Annex D.

6.3 Formal methods DO-333/ED216

The formal methods supplement is focussed mostly on verification and, as such, Section 6 is completely changed. There is a new set of objectives that require justification for the use of the specific formal method, the soundness of the analysis technique and the translation from the informal to the formal specification. It outlines what needs to be achieved for executable object code verification and coverage. Interestingly, if DO-333 is followed, the objectives for coverage in DO-178C are completely replaced.

7 Supporting information DO-248C/ED-94C

One of the targets set by RTCA/EUROCAE was to incorporate 'other guidance' into the main document wherever possible. To this end, some of the guidance in DO-248B was removed. However, some further frequently asked questions were identified and incorporated in the new DO-248C.

8 Forum on Aeronautical Software (FAS)

Finally, there is a follow-on committee comprising thirty or so invited members called the Forum on Aeronautical Software (FAS). This group was set up after the documents were accepted by RTCA and EUROCAE to assist in further clarifications to the documents. The group consists of previous chairs of subgroups and other major contributors. The group meets regularly (on-line) to progress issues raised as a result of contact with the material. More details can be found in (RTCA 2012h).

9 Summary

While not perfect, the documents were produced by a committee seeking a form of consensus, and the body of work that is the DO-178 suite of documents represents a comprehensive upgrade to previous guidance. All documents have been recognised by the FAA and EASA and it is therefore recommended that these documents are now used. Indeed, if it is intended that (e.g.) model-based development will be used, then it will be expected that any claims for credit as a result of their use will be based upon the relevant supplement. The core text in DO-178C has improved clarity on many topics and the new format in Annex A with objectives and activities has clarified matters.

References

RTCA (1992) DO-178B/ED12B – Software considerations in airborne systems and equipment certification. RTCA, Inc.

RTCA (2012a) DO-178C/ED12C – Software considerations in airborne systems and equipment certification. RTCA, Inc.

RTCA (2012b) DO-278A/ED109A – Software integrity assurance considerations for Communication, Navigation, Surveillance and Air Traffic Management (CNS/ATM) systems. RTCA, Inc.

RTCA (2012c) DO-330/ED-215 – Software tool qualification considerations. RTCA, Inc.

RTCA (2012d) DO-333/ED216 – Formal methods supplement to DO-178C/ED12C and DO-278A/ED109A. RTCA, Inc.

RTCA (2012e) DO-332/ED217 – Object-oriented technology and related techniques supplement to DO-178C/ED12C and DO-278A/ED109A. RTCA, Inc.

RTCA (2012f) DO-331/ED218 Model-based development and verification supplement to DO-178C/ED12C and DO-278A/ED109A. RTCA, Inc.

RTCA (2012g) DO-248C/ED94C – Supporting information to DO-178C/ED12C and DO-278A/ED109A. RTCA, Inc.

RTCA (2012h) Forum for aeronautical software. RTCA, Inc. http://www.rtca.org/content.asp?pl=28&sl=170&contentid=170. Accessed 15 November 2013

Re-Issuing Def Stan 00-55[1]

Graham Jolliffe

Jolliffe Associates

Amesbury, UK

Abstract   When Def Stan-00-55 (MOD 1997) was declared obsolete on 29 April 2005, there was an expectation that Def Stan 00-56 would provide guidance on how to develop and procure safety related software. That has proved elusive despite a number of attempts to provide the MOD with material that would assist its suppliers of safety related software. However, Def Stan 00-55 continued to be one of the most frequently downloaded defence standards and coupled with the MOD's need for clarity and consistency when procuring safety related software, it has been decided to re-issue the standard. This paper provides an insight into the rationale and main drivers behind its re-introduction and focuses on the principles and strategic intent of the standard compared with its predecessor.

1 Introduction

The UK Ministry of Defence (MOD) has had a long standing requirement for clarity and consistency when procuring safety related software and needs to be able to contract accordingly. Whilst Defence Standard 00-55 Issue 2 had its critics, its absence has not helped the MOD achieve its needs. Furthermore, as one of the most frequently downloaded defence standards, it would appear that others also still perceive a need for the standard.

However, a considerable amount of time has passed since Def Stan 00-55 was declared obsolete. In the meantime, methods and standards applied to the development of software and programmable hardware has moved on. Any re-issue of the standard needs to recognise this, and ideally avoid becoming obsolete due to further changes in technology.

---

[1] This document has been commissioned as part of the process of updating Def Stans 00-55 and 00-56 and is released to stimulate comment and debate. The information contained in this document should not be interpreted as representing the views of the MOD, nor should it be assumed that it reflects any current or future MOD policy. The information cannot supersede any statutory or contractual requirements or liabilities and is offered without prejudice or commitment to the MOD.

Some of these changes in technology have seen the reliability of hardware to improve, resulting in less frequent updates due to failures. Another driver for change is the rapid obsolescence of the programmable environment in systems that have a life of more than a decade. The change then is re-hosting the programmable hardware and software to a new environment yet retaining the same functionality, system level hazards and requirements. In these cases the upgrade is almost entirely off-the-shelf certified complex electronics and pre-certified software (operating systems) with a software/programmable wrapper as either an emulator or interface for the re-compiled logic.

Consequently, modifications often only require an update to software or programmable hardware. This in turn leads the MOD to require a software and programmable hardware safety standard that can be contracted separately, whilst still retaining close links to Def Stan 00-56.

Rather than continually refer to both software and programmable hardware, this standard uses the term Programmable Elements (PE).

1.1 Source material

In developing this standard, the author has utilised a lot of material from a variety of sources to supplement his own experience. This includes Interim Def Stan 00-56 Issue 5 (MOD 2013) which is effectively the parent of this standard. However, this standard has been designed to be able to contract separately from Def Stan 00-56, which is covered in more detail later in this paper. Other sources include:

- Principled Software Safety Assurance Tutorial (Kelly 2011), which identifies five principles for the achievement of PE integrity
- the Royal Navy Software Integrity Policy (MOD 2012), produced by the MOD naval authority to ensure the safety of any activity which relies on the integrated use of equipment or sub-systems that includes software. It contains a number of succinct policies which have been considered and adapted for this standard.
- the Niteworks Def Stan 00-55 Prototype (MOD 2012 – not published), which refers to Kelly's five principles and utilises the concept of a process diagram, which has been adapted for this standard
- other software standards referenced throughout this paper, which will provide significant input to the Part 2 guidance section of the standard
- the Software Systems Engineering Initiative – Statement of Best Practice (SSEI 2009), which contains a wealth of useful material, but proved too cumbersome for practical use. Nevertheless, much of the material remains valid and will provide a valuable contribution to the Part 2 guidance section of the standard.
- finally, consultation with stakeholders, which has included but not been limited to:

- the MOD System Engineering Integration Group
- the Military Aviation Authority
- the Defence Science and Technology Laboratory.

All of the above stakeholders continue to provide valuable comments which have helped shape this standard and should ensure that it is fit for purpose.

2 Strategic objectives and structure

In re-issuing Def Stan 00-55, the needs of the MOD are paramount, but to achieve success, the standard must take account of the criticism of its predecessor. This criticism included over prescription and the lack of recognition from applying other standards. Three strategic objectives address both this criticism and the MOD's needs and the structure is deliberately intended to follow that used in Def Stan 00-56 Issue 5.

2.1 Use of 'open' standards

Perhaps the single biggest change implemented by this standard is the use of 'open' standards, which recognises that a number of standards in widespread use already address safety of PE successfully. This approach has the additional benefit of avoiding prescription, since it is down to the contractor to propose a suitable standard to apply. It also means that the requirements Part 1 of the standard is relatively 'lite', although the guidance in Part 2 clearly has to be sufficiently robust to assist contractors make a suitable choice.

It is recognised that using a term such as 'open' requires definition. Currently, there is no commonly agreed definition, but this standard uses the European Interoperability Framework definition of 'There are no constraints on the re-use of the standard'. The important term 'no' means that this definition assumes no contractual access restrictions (including those relating to IPR) and full access to the process, irrespective of whether it is bespoke and/or company specific.

It is anticipated that a further benefit will accrue from this approach in making the standard technology agnostic. To achieve this, much will depend upon the interpretation of the term 'open', and hence a significant amount of guidance will be required both to ensure appropriate standards are suitable, but also to enable alternatives to be identified to cover new or novel technology.

2.2 Relationship to Def Stan 00-56

Although the MOD need to be able to contract separately for the safety of PE, it is clear that this standard must have the ability to use the approach within Def Stan 00-56 to avoid repeating numerous safety clauses in this standard. Def Stan 00-56 is currently being re-issued as Issue 5 to reflect the latest changes in the management of safety requirements. In doing so, there now is a dedicated annex covering design integrity, which includes five principles for achieving PE integrity. These have been captured as objectives in this standard and cover:

- PE safety requirements for their:
    - identification
    - traceability
    - satisfaction

- the impact from emergent hazard causes or unexpected behaviour
- establishing confidence that these objectives are addressed commensurate to the PE contribution to system risk.

These are covered in more detail in Section 3.

The origin of these principles was identified through work undertaken by Tim Kelly from the University of York and presented in a tutorial (Kelly 2011). However, these principles also align with the dependability1 and dependability2 view presented by Peter Ladkin at the IET International Systems Safety Conference, (Ladkin 2012). There is also overlap and alignment with the six generic safety claims details in MOD's Acquisition Guide for Complex Electronic Elements (CEE) Safety Assurance, issue 2-1 (MOD 2009).

2.3 Consideration of PE failure effect in a broader system context

PE failures may well impact features of the system that do not solely relate to safety. Whilst this standard first and foremost addresses PE safety, it is recognised that during the process of addressing the five principles above, it is likely that non-safety impacts may well be identified. Therefore, this standard makes some provision for this within the guidance section. Principally, this is likely to concern impacts to security and mission integrity. Although the standard has no normative requirements to cover this aspect, the guidance section will use the principles of MOD's JSP 440 manual of security to advise what steps should be taken in the event of such impacts being identified. This is covered in more detail in Section 4.

2.4 Structure

The proposed structure of Def Stan 00-55 is similar to that of draft Def Stan 00-56 Issue 5, which at the time of writing is about to be issued as an Interim Def Stan. In Def Stan Issue 5, key 'shall' requirements for achievement, assurance and management of risk to life are mandatory, with optional 'should' requirements and notes providing guidance and context. The draft Def Stan Issue 5 includes requirements for use of civil and open standards and competence, and guidance on how to meet the need for design integrity.

The proposed Def Stan 00-55 aims to be concise and deliberately does not regurgitate the safety management requirements of Def Stan 00-56. Whilst in most cases it is expected that Def Stan 00-56 will be the preferred safety management standard, this proposed standard does have provision for the use of open standards, which may include suitable alternate safety management standards.

3 Principles of PE safety assurance

To achieve its purpose and meet PE design integrity, this standard is based upon the five principles established in Annex D to Interim Def Stan 00-56 Issue 5 and outlined in Section 2.2 above. From these principles, this standard has derived five objectives and means of achievement as follows.

Objective 1: PE safety requirements are defined and valid. The purpose of this objective is to ensure that any contribution of PE to Product, System or Service (PSS) hazards are identified, understood and captured. This is met through activities that define PE safety requirements that are: valid, unambiguous, comprehensible, atomic, internally consistent, feasible and verifiable. This includes defining the PE safety requirement contribution to PSS hazards and validity.

Objective 2: PE safety requirement traceability is assured. This is met through activities that assure and demonstrate that the intent of PE safety requirements traceability has been established throughout requirements decomposition. Traceability must be established and demonstrated to an appropriate level of implementation abstraction and managed throughout the lifecycle.

Objective 3: PE safety requirement satisfaction is demonstrated. Perhaps the most obvious objective is that safety requirements satisfaction assures the correct implementation and provides evidence of the absence of errors. There will be various means of achieving this objective which will be elaborated in the guidance section of the standard. Ultimately, this is a verification issue and shares the challenges of requirements traceability above. The evidence has to be compelling and not only show that the requirements have been met, but that the evidence is traceable to those requirements.

Objective 4: impacts from emergent hazard causes or unexpected behaviour are mitigated. This is also related to Objective 2 and requires the contractor to ask if the PE functionality does anything else that is unsafe. Emergent hazards and/or properties may generate derived requirements. These derived requirements must be assessed and managed to ensure that they are adequately mitigated.

This can be addressed by the safety requirements from Objective 1 and by safety assurance and engineering processes and tools determined by the chosen standard, enhanced standards or recognised good practice.

Objective 5: confidence is established in addressing these PE safety objectives. The confidence established in addressing the (other) PE safety objectives needs to be commensurate to the contribution of the PE contribution to system risk. This cuts across the other four objectives. Perfect assurance of the achievement of the objectives is desirable, but cannot be fully achieved. For instance, it is not possible to prove that the safety requirements are complete. Therefore, this objective seeks to determine when enough is enough, through the concept of confidence.

Although it is easy to understand how the degree of confidence will impact the ability to meet safety objectives, it is a very subjective attribute and a difficult concept to capture contractually. This standard interprets confidence through the correct application of the following:

- identification of PE criticality from the PE failure assessment
- from which an appropriate standard can be chosen and proposed
- whose correct application should produce sufficient evidence whose extent should be commensurate with contribution of the PE to system risk.

This objective is another area that will require considerable guidance within Part 2. However, for PE safety this is usually achieved by applying and demonstrating criticality levels dependant upon the chosen standard. The level of criticality to be achieved should be identified by a PE failure assessment, which is discussed further in Section 5 covering the PE safety requirements process.

Section 2.4 above mentioned the possibility of a 'gap' between the desired design integrity and level of criticality achieved from applying the chosen standard. Some consideration will need to be given to identifying and mitigating these assurance deficits.

The strategy has been to translate the principles into objectives and refine the objectives into contractual 'shall' requirements supported by guidance.

4 PE related areas of concern

The design integrity Annex D of Def Stan 00-56 also highlights the growing concern with modern systems including cyber security and data integrity. As previously mentioned in Section 2.3, these aspects may not be safety related, but may well be identified through applying the processes required to achieve the objectives of this standard.

4.1 Cyber security

There have been a number of incidents where cyber attacks on systems have been safety significant, e.g. disabling protection systems. This is one of the reasons that Def Stan 00-56 Issue 5 requires that contractors should consider cyber security issues as potential causes of hazards. Annex D of Def Stan 00-56 states:

'The Complex Electronic and PE Integrity section refers to common concerns with regard to PE, but there are two further issues which relate to PE, both of which are of growing concern with modern systems: cyber security and data integrity. It is important that Contractors consider cyber security issues as potential credible causes of failure modes contributing to a hazard, and produce and implement appropriate mitigations.'

4.2 Data integrity

Data integrity is also an area of increasing concern. Annex D of Def Stan 00-56 states:

'Similarly, there is an emerging issue relating to data, both in terms of software processing critical data, e.g. target coordinates, complex data, e.g. terrain maps, or configuration data, e.g. defining the capabilities of a multi-role system. Errors in any of these classes of data can have a safety impact, thus there is a need to manage integrity. PSS can cause or contribute to, unsafe behaviour when its internal model of the world differs sufficiently from the actual state of the real world and those decisions or actions generated by the PSS (or recommendations given to operators) may be inappropriate.'

Although there are no requirements in Part 1 to cover these areas, Part 2 does consider the causes and consequences of such PE failures and advises contractors to consider such credible causes of hazards and PE failures and produce and implement appropriate mitigations based on this analysis, and report any findings to the MOD.

5 PE safety requirements process

5.1 Need for a process

One of the more useful aspects of the Niteworks Def Stan 00-55 Prototype (MOD 2012 – not published) was the use of a process diagram. Although the constraints on that prototype meant that the diagram had some flaws, the concept was still valid and the value of illustrating how the requirements relate to one another in a flow diagram is well recognised. The proposed Def Stan 00-55 PE safety requirements process diagram is shown in Figure 1 and illustrates the linkage between requirements clauses and their relationship with Def Stan 00-56.

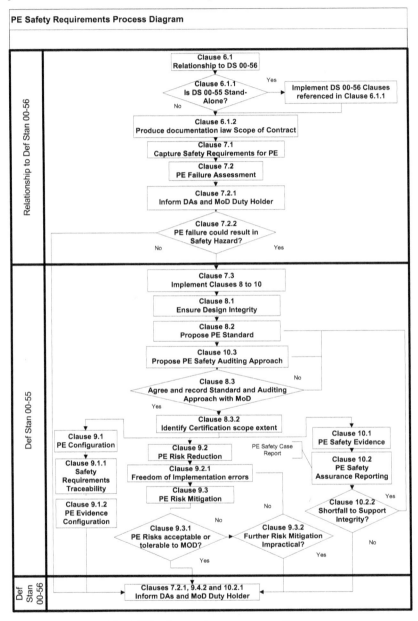

Fig. 1. PE safety requirements process diagram

5.2 Process overview

It is not intended to detail each requirements clause shown in the diagram in this paper. Such detail can be readily found within the standard complete with guidance material. Furthermore, it is quite likely that much of the detail will be amended before this paper is presented.

The process is intended to help users plan their PE safety activities. The first section, which relates to Def Stan 00-56 firstly identifies if the standard is to be used in conjunction with Def Stan 00-56 or not before capturing some preliminary contractual information and safety requirements identification in fulfilment of Objective 1. The final step is to undertake a PE failure assessment to determine the criticality of the PE (part of Objectives 4 and 5). It is quite possible that such an assessment may have been undertaken prior to implementing this standard, in which case this step may be omitted. It is also possible that the assessment identifies no safety related functionality, in which case this can be recorded, reported to the MOD and the process terminated.

Having captured the design integrity, the next section continues with the need to choose and agree a suitable standard to apply and a means of demonstrating compliance (possibly through auditing). There will be guidance in the standard but there is likely to be an option for the contractor to propose a standard and compliance method; however, it is for the MOD to agree both proposals.

At this point the process divides into three parallel processes which cover configuration control and traceability (Objective 2), risk reduction and mitigation (Objective 4) and collation of safety evidence and assurance (Objectives 3 and 5). Although these processes are shown in parallel, in practice Objective 3 can start but cannot be completed until Objectives 1 and 2 are complete. The safety evidence is collated and presented in a PE safety case report, which is the only specified deliverable from this standard. However, in practice, this may be incorporated within deliverables specified under Def Stan 00-56 if preferred.

Finally, MOD acceptance of completion provides a link back into Def Stan 00-56. It can also be seen that where there are shortfalls in integrity (assurance deficit) or further risk reduction is practical, there are return links back into the appropriate part of the process. It is recognised that these return links could result in constantly reviewing and updating, but in is expected that in practice, the combination of previously agreed standards and auditing will allow the process to reach a conclusion.

6 Contracting with Def Stan 00-55

The intent of this standard is that it can be contracted separately for PE projects. However, the preferred method of contracting is with the new Def Stan 00-56 Issue 5. This is because the interfaces are well defined and cover aspects such as scope of contract, safety committees, command summaries, information safety set summaries, and derived safety requirements of PSS.

However, if Def Stan 00-56 Issue 5 is not used, an interface needs to be defined to alternate safety requirements standards, such as Mil-Std-882 (DoD 2012) or even legacy issues of 00-56. Undoubtedly there will be gaps compared with aspects covered by Def Stan 00-56 Issue 5 and these should be dealt with in the contract to ensure that the scope covers any interface gaps.

7 Conclusions

Previous issues of Def Stan 00-55 have provoked a great deal of discussion and debate, having previously been viewed as both onerous and too prescriptive by some, and a source of good practice by others. However, during the time since Def Stan 00-55 was declared obsolescent, PE acquisition has become integral for every project team within MOD. Def Stan 00-56 Issue 4 (MOD 2007) does contain guidance on PE; however, this does require the whole standard on contract which reduces the flexibility provided by a standalone Def Stan 00-55. MOD's need for clarity and consistency when procuring safety related software is as pressing now as ever, due to off-the-shelf policies, changing technologies, obsolescence and greater emphasis upon regulatory compliance.

This rewrite attempts not only to address the criticisms of Def Stan 00-55 Issue 2, but also to highlight the potential for security aspects of PE to impact safety. Whilst at the time of writing there is still much to do, especially with respect to the provision of guidance, it is expected that the new standard will provide the MOD with a dependable method of procuring safety related PE and provide clarity and flexibility to industry, without excessive prescription.

Acknowledgments The core team responsible for the production of Def Stan 00-56 Issue 5 are thanked for their valuable comments and assistance.

References

DOD (2012) MIL-STD-882E System safety. US Department of Defense
Kelly T (2011) Principled Software Safety Assurance Tutorial
Ladkin P (2012) Some 'hot issues' in software safety standardisation. IET System Safety Conference keynote address
MOD (1997) Def Stan 00-55 Requirements for safety related software in defence equipment. Issue 2. Ministry of Defence
MOD (2007) Def Stan 00-56 Safety management requirements for defence systems. Issue 4. Ministry of Defence
MOD (2009) Acquisition guide for CEE safety assurance. Issue 2-1
MOD (2012) Royal Navy software integrity policy. 181776rrs01 Issue 02. Ministry of Defence
MOD (2013) Interim Def Stan 00-56 Safety management requirements for defence systems. Issue 5. Ministry of Defence
SSEI (2009) Interim standard of best practice on software in the context of Def Stan 00-56 Issue 4. SSEI-BP-000001 Issue 1. Software Systems Engineering Initiative

EMC Compliance for Functional Safety by adapting 61508's Techniques and Measures – New Guidance published by the IET

Keith Armstrong

Cherry Clough Consultants Ltd

Stafford, UK

Abstract   Until quite recently, all the work towards being able to achieve EMC compliance with functional safety standards, for IET guidance and IEC standardization, assumed that it would be the responsibility of EMC engineering personnel.

They would have needed to develop the necessary skills and expertise to achieve levels of EMC design confidence that were at least an order of magnitude (e.g. for SIL1) higher than is currently achieved.

This has not proved to be practical for several reasons, so instead the IET has now developed guidelines that only need practitioners of EMC engineering and functional safety hardware/software design (and its independent assessment) to develop their existing skills and expertise by a reasonable amount to achieve EMC for functional safety for any SIL.

1 Introduction

Complying with emissions and immunity ElectroMagnetic Compatibility (EMC) test standards has long been known to be insufficient for demonstrating compliance with functional safety requirements, even at Safety Integrity Level 1 (SIL1) or its equivalent in standards other than IEC 61508 (IEC 2010), see (Armstrong 2004, Armstrong 2009, Radasky et al. 2009, Armstrong 2010 and Armstrong 2012a).

The problem was that there was no published alternative that provided a set of requirements for achieving EMC for functional safety, which included methods for assessing whether those requirements had been met.

By the end of 2008 all of the guides, draft standards and IEC 'Technical Specifications' that had been written on how to achieve EMC for functional safety assumed that if big, heavy, costly 'grey boxes' (see later) were not used, was needed was to be clever enough in EMC design, and in EMC desig tion/validation (which included, but could not be limited to, EMC tes

However, since 2008, a number of companies who had tried to put these guides and other publications into practise had found that they fell far short of being practicable in real life.

The author's discussions since 2008 with these and other functional safety practitioners revealed the possibility of an alternative approach to achieving EMC for functional safety compliance, which after more than two years of work in the IET's working group on EMC for functional safety, has resulted in the very practical guidance document published on 23 August 2013 (IET 2013).

Converting the initial concepts into something that had practical utility and was accepted widely enough for the IET to publish required a huge amount of work by EMC experts and functional safety experts within the IET's working group. It also involved over 160 high-quality comments on its first draft from a very wide range of experts in functional safety and EMC throughout the UK.

These new IET guidelines provide, for the first time, a practical and cost-effective approach which doesn't require using military-style 'big grey boxes'. It has three parts, shown in Figure 1.

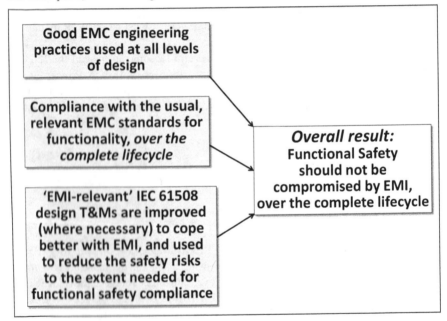

Fig. 1. Overview of the approach taken by the new IET guide

To use this new approach, the EMC community in general has a little more to learn to apply good EMC engineering practices to functional safety-related systems, and to equipment that is intended to be used in the assembly of such systems. It also has a little more to learn to design and construct such systems and equipment with sufficient confidence that they will continue to comply with their relevant EMC test standards throughout their lifecycles.

And designers and independent assessors in the functional safety community have a little more to learn too, to apply the IEC 61508 Techniques and Measures (T&Ms) they already know very well in slightly different ways to deal correctly with all reasonably foreseeable ElectroMagnetic Interference (EMI) over the anticipated lifecycle.

No EMC techniques and measures should be relied upon, on their own. The functional safety designer chooses a set of techniques and measures which ensure that, regardless of the EM disturbance that causes the error, malfunction or failure, the overall functional safety specifications are met. The lower the level of acceptable functional safety risk, the greater is the amount of work and documentation, and the higher is the competence, required in choosing EMC techniques and measures – just as has been the case for 61508's techniques and measures since 2000.

The IET's new guidelines (IET 2013) can be applied to complete safety-related systems, or to any parts of them, as shown in Figure 2.

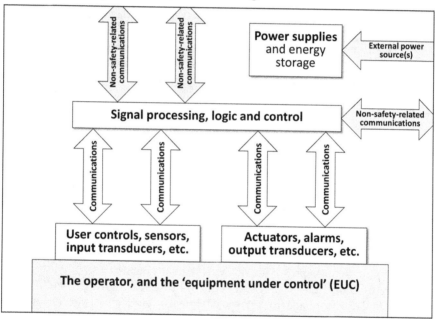

Fig. 2. Overview of a safety-related system and its constituent parts (in the clear boxes)

There is no reason why the traditional 'big grey box' approach (see later) should not be applied in combination with the techniques and measures described in (IET 2013).

For example, a complete safety-related system might be constructed from items of equipment supplied by third-parties (custom-designed, batch- or volume-manufactured) some of which use the 'big grey box' method, with the remainder using EMC techniques and measures from (IET 2013).

2 The 'big grey box' approach

This is a perfectly valid way of achieving EMC for functional safety that has been used for many decades, and requires no knowledge of the possible EM disturbances (i.e. EM 'threats') that could occur over the entire lifecycle.

It has been used for so long in the military and telecommunication sectors that there are many EMC engineers who are skilled in applying it, and many EMC component manufacturers who can supply appropriate parts for it, and even complete big grey boxes with everything in place ready to house electronic equipment.

The author is at a bit of a loss with naming this traditional EMC methodology, because it seems there is no single term or phrase that is in common use; hence his choice of the phrase 'big grey box approach'.

This rather colloquial phrase at least has the merit that everyone seems to understand what is being referred to: a 'brute force' approach that could well be over-engineered for most applications but provides very high levels of EMC confidence despite a lack of knowledge about the EM threats that could occur over the lifecycle, despite all foreseeable exposure to physical and climatic conditions.

The basic approach is to place the safety-related electronics in a shielded enclosure that provides at least 80dB of suppression for all radiated and conducted EM disturbances over the entire frequency range (e.g. 20Hz to 26GHz), and which is rugged enough to withstand the foreseeable physical/climatic environments over its lifecycle without significant degradation in the EM suppression it provides.

Such enclosures must be used with similarly rugged 'big grey power filters' and 'big grey power surge suppressors'. Signals enter and exit such boxes through 'big grey' military-style circular connectors fitted with filter/surge suppression pins, shielding, or both.

Suitable enclosures are generally made of very thick metal plates with seam-welded or conductively gasketted joints, hence the term 'big grey boxes'. Figure 3 shows some examples.

The problem with this 'brute force' approach is that it can be too large, heavy and/or costly for many modern safety-related systems, especially those made in high volumes, for example for use in civilian motor vehicles.

Where functional safety designers cannot (or choose not to) apply the 'big grey box' method described above, they should now use the IET's new techniques and measures (IET 2013).

3 Some more detail on EMC for functional safety

The basic standard on functional safety, IEC 61508, and the standards developed from it, are concerned with ensuring that complex electronic equipment[1] functions

---

[1] In this paper, 'equipment' is used to mean all types of electronic devices, modules, units, products, sub-systems, systems, installations, etc.

in such a way that safety risks remain within acceptable levels. For example, malfunctions in the flight control computers of passenger airliners can result in very high levels of risk (e.g. several hundred people killed).

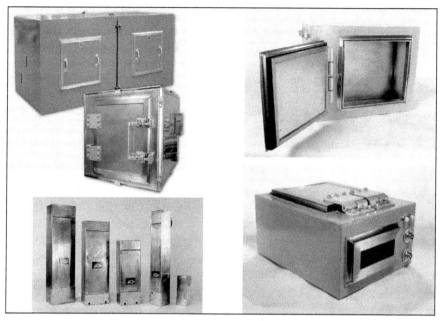

Fig. 3. Some examples of big grey boxes and their big grey filters and surge suppressors (these examples are from Universal Shielding, Inc., but there are several other manufacturers of such boxes and filters/suppressors)

IEC 61508 and related standards therefore require all reasonably foreseeable errors, malfunctions and faults (including, for example, bad solder joints) over the lifecycle, including those caused by aging, corrosion, accidental or intentional misuse, etc., to be detected and appropriate actions taken to ensure functional safety risks are kept lower than some (previously decided) maximum tolerable level.

In practice, the safety-related activities that occur on detecting an error, malfunction or fault in software or hardware fall into two broad categories:

1. Controlling the equipment concerned so that it becomes safe. This is typical of dangerous machinery, for example, by causing it to cease operating, and is called 'putting the equipment under control into a safe state'.

   It is important to note that, except for the availability requirements described later on, safety designers don't care if the equipment is damaged or otherwise made unusable – as long as it remains safe enough.

2. Correcting for the detected error, malfunction or fault so that the equipment continues to operate in a safe manner. This is typical of, for example, life support machinery, which of course doesn't have a 'safe state' – it has to keep

working as intended to keep the person alive. This might be achieved, for example, by switching from the malfunctioning control system to a backup system.

As well as the obvious medical life-support equipment such as ventilators and pacemakers, the second category includes rebreather-type diving suits and spacesuits. Most of us don't find ourselves underwater using rebreathers (instead of SCUBA diving gear), or making a spacewalk, but there is another category that has no safe state which almost all of us use daily – passenger transport by road or by air.

Cars and aircraft that are under way have no safe state, they cannot just be powered down like (for example) a production machine, so their safety-related control systems must be of the type that maintains driver or pilot control despite malfunctions and faults. (Fyfe and Dobel 2013) is an example of the safety problems that can arise when this fact is ignored or forgotten.

All electronic equipment can suffer errors, temporary malfunctions or permanent damage due to EMI, and so the ability to withstand EM disturbances is important for achieving acceptable levels of functional safety risk. For this reason, compliance with the IEC's basic publication on EMC for functional safety, IEC TS 61000-1-2 (IEC 2008), is now a normative requirement of IEC 61508. However, there is a problem with this: IEC TS 61000-1-2 has the same approach as the IET's 2008 guide (IET 2008) and so requires impractical levels of EMC expertise (if the 'big grey box' approach is not used).

The 2008 guidance (IET 2008) was based on IEC TS 61000-1-2, and so both documents base EMC design – and its verification and final (usually independent) validation by an accredited functional safety assessor – on a detailed assessment of the worst-case EM environment over the anticipated lifecycle. Unfortunately, there are large practical difficulties with determining the lifecycle EM environment well enough.

Both IEC TS 61000-1-2 and (IET 2008) also list numerous techniques and measures that may be used for design, verification and validation, but neither provides detailed information on how to make an EMC design comply with a specified level of functional safety risk; or on how an independent functional safety assessor could validate that it had achieved that specification.

In consequence, EMC engineers typically focus on what they know best: using EM mitigation techniques in design (filtering, shielding, surge suppression, galvanic isolation, etc.) and on immunity testing for its verification/validation.

Unfortunately, the design confidence required to achieve acceptable levels of functional safety risks according to IEC 61508 is between one and four orders of magnitude greater than most EMC engineers and EMC testers have expertise in achieving. So, although this approach seemed like a good idea when IEC TS 61000-1-2 and (IET 2008) were written, in practice it has been found to suffer severe difficulties.

It is important to understand that IEC 61508, IEC TS 61000-1-2 and their related and alternative standards, are safety standards, and so are very different from

EMC standards. Complying with them requires expertise in achieving functional safety – an engineering discipline developed in total isolation to the discipline of EMC, with which it shares no concepts or terminology.

This great difference between the two disciplines adds hugely to the difficulties faced by any EMC or functional safety engineers who are expected to ensure that equipment achieves an acceptable level of functional safety risk over its entire lifetime despite all EMI.

As briefly discussed in Section 1, the practical difficulties that have been experienced in attempting to apply (IET 2008) and IEC TS 61000-1-2 spurred the IET's WG on EMC for functional safety to create its new guidance (IET 2013).

All EM disturbances that are not sufficiently attenuated by mitigation such as shielding, filtering, surge suppression, etc., result in EMI problems. All such EMI appears as problems with signal, data or power integrity in hardware, software or both, where they can be dealt with by the techniques and measures that designers of functional safety-related hardware and software are very familiar with. These techniques and measures have (mostly) been listed in IEC 61508 since 2000, and are all very well-proven and well-understood through having been developed and used in practice for many years (even decades) before then.

Functional safety designs are always subjected to independent safety assessment, and if the independent assessor doesn't like a design, or thinks the verification and validation it has been subjected to do not prove it is safe enough, he or she has an absolute veto on that design being manufactured. So, independent functional safety assessors are already very familiar with the design techniques and measures listed in 61508.

Although these design techniques and measures have been found to be quite effective against the effects of EMI on hardware and software, they were not originally developed to deal with EMI and so, as was mentioned in Section 1, the new IET guidance recommends how they may be improved so that a designer may, for the first time, satisfactorily demonstrate to an independent functional safety assessor that errors, malfunctions and faults caused by EMI should not cause functional safety risks to rise above the specified tolerable levels.

For example, a common 61508 T&M is to have two identical sets of hardware and software with the same inputs, and performing the same operations on that data. If an error, malfunction or fault occurs in one of these 'parallel channels', a comparator detects that their outputs no longer agree and triggers appropriate actions to maintain safety.

However, the effects of a given EMI in circuits or software are 'systematic' and not random, so the errors, malfunctions or faults it creates in identical channels can easily be so similar that the comparator cannot tell that there is a problem at all. Such systematic errors are often called 'common-cause', and the IET's new guide recommends that when using parallel channels, one of them should be run on inverted data with respect to the other.

Now the common-cause systematic effects of EMI will have different effects on the data in the two channels, making it very much more likely that the dual-channel technique will detect errors, malfunctions and faults caused by EMI. Note that inverting the data in one channel and re-inverting it back for comparison adds nothing to the cost of manufacture when using FPGAs, as most designers do.

The IET's new guide also recommends that when using parallel channels, they are realized using different architectures for their hardware and their software, which achieve the same end-result. This is an especially valuable technique when using three or more parallel channels with voting to maintain safe operation where there is no safe state, and, for example, this technique is commonly used for the flight control electronics of modern passenger aircraft. Often thought of as an expensive 'high-end' technique, when realized in volume-manufactured silicon chips it adds little extra cost.

There is, of course, a very wide range of safety-related systems, and so the functional safety actions that are triggered by the detection of an error, malfunction or fault can be very different. The safety case describes what actions are taken, and how/why they maintain a tolerable level of safety risk, and is also assessed by the independent functional safety assessor.

EMI is identified by IEC 61508 and IEC TS 61000-1-2 as a 'systematic failure mode', meaning that it is not statistically random, but instead is a feature of a given design, in the same way that software 'bugs' are considered to be a feature of a given software design.

The SIL concept applies to the operation of a completed safety-related system, which may use not just electronic, but also electro-mechanical, mechanical, building works (e.g. protective barriers) and personnel management (e.g. restricting access to the area within protective barriers). The author understands that the EMI contribution to any SIL is no more than 10% of the total risk it represents.

Systematic failures (including: errors; recoverable malfunctions, and permanent faults) can only be dealt with by the use of well-proven design techniques, plus well-proven verification and validation techniques. Together, these must achieve the confidence in the design, and in its (usually independent) validation, that is required by the SIL specified for the safety function concerned.

Trying to anticipate the rates of occurrence of EM disturbances is generally inappropriate when trying to achieve a specified SIL. For example, even if an especially extreme EM disturbance happened only once every ten years on average, the SIL corresponds to the level of confidence that the safety function will withstand this rare EM event without failing whenever it happens.

This is an important aspect of EMC risk management that is often misunderstood. The author often sees EMC engineers incorrectly attempting to achieve SILs (or ASILs, under ISO 26262) by using statistical reasoning for the rate of occurrence of EM disturbances. It is significant that by removing from EMC practitioners the need to understand functional safety engineering, (IET 2013) helps to avoid dangerous mistakes caused by lack of knowledge.

4 Practical difficulties in determining the worst-case EM environment(s)

(IEC 2010) requires safety-related equipment to be designed, and for its design to be verified and validated, to cope with the worst-cases of all its environmental exposures over its anticipated lifetime. For this reason, IEC TS 61000-1-2 and (IET 2008) require EMC design and verification/validation to be based upon an accurate determination of the worst-case EM environment(s) that could be experienced over the anticipated lifetime. Unfortunately, there are significant practical difficulties in doing this.

Most industries have only very general guidelines on EM environments to follow, such as IEC 61000-2-5 (IEC 2011) and the IEC 61000-4 series of immunity testing standards (IEC various). These are based on so-called 'economic/technical compromises' that ignore any considerations of safety-related or other risk-managed applications. Depending on which standards team members one talks to, the types and levels of the EM disturbances in these documents are estimated to cover between 80% and 95% of what can be expected in 'normal' EM environments.

Worst-case (i.e. most extreme), rare or unusual EM disturbances are very important indeed when trying to improve the normal immunity to EMI by, say, 10,000 times for a safety function that prevented a vehicle's speed from going out of driver control – but are not considered at all in IEC 61000-2-5or IEC 61000-4.

Many manufacturers of safety-related systems, and independent functional safety assessors, have told the author that they cannot even begin to comply with IEC 61000-1-2, because they have no expertise in assessing worst-case EM environments over the anticipated lifetime of their equipment, and cannot afford to employ such expertise.

There are also significant problems concerning the ability of anyone to predict what the worst-case EM environment will be for a given location, number of locations, or vehicle route over the next 10, 20, 30 or more years (for example, railway trains are currently being designed for a service life of 50 years or more).

Military and aerospace EMC designers have the big advantage that a lot of work has gone into (and is still going into) characterizing their EM environments and their corresponding immunity tests, having regard to mission-criticality. However, even they might baulk at predicting their critical systems' EM environments over the next 30 or 40 years, or assessing the possibilities for any of the foreseeable EM disturbances to happen simultaneously or in some time-sequence that is critical for the equipment concerned (Grommes and Armstrong 2011, Armstrong 2012b).

A very big advantage of (IET 2013) over the lifecycle EM environment assessment required by (IET 2008) and IEC TS 61000-1-2 is that its techniques and measures ensure that the required design confidence for the specified SIL is achieved as regards any/all EM disturbances.

Because they cover all signal/data/power integrity issues, they also cover all EMI, even from EM disturbances and combinations of them which were unforeseen, or even unforeseeable, during the design of the system, so they cope with any/all possible future changes to the EM environment.

5 Practical difficulties with EM mitigation

EMC designers who use the 'big grey box' approach described in Section 2 can provide evidence – usually obtained from the suppliers of their big grey boxes, big grey filters and big grey surge suppressors – that satisfies independent functional safety assessors that the design of their EM mitigation is so comprehensive and reliable that all risks due to EM disturbances would be low enough for the chosen SIL over the anticipated lifecycle. However, as was said earlier, such 'brute force' EM mitigation approaches can be too large, heavy or costly for volume-manufactured safety-related systems, or equipment intended for use in them.

Filters made from chokes and capacitors, and shielding, suffer from resonant frequencies at which they provide gain (amplification) rather than attenuation (suppression). Filter resonances are affected by their real-life source and load impedances – which are not tested by standard EMC tests.

Shield resonances are affected by the size of the gaps at their inevitable joints and seams no matter how narrow those gaps are (the film of oxide that naturally forms on plain aluminium is more than sufficient to create a resonant aperture).

A knowledgeable EMC designer will ensure that these resonances occur at frequencies outside those at which there could be any reasonably foreseeable threats in the EM environment(s) over the lifetime. But component values can change over time, due to internal degradations and/or temperature, and soldered joints and other kinds of electrical connections can also degrade or fail over time, for example due to shock, vibration, galvanic corrosion, etc. Some low-cost class X2 mains filter capacitors fully compliant with the relevant IEC standard lose 10% of their value for every 1000 hours of operation!

The result is that filter and shield resonant frequencies will change over time and so can cause gain (or at least, insufficient attenuation) in the frequency ranges where significant EM threats can occur in the EM environment.

Using two or more different types of filters or shields in a redundant combination makes it possible to mitigate the effects of such resonance shifts, but interactions between the multiple filters or shields adds additional possibilities for resonances to arise, which must also be dealt with. Taking all these foreseeable issues into account soon makes design intractable.

The IET's new guide (IET 2013) avoids this whole problem, by making it practical to deal with most/all the effects of EMI by hardware and software techniques and measures, so that special EMC expertise is very rarely needed.

6 Practical difficulties with verifying and validating the SIL of an EMC design

(Armstrong 2004, Armstrong 2009, Radasky et al. 2009, Armstrong 2010 and Armstrong 2012a) show that any affordable immunity test plan is unlikely, on its own, to provide sufficient confidence in design verification or validation, even for SIL1, for reasons far too numerous to list here.

(Grommes and Armstrong 2011, Armstrong 2012b) discuss ways of extending the 'coverage' of immunity tests, perhaps even to the point of being able to prove compliance with SIL1, for new equipment assembled correctly with nominal components. But such testing would still leave uncontrolled the important EMC issues of component tolerances, degradations, bad batches and counterfeits, assembly errors, ageing, corrosion, foreseeable faults, use and misuse, etc.

IEC 61508 has always understood that very few aspects of a functional safety design can be completely verified or validated for compliance with the specified SIL by using testing techniques alone, and this applies to testing EM immunity just as much as it does to testing software for bugs.

To achieve design verification/validation with the confidence levels required by the SILs, IEC TS 61000-1-2, IEC 61508 and (IET 2008) specify the use of a wide variety of design assessment techniques and measures, including, for example:

- demonstrations
- checklists
- inspections
- expert reviews and assessments
- audits
- 'walk-throughs'
- validated computer modelling, simulation, etc.
- testing (which cannot be sufficient on its own).

The new IET guidance avoids this whole problem area, by moving most of the EMI risk management issues to the choice of appropriate hardware and software design techniques and measures, in which most independent functional safety assessors have developed considerable expertise since IEC 61508 was first published in 2000, if not earlier.

7 The 'T&M' solution to the above practical difficulties

Hardware and software design techniques and measures have been developed over at least two decades specifically to deal with all reasonably foreseeable degradations and faults, as well as software bugs. These were never intended to deal with EMI, and yet many of them are very good at doing just this and the new IET guidance extends their application specifically to cover all of the errors, temporary/intermittent malfunctions and permanent failures that could be caused by EMI.

Depending on the thoroughness with which the new IET guide's techniques and measures are applied, the confidence that a design will withstand EMI can be increased to whatever extent is required to achieve the required SIL.

The key issue in understanding the approach in (IET 2013) is that the effect of EMI on electronic hardware and software is always a degradation of, or temporary or permanent damage to, signal/data integrity (SI) and/or to power integrity (PI). SI and PI degradations and failures can always be dealt with by applying appropriate techniques (including error detection and/or correction) in the design of the hardware, software and DC power supplies.

Where equipment has a 'safe state' (e.g. powered down), error detection techniques and measures can be used to control putting it into that safe state (e.g. by switching it off, in some applications) whenever they detect an error, malfunction or failure.

Where there is no safe state, error correction techniques can be used to restore the correct signals, data processing and power rails, so that the equipment continues to work as intended by its designers. In some circumstances where continuous full-specification operation is necessary, EMC expertise in preventing permanent damage from overvoltages, overcurrents or excessive power dissipations may be required. Such EMC requirements should be specified by the hardware or software functional safety experts.

Most of the 'design hardening' techniques and measures described in (IET 2013) have been listed in IEC 61508 since 2000, and so are very familiar to the designers of functional safety-related equipment, and their independent assessors. The few techniques and measures not already listed in IEC 61508 are mostly well-established good practices in functional safety engineering, and so are also familiar to designers and their assessors. One or two techniques and measures are completely new, but they should not cause any difficulties for designers or assessors.

The knowledge that permits these well-proven 'hardening' techniques and measures, which are already used for compliance with IEC 61508 and its related standards, to be extended to cover EMI for the specified SIL, is that EMI can cause:

- a nearly infinite variety of degraded, distorted, delayed, altered-priority, false, etc., signals/controls/data at one or more of the system's ports (including the enclosure port)
- plus under/overvoltages, intermittencies, interruptions, noise or even permanent damage on one or more of its signal/control/data lines and DC power rails
- any/all of the above occurring simultaneously or in any time-sequence.

What this means in practice is that the new IET guide's hardware and software techniques and measures will generally need to be applied more rigorously than has been typical for the regular techniques and measures listed in IEC 61508.

8 The great importance of 'availability'

The author has been told of a (SIL4) railway signalling system that was designed without any EM mitigation. It had a safe state: when its signal was at red, a train on that line may not proceed beyond that signal. Whatever errors, malfunctions or failures arose in its electronic hardware or software, for whatever reasons (including EMI) its signals always failed to red, which the rail industry calls a 'right-side failure' (RSF).

However, when the system was deployed on an actual railway, at least once a minute on average EMI caused by its normal EM environment would make it fail to its safe state (red light, RSF) – and no trains could run. The signalling system was perfectly safe – unfortunately it made the railway inoperable by stopping all of the trains, all of the time!

Equipment that 'fails safe' too often can be expected to suffer unauthorized modifications to reduce its downtime, for example by disconnection of its safety-related systems, in an attempt to improve availability and improve productivity. Manufacturers who fail to take this into account are at increased risk of liability under European product liability legislation, at least.

Because low-enough levels of downtime are necessary, (IET 2013) recommends passing tests to the relevant emissions and immunity standards for the normal EM environment expected for its application. These standards may be those required for compliance with the EMC directive, or they may be customer-specified EMC standards (typical of military, underground railway, and automotive applications, for example).

This is, of course, what is already done at the moment – except that this level of EMC performance needs to be maintained over the entire lifecycle.

To ensure that equipment continues to be compliant with its relevant EMC standards over its lifecycle, some manufacturers take equipment that complies with its usual EMC emissions and immunity test standards, artificially age it using well-established acceleration techniques, and then retest the aged units to check that they still comply with those EMC standards.

Another approach, sometimes used in large installations or costly military vehicles, is to inspect and/or test all of the EM mitigation measures at regular intervals during their lifecycles, refurbishing or replacing anything that is found to have degraded significantly or is close to its individual, planned, end-of-life. (There is at least one manufacturer of equipment designed for in-situ testing of filters and surge suppressors to see if they have degraded unacceptably and need replacing.)

Although it was said earlier that passing tests to the relevant emissions and immunity standards for the application and its normal EM environment is what is already done at the moment, this is not quite correct. For example, most EM environments now contain close-proximity radio transmitters, such as cellphones, datacommunications that use the cellphone networks (e.g. M2M (Wikipedia, M2M)), Bluetooth earpieces, Wi-Fi, etc. but the normal immunity test standards do not cover this situation.

Indeed many modern work environments (including healthcare) actually now rely on the close proximity of radio transmitters! Testing using the usual far-field RF immunity tests such as IEC 61000-4-3 cannot simulate close-field RF transmitters, so – where close-proximity radio transmitters cannot be reliably kept away from the safety-related system – it should comply with IEC 61000-4-39 (IEC future), see Figure 4.

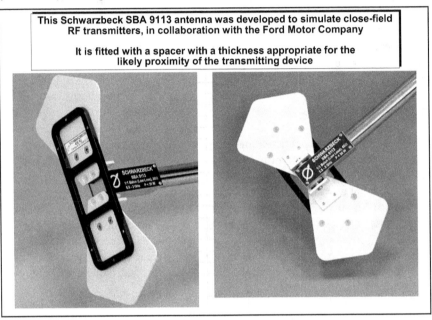

This Schwarzbeck SBA 9113 antenna was developed to simulate close-field RF transmitters, in collaboration with the Ford Motor Company

It is fitted with a spacer with a thickness appropriate for the likely proximity of the transmitting device

Fig. 4. The antenna used when testing to (IEC future) for close-proximity radio transmitters

Locations that are exposed to radar pulses from airports, harbours, military airbases, naval bases, weather radars, etc., might need to apply the immunity test (Ford Motor Company 2009).

In general, for reasons of maintaining appropriate levels of availability, wherever an EM environment suffers from significant levels of EM disturbances that might cause unacceptable downtime when the EMI they cause triggers the operation of a safety-related system, safety-related systems should be designed and tested to ensure that they comply with the relevant immunity test standards over their lifecycles.

9 Conclusions

Previous guidance in IEC TS 61000-1-2 and (IET 2008) on managing functional safety risks assumed the use of very high levels of EMC expertise to accurately determine worst-case EM environments, and to improve the effectiveness of EMC design by between 100 and 100,000 times more than is normally achieved – over the entire lifetime of an equipment, not just when it is new.

The lack of such EMC expertise, and the apparent lack of any interest in obtaining such EMC expertise, plus the many practical difficulties associated with this EMC-engineering-based approach, are currently preventing EMI from being taken fully into account in functional safety-related systems (unless they are using the 'big grey box' approach).

Indeed, it seems very unlikely that the approach assumed by IEC TS 61000-1-2 and (IET 2008) could ever be made to work in practice, even if the assumed EMC expertise magically became available.

For these reasons, the latest guidance from the IET's working group on EMC for functional safety (IET 2013) avoids any need to develop or employ greater EMC expertise than is necessary to ensure compliance with the relevant emissions and immunity test standards over the lifecycle.

It does this by moving part of the work onto the existing base of experienced hardware and software functional safety designers, and their experienced independent functional safety assessors.

(IET 2013) makes it practical and cost-effective for this community of designers and assessors to manage functional safety risks as regards EMI, by extending the use of their existing, well-proven and well-understood 'design hardening' techniques and measures in both hardware and software.

The effects of EM disturbances that exceed what can be coped with by compliance with the relevant immunity test standards will be detected by the hardware and software techniques and measures and appropriate actions taken to maintain the functional safety risks at acceptable levels, according to the safety case.

References

Armstrong K (2004) Why EMC immunity testing is inadequate for functional safety. IEEE International EMC Symposium, Santa Clara, CA, Aug. 9-13
Armstrong K (2009) Why increasing immunity test levels is not sufficient for high-reliability and critical equipment. IEEE 2009 International EMC Symposium, Austin, TX, August 17-21
Armstrong K (2010) Including EMC in risk assessments. IEEE 2010 International EMC Symposium, July 25-30, Fort Lauderdale, FL
Armstrong K (2012a) Including EMI in functional safety risk assessments. In: Dale C, Anderson T (eds) Achieving systems safety. Springer
Armstrong K (2012b),Testing for immunity to simultaneous disturbances and similar issues for risk managing EMC. IEEE International EMC Symposium, Pittsburgh, PA, August 5-10
Ford Motor Company (2009) RI 114 RF Immunity 400MHz – 3,100MHz, in EMC-CS-2009.1 EMC Specification for electrical/electronic components and subsystems. Many EMC test labs around the world are equipped for, and familiar with doing this 'radar' test. http://www.fordemc.com/docs/download/EMC_CS_2009rev1.pdf. Accessed 3 October 2013
Fyfe M, Dobell G (2013) Outcry on safety forces VW recall. The Age, Sydney, Australia. http://www.theage.com.au/drive/motor-news/outcry-on-safety-forces-vw-recall-20130611-2o28i.html. Accessed 3 October 2013
Grommes W, Armstrong K (2011) Developing immunity testing to cover intermodulation. IEEE International EMC Symposium, Long Beach, CA, August 15-19

50   Keith Armstrong

IEC (various) IEC 61000-4-x Electromagnetic compatibility (EMC) – Part 4: Testing and measurement techniques. There are many parts in this series, with different publication dates

IEC (2008) IEC TS 61000-1-2, Ed.2.0, 2008-11, Electromagnetic compatibility (EMC) – Part 1-2: General – Methodology for the achievement of the functional safety of electrical and electronic equipment with regard to electromagnetic phenomena. IEC basic safety publication

IEC (2010) IEC 61508 Ed.2:2010, Functional safety of electrical/electronic/programmable electronic safety-related systems. IEC basic safety publication, in seven parts

IEC (2011) IEC 61000-2-5 Ed.2:2011, Electromagnetic compatibility (EMC) – Part 2-5: Environment – Description and classification of electromagnetic environments

IEC (future) IEC 61000-4-39 Measuring methods for radiation sources in close proximity, immunity to radiated fields in close proximity, 9kHz to 6GHz. At the moment the closest to this standard is ISO 11452-9.2 Road vehicles – Component test methods for electrical disturbances from narrowband radiated electromagnetic energy – Part 9: Portable transmitters. This is in turn based upon the Ford Motor Company's Test Method RI 115 RF Immunity to hand portable transmitters in their EMC-CS-2009.1 EMC specification for electrical/electronic components and subsystems. http://www.fordemc.com/docs/download/EMC_CS_2009rev1.pdf. Accessed 3 October 2013

IET (2008), EMC for functional safety. Edition 1. http://www.theiet.org/factfiles/emc/emc-factfile.cfm or http://www.emcacademy.org/books.asp. Accessed 3 October 2013

IET (2013) Overview of techniques and measures related to EMC and functional safety. http://www.theiet.org/factfiles/emc/emc-overview.cfm. Accessed 3 October 2013

Radasky WR, Delaballe J, Armstrong K (2009) 7b) Testing EM for Safety. Part of the Workshop on EMC & Functional Safety, IEEE 2009 International Symposium on Product Safety, October 26-28, Toronto, Canada

Wikipedia (M2M) Machine-to-Machine communications. http://en.wikipedia.org/wiki/Machine_to_machine. Accessed 3 October 2013

Stopping Data causing Harm: towards Standardisation

Mike Parsons and Paul Hampton

CGI UK

London, UK

Abstract It is increasingly clear that data, not just systems and software, can be a safety problem and the SCSC has recently promoted efforts to look at the issue of data in safety systems. This started with a seminar *'How to stop data causing harm'* held in December 2012 and has progressed with 6-weekly meetings of a working group during 2013. The group, comprising industry, academic, government and independent consultants is producing a guidance document, entitled *'Guidance for management of data where safety is an issue: managing the risks of dataware in safety-related and safety-critical systems'*. The objective of the guidance is to describe the safety data problem, and initially, for key data types and lifecycles, provide methods for defining the level of risk and recommended strategies for safety risk reduction. This paper presents the progress in developing this guidance, and provides an outline of the next phase of this work, which will include production of supplementary material for incorporation into existing safety standards.

1 Introduction

1.1 Background

System safety depends not only on the hardware and software comprising a system, but also on the data within it and in its environment. This data takes many forms: it might be for the application, e.g. patient medical records in a hospital; about the system itself, e.g. configuration data for a satellite navigation system; or about users of the system, e.g. operator competence data in a nuclear power plant.

Incorrect data could clearly have serious safety consequences for the people or other systems using it. Data could become hazardous in many ways, for instance it could be corrupted, lost, not in the right place, or out-of-date. In many cases the implications of the data being wrong are the same as for serious system failure.

Current safety standards and regulations focus strongly on systems, hardware and software development with data aspects poorly covered. Yet, increasingly, data is at the heart of the system, and, therefore, at least as important as the hardware and software used to store and manipulate it. A new approach is needed, together with standards and guidelines, to ensure that safety data is created, maintained, used and protected appropriately.

Data has to be seen as a 'first-class citizen', i.e. data has its own risks, and it can become an asset or liability for the organisation. There is a need to justify the safe handling of the data in the safety case in the same way as the hardware and software comprising a system. If we cannot be sure that the data (in its many forms) is generated, stored, manipulated, distributed and destroyed safely, then all of the other aspects of the safety case could be undermined.

A task to produce guidance material on managing the safety risk of data was therefore taken on by a working group of the UK Safety Critical Systems Club (SCSC). A series of collaborative meetings were held during 2013 and this document presents the consensus position of the group at the end of October 2013.

This work aims to provide guidance for eventual incorporation into existing safety standards. This may take some time, so the initial work is focused on production of a separate guidance note. How this note fits with each standard is an activity planned for 2014.

1.2 Origins

Back in December 2012 the SCSC held a seminar in London entitled '*How to stop data causing harm*', bringing a variety of speakers to talk specifically about *data as a source of safety risk*. Up to this point, although safety risks from data had been considered by several authors for some years (Storey and Faulkner 2003a, Faulkner 2004, Knight et al. 2004), this work had generally taken a low profile.

At the seminar, significant and cross-sector interest was expressed by the attendees, and it was thought that the time was right for a wider initiative to look at the effects of data on safety and improve the awareness and management of risks that it poses.

One of the authors asked for volunteers to join a working group and the SCSC agreed to sponsor the activity. The SCSC Data Safety Initiative Working Group (DSIWG) was subsequently formed.

The first kick-off meeting held at CGI, Kings Place, London in January 2013 was well attended and remarkably productive. At this meeting the following aim was agreed:

> to have clear guidance on how data (as distinct from software and hardware) should be managed in a safety-related context, which will reflect emerging best practice

and the following objectives for 2013:

- Produce cross-sector guidance by the end of the year including a clear statement on handling of data as a separate component within safety related systems.
- Produce a high level strategic plan by the end of the year for fuller adoption, e.g. into existing standards or a new standard.
- Influence standard updates currently in progress where we can.
- Actively promote and disseminate objectives and outcomes of the initiative to the wider community, professional bodies, etc.

The intended audience of the guidance document was agreed as:

- developers of systems involving data where the system stores, processes or distributes data which has safety aspects
- users or operators of systems involving safety-related data
- managers of businesses or organisations dependent on safety data
- assurers of safety data
- regulators of sectors where data can have safety implications.

An overall roadmap for the data safety activity was derived later and is shown in Figure 1.

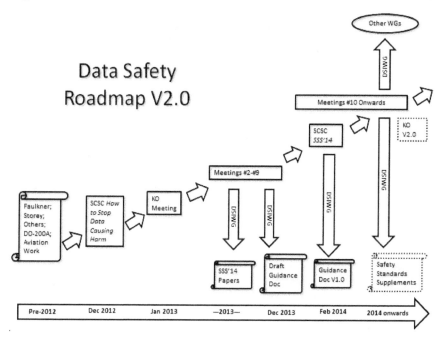

Fig.1. Data safety roadmap

The first issue of the guidance note will be available at SSS '14.

1.3 DSIWG meetings

At the date of writing, eight meetings have been held at a variety of locations. Representation has been from commercial companies, independent consultants, academic and industry bodies and the following sectors have been represented:

- defence
- pharmaceuticals
- rail
- aviation
- air traffic control
- nuclear power
- hydrographical charts
- aero engines
- health
- government
- space
- satellite navigation
- energy and utilities.

Three more meetings are currently planned running into March 2014.

The mailing list for the data safety activity now has over 50 members. More are always welcome – contact either of the authors[1] if you are interested in joining.

1.4 Literature

Several authors, in particular Neil Storey and Alastair Faulkner, have been active in this field for some years, producing informative papers (Faulkner et al 2000, Storey and Faulkner 2001, Storey and Faulkner 2003b, Faulkner 2004, Knight et al. 2004, Inge 2011). They have proposed over the years that data itself should be subject to hazard and risk assessment and intuitively this appears correct: instead of focusing primarily on the software or hardware of a system we should also include consideration of the data and its usage.

One of the few standards that has specific guidance on data is DO 200A (RTCA 1998), which is concerned with aeronautical data. This identifies a number of aspects of data quality including accuracy, resolution, confidence, traceability, timeliness, completeness, and format of the data. It also proposes a concept of data processing assurance level related to the Data Integrity Level (DIL) scheme proposed later. Work has also been conducted in the nautical navigational field which is highly relevant.

---

[1] mike.parsons@cgi.com or paul.hampton@cgi.com

2 The problem

2.1 The change in safety systems

Safety-related systems are becoming more data-intensive or data-centric, often using large and complex data sets. In addition there are many more safety-related systems that are constructed using generic Commercial Off-The-Shelf (COTS) products, not developed to any formal assurance or integrity level, and whose criticality is *inherent in the data* rather than in a directly controlling function. These typically make use of commercial database products.

These new data-intensive systems are often used as decision support or advisory systems in a safety context, where there is an experienced operator who, in theory, is able to detect and correct data problems. However, data is now so complex and of such a large volume it is becoming increasingly unlikely that a user would spot the data errors, and unreasonable to expect them to do so.

A current example is in the medical field, where the amount and complexity of medical data stored for a patient in a major hospital is increasing to form a 'data explosion': there is no way a busy clinician could be expected to spot subtle and yet critical data errors, for instance a believably corrupt value in a diagnostic test result.

There are industry trends which make this initiative very timely: the push for 'big data' systems means that safety data will be used in more and varied ways, and as part of very large *aggregated* databases, often via web services.

Increasing use of systems of systems technology means that data systems are becoming more and more connected using data from a variety of disparate, distributed sources. This means that mapping and translation of data between diverse systems becomes an issue, as well as dealing with data conflicts across multiple systems. The usage of the data is hard to predict in some of these applications; there is also a danger that the safety aspects of the data will become lost due to the nature and scale of these systems.

There is also a big push towards much more distributed access to data, e.g. via mobile devices and the internet of things, which means that it is much harder to establish the overall data integrity picture.

Many organisations are becoming highly *data-dependent*: if their data is incorrect or unavailable then the organisation cannot function sensibly. This is particularly pertinent to the case for users of safety-related data, where lack of availability may lead to increased risk of harm. Also, this dependency increases over time due to the emergence of a 'safety dependency gap' (Hampton 2012), a slow but increasing gap between the integrity of the safety data and the ambitions for its use.

2.2 Current guidance situation

In most safety-related industry sectors there are extant formal safety standards and guides for development of systems, with supporting materials to assist in their application (IEC 2010, MOD 2007, RTCA 1992). This approach is well established and focuses on demonstrably assured techniques for both production and verification, e.g. detailed requirements-based testing. There is remarkably little guidance available for data; although some more recent revisions of standards, e.g. (IEC 2010) do make reference to the data problem, they offer few solutions or guidance on how to manage the risk.

2.3 Data risks

There are several attributes of data that can lead to safety risks. These include:

Correctness. The data has to be correct to be safe. Corruption can cause the most severe types of safety risk, especially when the changes are believable: if corrupt data is used as valid data the consequences could be severe. Examples might be: corrupted ID leading to maintenance of the wrong railway asset, or a corrupt allergy coded on a patient record leading to administering a drug with a severe reaction, etc.

Completeness. Data has to be complete to be safe. If data is completely lost or deleted then this presents a significant safety issue, especially if the loss is silent or undetectable. Examples might be: criminal record entry lost from vetting and barring list, leading to inappropriate appointment into a child minding or teaching post.

Availability. Data has to be available and usable to be safe. Data which is not available when needed presents the same issues as data which is missing; at the very least this could cause operational difficulties and may lead to cancellations or delays with safety impact (e.g. hospital cancer treatments).

Currency. Data has to be current to be safe. Use of old or out of date data could produce completely incorrect results, with impact similar to believable corruption.

A complete list of data safety characteristics is given later (see Section 4.3).

2.4 Types of safety data

Which types of data are to be covered by this guidance? The field is potentially large, with many types of data influencing the final operation of any system. For the first version of the guidance document we have decided to focus on the subset shown in Table 1[2].

Table 1. Initial set of safety-related data types

Data type	Description
Verification	Data used to test and analyse the system
Configuration	Data used to configure, tailor or instantiate the system
Application	Data used in the system during live operations that has end-user meaning
Operational	Data collected or produced about the system during trials, pre-operational phases and live operations
Justification	Data used to justify the safety position of the system, e.g. in a safety case report

The full list (for future consideration) is outlined in Table 2.

Table 2. Full set of safety-related data types

Data type	Description	Explanation	Typical containers
Prediction	Data used to model or predict behaviours and performance	Data for studies, models, prototypes, initial risk assessments, etc. This is the data produced during the initial concept phase which subsequently flows into further development phases	Prototype results, evaluations, analyses, etc.
Assumption	Data used to frame the development or operations, or provide context	Restrictions, risk criteria, usage scenarios, etc. explaining how the system will be used and any limitations of use	Concept of operations document, system safety requirements document
Requirements	Data used to specify what the system has to do	Data encompassing requirements, specifications, internal interface or control definitions, data formats, etc.	Formal specifications, Interface Control Documents (ICDs), user requirements documents
Interface	Data used to enable interfaces between systems: for operations, initialisation or export from the system	Data that exists to enable exchange between systems. Covers start-of-life operations (data import or migration), end-of-life operations and ongoing operational exchange of data between systems.	Protocols, interface spec, schemas, ICDs, transition plans, extract, transform and load tool specs, cleansing and filtering rules

---

[2] Note that system here is used in a generic sense: it could be an IT system, manual data system or a mixture of both.

Data type	Description	Explanation	Typical containers
Design and development	Data produced during development and implementation	This is data encompassing the design and development process artefacts: everything from design models and schemas to document review records. It also includes test documents (specification and results) but not the test data itself.	Design documents, review records, hardware, software and design, test scripts, code inspection reports, etc.
Verification	Data used to test and analyse the system	This is data comprising the test values and test data sets used to verify the system. It may include real data, modified real data or synthetic data. It includes data used to drive stubs, and any data files used by simulators or emulators.	Test data sets, stub data, emulator and simulator files
Configuration	Data used to configure, tailor or instantiate the system	Data used to set up and configure the system to perform a particular function, for a particular installation, product configuration, behaviour or usage	Configuration files, initialisation files, hardware pin settings, network addresses, passwords, etc.
Application	Data used in the system during operations	This is the data processed or produced by the system which has end-user meaning. It may be displayed and used within the system or may be for transfer or distribution to other systems or downstream users. It is data that has some real 'application' meaning, i.e. it is not to do with the system internals.	May be stored internally within the system (e.g. in databases or text files), or transferred into or out of the system through interfaces (e.g. Ethernet)
Instructional	Data used to warn, train or instruct users about the system	This is data that explains to users the risks of the systems and gives any mitigations that may be required to be implemented by users, e.g. by process, procedure, workarounds, limitations of use.	Manuals, standard operating procedures, online help, training courses, etc.
Release	Data used to ensure safe operations per release instance	Explanation of particular features or limitations of a release or instance. May include specific time-limited workarounds and caveats for a release.	Release notes, certificates of design, transfer documents

Data type	Description	Explanation	Typical containers
Operational	Data collected or produced by and about the system during trials, pre-operational phases and live operations	Includes fault data and diagnostic data. This may be the results of various phases of introduction and may include trend analysis to look for long-term problems.	Field data, support calls, bug reports, non-conformance reports, data reporting and corrective action system data
Evolution	Data about changes after deployment	This is data that covers enhancements, formal changes, workarounds, and support issues. It also covers data produced by configuration management activities, such as baselines or branch data.	Change requests, modification requests, issue and version data, configuration management system outputs
System	Data about the installed or deployed system and its parts, including maintenance data	Data related to location, condition and maintenance requirements of the system under consideration. This may cover hardware, software and data.	Inventory, asset and maintenance database systems
Justification	Data used to justify the safety position of the system	Data used to explain and make the case for starting or continuing live operations and why they are safe enough. Often passed to external bodies for review.	Safety case report, certification case, regulatory documents, COTS justification file, design justification file
Staffing and training	Data related to staff training, competency, certification and permits	Data which allows staff to perform a function within the wider context of the safety-related system. This may include training records, competency assessments, permits to work, etc.	Human resources records, training certificates, card systems
End of life	Data about how to stop, remove, replace or dispose of the system	This is data covering all activities related to taking the system out of service or mothballing, storage or dormant phases.	Transition, disposal and decommissioning plans
Investigation	Data to support accident or incident investigations	Data collected or produced during an investigation which may be used in formal investigation reports, lessons learnt or prosecutions. This can be source data (e.g. photographs) or may be derived (accident simulations, analyses, etc.).	Accident investigation reports and supporting documents

3 Structure of the guidance document

The structure of the guidance document was agreed early on in the activity. The sections are intended to cover all the main issues of data in a safety context:

1. Background

    –   History
    –   Aims
    –   Intended audience
    –   Current situation
    –   The change in safety systems
    –   Literature
    –   The data-centric picture
    –   Types of data
    –   A way forward
    –   Vision
    –   Roadmap
    –   References

2. Guidance for use
3. Definitions, acronyms and glossary
4. Scope and applicability

    4.1 Coverage
    4.2 Intended audience
    4.3 Indirect and direct control systems
    4.4 Types of safety-related data
    4.5 Relationship between safety and security regulation of data

5. Data Issues

    5.1 Why data safety different – data lifecycle
    5.2 Properties
    5.3 Common data safety issues

        5.3.1 Reuse
        5.3.2 Aggregation
        5.3.3 Ageing
        5.3.4 Confidence
        5.3.5 Storage, archiving and legacy data

6. Risk model

    6.1 Usage scenarios
    6.2 Hazard identification

        –   Function based (top-down)
        –   Data based (bottom-up)

A Wiki is used to hold the working document.

4 Important concepts

At the time of writing the guidance document is still in development, but some work on concepts is worth highlighting.

4.1 DILs and IDILs

Early on it was decided that the concept of a *Data Integrity Level* (DIL) representing the 'level of trust' required in data was a useful one, and DIL has continued as a basis for discussion through the meetings. Four levels of DIL (1-4) have been used, plus a DIL 0 representing no reliance and hence no safety risk.

    The DILs would normally apply to data sets and their associated data properties (see Section 4.3) but it could also be applied at the individual field level on the basis that lower DIL fields within a high DIL dataset would be subject to the same (higher) level of assurance.

It is anticipated that much of the guidance within the document will be parameterized by DIL, similar to existing hardware and software standards. There will likely be a linkage between the existing concepts of SILs, DALs and Software Levels and DILs, for instance to manipulate data at DIL X, a software system should be built to SIL Y.

The concept of *IDIL* (Initial DIL) was used until recently, representing a preliminary assessment of the DIL. However, this has now been replaced with the concept of organisational data risk.

4.2 Organisational data risk

The concept of *Organisational Data Risk* (ODR) evolved from the IDIL, representing a risk level that an organisation holds due to the safety-related data it has responsibility for (e.g. holds or owns). Again, four levels of ODR (ODR 1-4) are defined, plus a zero value. The key idea behind ODR is that the risk is not restricted to harm to people or the environment, other organisational risks such as loss of reputation, fines and liabilities are also included in the composite risk calculation. The ODR assessment form is discussed in Section 4.4.

4.3 Safety data properties

To date some 22 possible properties of safety data have been identified. These are:

- integrity
- resolution
- availability
- non-accessibility / unavailability (i.e. no access intentionally)
- history
- completeness
- currency
- destination
- lifetime
- correctness
- traceability
- fidelity (how well it represents the real world entity)
- format
- timeliness
- priority
- confidence level
- accuracy
- verifiability

- sequencing
- accessibility
- consistency
- disposability.

The concept that all safety-related data has a specific lifetime is likely to be a useful one. Data does become 'stale' and this may cause problems in any system; in a safety-related system it could give rise to safety risk.

4.4 ODR assessment

One of the first concrete outputs from the DSIWG meetings was the ODR assessment form. The aim of this form is to quickly assess the safety risk a particular organisation is exposed to in a specific data usage situation. This could, for instance, be a contractor delivering a system or an organisation making operational use of the system: it takes the view of one organisation only.

The form is intended to be simple and quick to use. The eight questions are answered and then an ODR level is calculated. This has been trialled on two example case studies, but likely needs further calibration. The main use foreseen for this form is in the initial stages of a proposal or a deployment when a rough idea of the risk being taken on is needed.

The first question from the assessment form is shown in Figure 2.

4.5 Dataware framework assessment report

The ODR assessment form is a useful and relatively quick way of assessing the risks associated with data in the organisation. However, once this initial risk is established, a more detailed analysis is required to explore tangible hazards in the use of data[3]. This hazard analysis will then inform a better understanding of key areas of concern (e.g. specific data exchanges or processing in the scope of supply or operational system) and to help set the direction for further in-depth analysis to develop and implement appropriate mitigation strategies.

However, it was felt that there was a need for this initial analysis to be structured in a way that ensured a level of consistency between assessments that would make them easier to produce, review and compare with other safety related supplies and operational systems.

To this end, a document template (Faulkner and Nicholson 2013) has been produced along with several worked examples to demonstrate how the report could

---

[3] The first question from the ODR form is worth noting as it is now proposed as the basis for formally deriving a DIL with answers a) to e) mapping to DIL 0 to DIL 4 respectively.

be implemented. These exercises have shown that the concept is promising but further refinement and calibration is necessary to maximise the value that the report will add.

QUESTION 1 – SEVERITY AND PROXIMITY			
How severe could an accident be that is related to the data? Could it be caused directly by the data?			
This question considers the safety consequence, the proximity and contribution of the data to the accident sequence.			
1a	All currently foreseen uses of the data could not contribute to an accident. The data is not relied upon for safe operation. Negligible environmental impact.	1	☐
1b	A possible use of data could contribute to a minor accident, but only via lengthy and indirect routes. Could lead to minor injury or temporary discomfort for 1 or 2 people. Many other people/systems are involved in checking the data Some aspects of safe operation rely very indirectly on the data. Minor environmental impact only via indirect routes.	2	☐
1c	A use of the data could lead to a significant accident resulting in minor injuries affecting several people or one serious injury. Several other people/systems are involved in checking the data. There is a dependency on the data for safe operation. Environmental impact is possible.	4	☐
1d	A likely use of the data could directly lead to a serious accident resulting in serious injuries affecting a number of people, or a single death. One human or independent check is involved for all data. There is major dependency on the data for safe operation. Major environmental impact possible.	8	☐
1e	An intended use of the data could easily lead to an accident resulting in death for several people. The accident could be caused by the data with little chance of anything else detecting and mitigating data issues. The accident could affect the general public or have wide and could cause catastrophic environmental impact.	16	☐
Justification:			

Fig.2. First question from ODR assessment form

4.6 Terminology and ontology

Early on in the process, it emerged that there are issues and potential pitfalls with terminology that would make it difficult to articulate the data safety problem and the mitigating strategies required to manage the attendant risk. For example, many terms such as 'data integrity' are overloaded in the industry and so a well-defined vocabulary was seen as essential input to formulating the guidance.

A dictionary of terms for the data safety initiative is therefore being maintained that borrows terminology from the hardware and software domains where meaning is unambiguous but takes care in defining overloaded terms precisely for their use in the context of data safety.

As well as a dictionary of terms, the relationship between terms and associated concepts is also key to conveying intended meaning in an unambiguous way. Work has therefore been done in establishing a formal model for the relationship between concepts as shown in Figure 3.

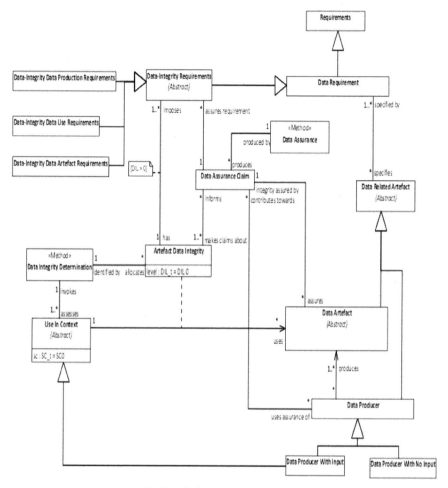

Fig.3. A draft data assurance model

4.7 Mitigations

Historically various methods have been suggested to mitigate the risks due to data. These include: redundancy, formally designing data storage, and structuring data in ways more amenable to checking and correction, all of which appear sensible and pragmatic.

The working group has proposed an initial list of techniques (see Table 3). These techniques now need filtering and mapping to particular DILs.

Table 3. Initial list of techniques

	Techniques
Design and development	BIT/BITE testing (especially for configuration data) Parity bits Checksums Cyclic redundancy checks Hashes Digital signatures Sequence numbers Auditing Logging Encapsulation Authorisations/authentication Tracing (to original sources) Sanity checks Multiple stores Multiple channels Diversity/different technologies Separate implementation teams Comparisons/voting Range checks Expiry dates Confidence levels
Assurance	Review/inspection Sanity check Statistics-based sampling 'Ground truth' check i.e. cross-check with real world Auditing Tracing Frequency of verification Data quality measuring Trend analysis
Verification	Simulation Cross-check
Procedural	Defined data owner Authorisations Responsibilities Process definition Training Competence Client sign-off Data quality correction mechanisms
Paper/environment	Physical environment Lock and key Manual inspection Repair/restoration Preservation Indexing Duplication

	Techniques
Machine media	Storage/handling
	Lock and key
	Physical environment
	Sample restores
	Backups/duplication
	Resilience/redundancy
	Obsolescence-proof
	Re-write of media (especially magnetic)
Usage	Beta testing
	Widespread distribution
	Open source techniques
	Non-critical trialling
	Limited/pre-op deployment

4.8 Lifecycles

Earlier sections have discussed the tools and technique for assessing data risk, establishing the level of assurance required and the range of techniques available to mitigate the risks. Further guidance is also required to link these aspects together to answer two fundamental questions:

1. For a given data lifecycle; whether this be part of, for example, a data supply chain, development or operational lifecycle, at which point in the lifecycle should particular techniques be applied?
2. For a given assurance level and data type, what assurance techniques are recommended to reduce the safety data risk?

To provide an answer to the first of these questions, the group is working to develop high level 'model' lifecycles that will reflect the typical processes in play for the vast majority of real life implementations across all domains. The intention is not to produce models that cover all potential circumstances exactly, but that are sufficiently detailed, relevant and meaningful to clearly inform the reader as to when in their specific lifecycle a particular data type is important, and hence when assurance techniques should be applied.

Figure 4 shows an example of a typical operational lifecycle and illustrates the points in the lifecycle when assurance activities should occur for a given data type.

4.9 Assurance recommendation tables

To address the second of the questions posed, the group is developing a set of tables that will provide, for each lifecycle and data type, recommendations for the assurance technique appropriate at each DIL level. This is a similar approach to that adopted in other established safety standards, and so it is hoped these will make the guidance easier to understand and apply. Figure 5 shows an example of a table currently in development.

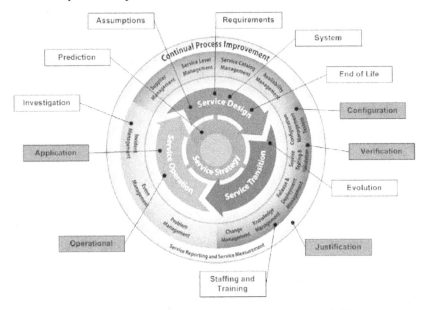

Fig. 4. Assurance activity touch points for a typical operational lifecycle

Methods and Approaches – System Design					
Technique	DIL 1	DIL 2	DIL 3	DIL 4	Notes
Built-in-Test (BIT/BITE)	-	R	HR	HR	On data
Cyclic / Continuous BIT	-	-	R	HR	On data
Parity Checks	R	R	HR	HR	Within data
Checksums / CRCs / Hashes	-	R	HR	HR	On data
Digital Signatures	-	R	HR	HR	On data
Sequence Numbers	R	R	HR	HR	On data
Auditing Facilities		R	HR	HR	To show data changes
Logging Facilities	R	R	HR	HR	To show data changes
Encapsulation	R	R	HR	HR	Of data
Multiple Stores	-	-	R	HR	Of data
Multiple Channels	-	-	R	HR	Of data processing
Diverse Technologies	-	-	R	R	Of data processing
Independent Processing	-	-	R	HR	Of data
Comparisons / Voting	-	-	R	R	Of data
Range Checks	R	R	HR	HR	On data
Expiry Date Checks	R	R	HR	HR	On data

Fig. 5. Recommended techniques by DIL

The guidance will not mandate a particular technique but will provide recommendations on how appropriate the technique is for reducing risks for the given DIL.

The expectation is that the guidance will be refined over time and come to reflect industry best practice.

5 Conclusions

From the work the group has done to date we can begin to see the shape of the toolset of components required to manage data safety risk, as we now have:

- a language, dictionary and ontology for articulating ideas and concepts across different sectors in an unambiguous way (Section 4.6)
- techniques for quickly assessing the organisational risk of data, so that an organisation can understand its risk exposure, and to inform and justify further activities (Section 4.4)
- a framework for conducting a more detailed analysis exploring tangible hazards in the use of data in a structure that aids review and comparison between systems (Section 4.5)
- a classification scheme for assessing and categorising the criticality of data and its properties (Sections 4.1 and 4.3)
- models of different data lifecycles and guidance on when assurance techniques should typically be applied for a given data type (Section 4.8)
- recommendations for assurance techniques to be applied for a given data type and data integrity level (Section 4.9).

The data safety work is therefore progressing well with a high degree of motivation and conviction. Data is clearly an issue in safety systems and it has been largely ignored to date by existing safety standards; guidance on assessing data risk and management of the risk is needed. The DSIWG is on track to produce a draft guidance document by the end of 2013 and launch the first issue at SSS '14 in February.

6 Future work

It is anticipated that the bulk of the work in 2014 will be in the following areas:

1. dissemination of the initial guidance into the wider safety world, in particular influencing revisions of existing standards to ensure data is properly considered
2. production of V2.0 of the guidance document, covering additional data areas.

Acknowledgments   The authors acknowledge all the hard work of the DSIWG members for giving up their time and participating in the meetings, and also the organisations that have generously hosted the meetings. The authors would also like to thank Brian Jepson for creating and maintaining the DSIWG working group site within the SCSC website.

References

Faulkner A (2004) Data integrity – an often-ignored aspect of safety systems. EngD thesis. http://wrap.warwick.ac.uk/1212/. Accessed 11 October 2013

Faulkner A, Nicholson M (2013) Data framework report template. http://scsc.org.uk/file/gd/158-002%20Dataware%20Framework%20Report%20v0-01-20.doc. Accessed 11 October 2013

Faulkner AG, Bennett PA, Pierce RH et al (2000) The safety management of data-driven safety-related systems. 19th International Conference on the Reliability, Safety and Security of Critical Computer Application (SAFECOMP). http://www.eng.warwick.ac.uk/~neil/papers/safecomp%202000.pdf. Accessed 11 October 2013

Hampton P (2012) Survey of safety architectural patterns. In: Dale C, Anderson T (eds) Achieving systems safety. Springer

IEC (2010) IEC 61508 Functional safety of electrical/electronic/programmable electronic safety-related systems. Edition 2.0. International Electrotechnical Commission

Inge J (2011) Safe data: recognising the issues. Safety-Critical Systems Club Newsletter 21(1). http://scsc.org.uk/news.html?v=21&n=1&a=b&pap=877. Accessed 11 October 2013

Knight JC, Strunk EA, Greenwell WS et al (2004) Specification and analysis of data for safety-critical systems. 22nd International System Safety Conference, Providence RI. http://www.cs.virginia.edu/~eas9d/papers/issc.04.pdf. Accessed 11 October 2013

MoD (2007) DEF STAN 00-56 Safety management requirements for defence systems. Issue 4. Ministry of Defence

RTCA (1992) RTCA/DO-178B Software considerations in airborne systems and equipment certification

RTCA (1998) DO-200A, Standards for processing aeronautical data. http://www.rtca.org/onlinecart/product.cfm?id=238. Accessed 11 October 2013

Storey N, Faulkner A (2001) The role of data in safety-related systems. Proceedings of the 19th International System Safety Conference, Huntsville AL. http://www.eng.warwick.ac.uk/staff/ns/papers/data-based%20systems%20paper.pdf. Accessed 11 October 2013

Storey N, Faulkner A (2003a) Data – the forgotten system component? Journal of System Safety. http://www.eng.warwick.ac.uk/~neil/papers/forgotten%20component%20paper.pdf.   Accessed 11 October 2013

Storey N, Faulkner A (2003b) The characteristics of data in data-intensive safety-related systems. Lecture Notes in Computer Science 2788:396-409

Accident Sequence Based Method for Combining Safety Standards

Stephen Bromage

MIRA Ltd

Nuneaton, UK

Abstract   With the increase in commercial off-the-shelf components being used to produce complex systems the safety engineer is presented with a variety of standards on which to base a cohesive safety case. Low volume suppliers also do not have the leverage with suppliers to produce high integrity versions of components and sub-systems. Compressed timescales do not allow for reverse engineering to allocate an integrity level. This paper discusses a risk management process based around accident sequencing. This uses event trees as a framework on which to place controls or mitigations conforming to a variety of standards.

1 Introduction

1.1 Background

The safe use of a product can require action from multiple stakeholders. The stakeholders include the supplier of the product, the owner of the product, the user of the product and the controller of the environment where it is used. The legislative framework for safety reflects this.

In the automotive field there is the Road vehicles (Construction and Use) Regulations (HMG 1986b) where statutory requirements incorporated through type approval are placed on the suppliers of vehicles placed on the market and on the drivers or operators of the vehicle. Other parts of the Road Traffic Act (HMG 1991) place further requirements for driver's skills and use of the infrastructure provided. Taken as a whole, these determine the level of safety required on the roads in the UK today.

For work equipment, there is a similar allocation of responsibilities. The supplier has to meet certain obligations such as those in the Supply of Machinery (Safety) Regulations (HMG 2008). The purchaser and the user have to ensure that they have the correct work equipment, e.g. by purchasing CE marked machinery. CE marked machinery on its own is not a guarantee of safety unless the correct machinery for the task is purchased and used in the correct way by appropriately trained personnel, covered by the Provision and Use of Work Equipment Regulations (HMG 1986a). Further regulation under the Health and Safety at Work Act (HMG 1974) then determines the level of safety.

For some products, such as automotive or white goods, the supplier has no control over the use. Only the framework placed on the user controls how the product may be used. Even then, users operating outside of the framework have to be protected against reasonably foreseeable levels of misuse.

In other areas, the user places a full specification on the equipment supplier for a bespoke product, and has control over its use and over the environment in which it is used. For these products a risk based approach can be used. The product may not be intrinsically safe, but is used in such a way that this is mitigated outside of the boundaries of the product. For example, large process plant machinery may be assembled in the plant from multiple suppliers. Each supplier would generally place a guard around moving parts which could compromise its performance in the context of the plant. The plant operator can then operate the plant in a protected and interlocked area thus mitigating the risks normally mitigated by guards.

Two broad types of regulation have grown up around these two approaches: prescriptive and risk based. Until relatively recently, automotive safety was prescriptive with a vehicle being considered to be safe on the road if it passes type approval. Type approval was granted on the basis of the incorporation of some pieces of equipment such as the horn, and the performance of others such as the brakes. With the advent of complex computer based processing now controlling vehicles, standards are now using a risk based approach in the area of functional safety. The recent introduction of ISO 26262 (ISO 2011) for passenger cars (i.e. M1 class vehicles) is a good example. Only some of the type approval requirements require a consideration of functional safety (e.g. brakes and steering), but ISO 26262 now represents the state of the art for any safety-relevant electronic system in a car.

An example of the risk based approach is in the UK MoD's equipment procurement where safety management to Def-Stan 00-56 (MOD 2007) is a requirement placed on the supplier.

Manufacturers of high and medium volume equipment are well served by standards that can be used to assure safe products. However, the overhead imposed by the use of some of the standards is high and without the volume of sales, or an extremely high sales price, is difficult to amortise on low volume or custom products. ISO 26262 is for the M1 class vehicle, which is the type of private vehicle seen in large numbers on the roads, each logging high usage time.

Who can visualise what a failure in 10 million hours on a custom snow plough used twice a year in the British Midlands actually means?

The risk based approach used in Def-Stan 00-56 has changed to now recommend the use of a suitable commercial standard for safety integrity. This has given the product supplier the problem of selecting a standard for a system which may not have a suitable standard.

Even large organisations that in the past have been able to tailor the product to their own requirements seemingly regardless of cost are being economically squeezed. There is a greater pressure to purchase off-the-shelf and modify to meet requirements or for bespoke complex systems to string together multiple off-the-shelf sub-systems. These off-the-shelf components and sub-systems have been developed to standards to meet requirements in their own domain. This is acceptable if the new domain is very similar. However, what if the manufacturer wants to incorporate the off-the-shelf sub-system in a novel way? Does the sub-system certificate of conformity give any guarantee? The manufacturer of a piece of consumer electronics is not going to undertake the tests to show that it is still appropriate in a harsh high performance environment where the failure may involve more than the loss of your phone connection. The purchaser of the item of consumer electronics for use in a one-off system is unlikely to have the time to fully re-qualify the item in its new environment.

1.2 The risk based approach

This paper discusses a method that can be used by the low volume or specialist supplier to assure the safety of their product. It can also be used for the accelerated development of complex systems assembled from off-the-shelf systems. The method is risk based, which enables it to be used when there is an acceptability of risk target that can be defined.

By assessing the risk, comparing it with the acceptability requirement, reducing the risk and testing again to the acceptability requirement, the risk can be iteratively reduced until the requirement is satisfied.

The risk based approach is particularly useful when there is influence over the user through health and safety methods and over the equipment using product safety methods. The supplier of machinery to a closed environment such as a factory or a process plant has some assurance that the user will use the equipment in a certain way and the environment is suitable for its use. The supplier of white goods to the home has no such assurance.

1.3 Introduction to the method

The risk-based approach is usable when combining prescriptive requirements with standards based on risk assessment. An example of this can be found in the Supply of Machinery (Safety) Regulations. Under the essential health and safety requirements of the regulations, there is a requirement for provision of an emergency stopping device. However, the control system for such machinery may be based on a standard with a safety integrity based approach. By applying the safety integrity level (SIL), the machine may be controlled sufficiently reliably to not need an emergency stop. To see how the empirical approach of applying an emergency stop to all machinery combines with the analytical approach of a SIL controlling the failure rate, the system can be modelled in an event tree as an accident sequence.

The method combines integrities from multiple standards with layers of protection within an event tree or accident sequence framework.

2 Standards

The standards applicable to product design and use can be viewed within a legislative framework. An example for the UK market is shown in Figure 1.

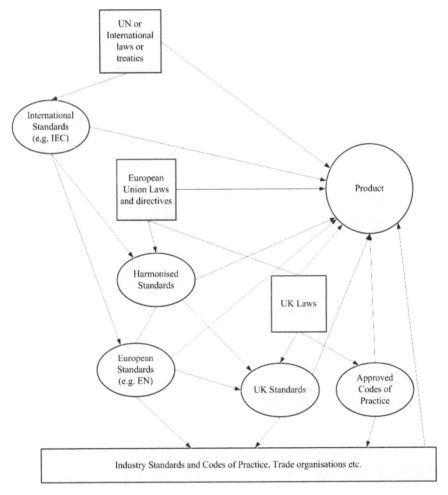

Fig. 1. Legislative and standards framework for a product

In low volume or custom equipment, there is a temptation to use standards out of context. In the absence of a standard for the particular product, this may represent good guidance, but may also give a false sense of security. For example, an off-road vehicle type-approved for use on the road is acceptable on the road because all of the type approval testing carried out. Taking a type approved vehicle into a different arena may negate some of the thinking behind those type approval tests. Such vehicles have been used for transport in mines. Are the type approved lights suitable for that environment? Can the tyres cope with the surface within the mine? Does the dust build-up compromise the performance of the braking system? Does the maintenance advice suit a 24/7 alien working environment? The type approval testing cannot answer these questions and so more work may be required before the user is confident that the change in use is acceptably safe.

A second issue with standards is the level at which they operate. Standards that are aimed at applying safety at a sub-system level may not give suitable advice at a systems or a system of systems level. Similarly, higher level standards may not offer the level of advice for individual component design. Consequently, standards have to be used together to achieve an appropriate level of safety.

3 Accident Sequence Analysis (ASA)

The accident sequence is the familiar event tree. The event tree for the accident follows the course from causes, through hazards and accidents to consequences. For this discussion, the event tree is taken as being centred on the accident with multiple inputs and consequences, as shown in the bow tie model (Figure 2).

The application of frequencies and probabilities to the event tree and a severity to the consequence enables a risk to be assigned to the accident. The model can be used for two basic measures of risk. For the risk usually assessed in the form of an integrity level, the risk reduction measure is assigned an integrity level and then the product development is to a standard compatible with that level. The integrity level associated with the original risk does not actually reduce as a result of implementing the risk reduction measure. In defence and other areas where the risk is a combination of inherent, functional and environmental, a risk class can be used. In risk reduction, the risk class itself is reduced.

The measure of acceptability is hence different in the two cases:

- For SILs, the product is acceptably safe when the safety development of the product matches the standards imposed by the integrity level, with increasing levels of redundancy, detection and process checking for higher risks.
- For risk classes, the mitigations and controls are applied reducing the risk class until it meets a form of acceptability criteria.

The event tree frequencies may be qualitative or quantitative. When dealing with systems made of Commercial Off-The-Shelf (COTS) and custom units, both may have to be combined.

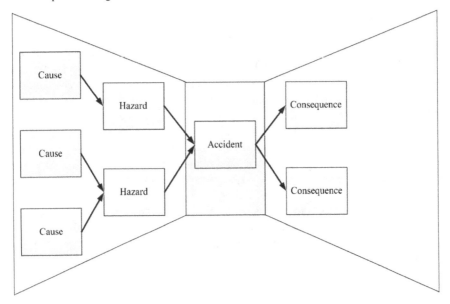

Fig. 2. Bow tie model centred on the accident

The event tree has to be assessed at least twice, once prior to risk reduction and again following risk reduction. Intermediate iterations may be required if trade studies are to be carried out on competing mitigations or to support an ALARP cost-benefit analysis.

Qualitative frequencies are extremely difficult to assess in the lower frequency ranges in that these frequencies are out of the realm of personal experience. Unless there are good statistical data on the events it can be difficult to decide on a frequency to use even within the factor of 10 used to define the bands. However, the causes of hazards, which are often high frequency relative to the harm that occurs in the accident, can usually be allocated a realistic frequency based on the input of suitably qualified and experience personnel. After the hazard, the event tree enables a probability to be applied at each branch in the tree as the accident sequence proceeds, with higher probabilities that can be visualised combining to produce the desired low accident frequency. From this a guidance table can be produced for use in the process. An example of comparative frequencies, based on Def-Stan 00-56 terminology, is given in Table 1.

Thus in a chain of events in an accident sequence, all assessments at each stage can be understood, but combine to create the desired low numbers as in the example that follows:

- Use is frequent (occurs continuously).
- Failure is occasional (1 per annum).
- Hazardous failure as a proportion of all failures is occasional ($P = 0.1$).
- Impact with a person in low a population area is occasional ($P = 0.1$).
- The impact leads to an fatal injury of the person is remote ($P = 0.01$).

Table 1. An example of comparative frequencies

Qualitative term	Description	Frequency (per equipment per annum)	Probability
Frequent	Occurs continuously	50	
Probable	Likely to occur in each equipment each year	5 – 50	1
Occasional	Likely to occur to one equipment each year	0.5 – 5	0.1
Remote	May occur to one equipment within the lifetime of all equipments	0.05 – 0.5	0.01
Improbable	May occur but not likely	0.005 – 0.05	0.001
Incredible	Extremely unlikely to occur	< 0.005	0.0001

From the above events, the frequency of a fatal injury from this hazard is 1 x 0.1 x 0.1 x 0.01 = 0.0001 per annum. This is then translated from the table as incredible and is extremely unlikely to occur.

In this case it was possible to estimate a failure rate, so a probability did not have to be applied to the use figure, but by using the probability throughout the accident it is possible to have a figure for the injury that could not be easily visualised.

One point to be aware of is that too many steps with order of magnitude probability bands may lead to over-optimistic reductions.

By combining the accident sequence with a method of allocating frequencies and probabilities, an event tree can be produced, such as the example shown in Figure 3.

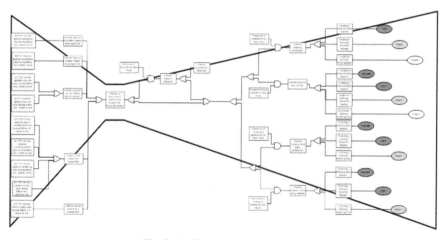

Fig. 3. Accident sequence event tree

In this example, the causes are not shown as they are modelled on fault trees and the frequency information is inserted into the hazardous event and combined with a scenario to produce the hazard at the 'knot' of the bow tie. From the hazard, the tree shows multiple possibilities arising from the hazard culminating in a level of harm. In this example, the level of harm is divided by a severity split as the last stage as the accident could lead to different injuries. At this stage, the event tree can be used to populate a risk class for the accident sequence.

To calculate the risk (severity x frequency) a simple spreadsheet can be used, as shown in Figure 4, although there are suitable dedicated tools available for modelling event trees.

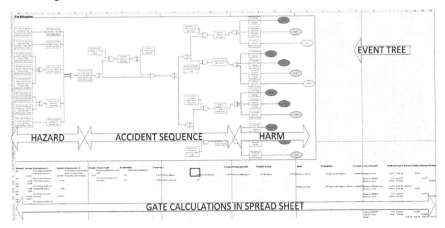

Fig. 4. Accident sequence spreadsheet

If the risk does not meet acceptability criteria after this first pass, further iterations are necessary and additional risk reduction will be required.

4 Risk reduction

The risk reduction process is the heart of the technique in this paper. This process would not be used for designing a single automotive unit for functional safety where the ISO 26262 standard is applied directly. For that, the Automotive Safety Integrity Level (ASIL) would be allocated to the safety requirements and the design process followed through to that level.

The risk reduction process will be illustrated by means of an example. The example is taken from work carried out for the steering function of an autonomous ground vehicle concept.

Autonomous ground vehicles need to take in information from the outside world and convert it into vehicle control actions. This is the role that is normally played by the human driver. At the current stage of development of this type of vehicle, volumes are low with the consequence that any high development costs have to be amortised over few products. There is a commercial incentive to use off-the-shelf equipment developed for similar purposes. For the private car market, many companies have developed steering features such as lane assist, lane keep and parking assist. All of these features monitor conditions and apply varying levels of control input to the steering. It would be attractive to the autonomous ground vehicle manufacturer to be able to fit just one of these systems to their vehicle, with a higher torque output to replace the driver rather than merely assist the driver.

If it is to be sold in the United Kingdom, the vehicle that is fitted with these features would be type approved. As part of the type approval, the manufacturer would analyse the functional safety of the system to ISO 26262 as best practice and applicable to the domain. ISO 26262 safety is based on ASILs to avoid confusion with SILs used in IEC 61508 (IEC 2010) for example. ASILs are classified from A to D, with D representing the highest level of requirements for safety integrity.

A typical hazard associated with malfunction of a simple lane assist device (Figure 5) is likely to be classified ASIL A. The device has no control over the steering but does present feedback to warn the driver of lane departure. This can be achieved visually, audibly or with tactile feedback through the steering wheel. As this does not directly control the steering, it cannot be used for autonomous control, but may provide data input and processing for the autonomous controller.

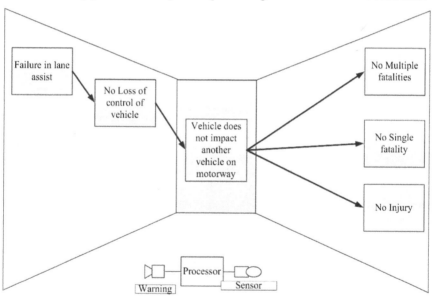

Fig. 5. Lane assist

A lane keep device (Figure 6) provides more control. In this, the steering is driven to encourage the driver to keep in lane. With increased torque, this could be used as a basis for our autonomous vehicle (Figure 7). However, in the event of a failure leading to the system providing an unrequested steering input, the driver can easily overcome the steering torque and bring the vehicle back under control. Such systems usually monitor driver input to ensure that the driver is actively driving and not relying on the steering. There remains a low probability that the driver will not regain control which may lead to a typical hazard associated with the function being classified as ASIL C.

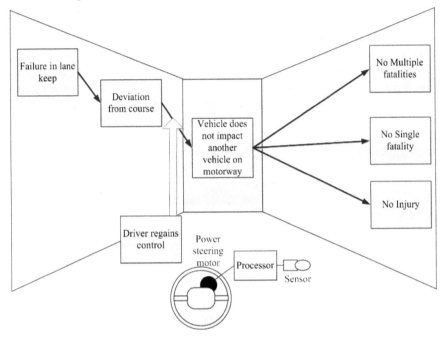

Fig. 6. Lane keep

The autonomous vehicle would not have the benefit of driver input and so could not tolerate the failure leading to the unrequested steering. Without a driver initiated recovery technique, the associated hazard would be classified as ASIL D. Furthermore, societal demands may be less forgiving of an autonomous driver than the human version and even a single unit developed to ASIL D would need to be backed up by additional risk reduction such as large scale redundancy to be acceptable.

Clearly, an off-the-shelf unit developed to implement ASIL C requirement does not meet the risk acceptability criterion of (at least) an ASIL D requirement. Risk reduction is now required.

Risk reduction may be applied at any stage through the accident sequence. Many standards provide risk hierarchies where greater weight is given to reducing the risk at source by removing the cause of the hazard. Where the use of the machine is controlled as well as its product safety, risk can even be controlled post-accident, by providing first aid, for example. This is clearly undesirable as the only risk reduction.

In the autonomous vehicle steering system example, it is preferable to develop the control system to implement ASIL D safety requirements as this is a risk reduction at the cause. This matches the implementation to the requirement. The cost of developing higher integrity control systems rises considerably with the higher integrity, which may make our low volume vehicle uneconomic.

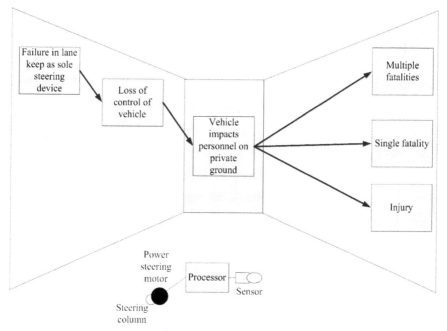

Fig. 7. Lane keep used as the sole autonomous steering device

A useful risk reduction technique is redundancy. By applying a second sensor and processor, as shown in Figure 8, the failure rate at the cause is reduced. Some standards apply a technique of decomposition whereby two sub-systems or components of a lesser integrity can be combined to produce a higher integrity. By using two sub-systems to the same standard, decomposition may be possible.

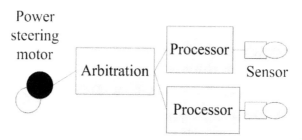

Fig. 8. Redundancy

Two identical processors and sensors provide some improvement as the random failure modes are unlikely to occur at exactly the same time (Figure 9). This does not address the systematic failure modes addressed by the application of the standard to the appropriate ASIL. Therefore, it is preferable to employ two different processors and sensors. It is now less likely that two suitable off the shelf solutions would be found to the same standard. Decomposition of the integrity level cannot now be performed to either of the standards. At this stage, the accident sequence event tree is used.

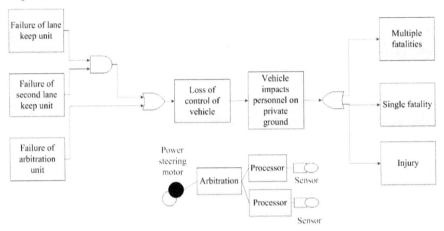

Fig. 9. Redundant system event tree

The failure rate of the first unit is entered into the tree from its ASIL classification. The failure rate of the second unit is entered from, say, manufacturer's information as it is not to a standard. The event tree can now be calculated through to produce a value for the risk, which can be compared with the acceptability value. Also, if the differing control commands are output from the two processors, some form of arbitration is needed. This would take on the ASIL for the function if the design is all to the one standard and would require more development. It is likely to have to incorporate error detection for latent failures. In the accident sequence method, its contribution is modelled directly into the event tree. As it is adding to the failure rate (through the OR gate) and off-setting the gains made through redundancy, it is still likely to require development to a high integrity.

In this case, the accident sequence now enables us to look for risk reduction further along the event tree. Our example now returns to the lane assist system, which is only developed to ASIL A.

The lane assist sensor, already configured for recognizing departures from the route, could be attached, not to a warning system, but to the vehicle's brakes (Figure 10). On its own, this feature is not very practical. The vehicle needs to navigate the lane, not stop every time it attempts to depart from the lane. With correctly set limits outside of the operating limits of the steering system, the secondary system does act as a safety mechanism for when the primary steering device fails.

Now the system has to be tested for acceptability. As this is not integrity decomposition in the normal sense in the standards, the combination of a protection system (brake) developed to implement the safety requirements of ASIL A and a primary control system developed to implement the safety requirements of ASIL C cannot necessarily be interpreted as giving the ASIL required. The secondary system may also be sourced from a different domain and not have its safety integrity specified in a way suitable for combination. Also, as previously stated, the highest integrity level for a human driven vehicle may still be too low for society to accept an autonomous vehicle into service, especially into populated areas. So the system must be tested against the overall acceptability set for the project. This test is carried out in the accident sequence event tree model.

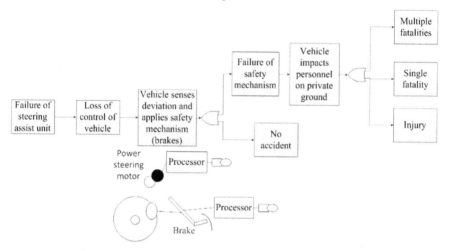

Fig. 10. Primary system with additional layer of protection

The sequence in Figure 4 is now extended to record layers of protection. Figure 11 shows four layers of protection. Each layer contains all of the controls to manage the protective function in that layer. The controls may be for the design of the device, of instructions on use, or for detection of its failures. The sequence aligns the controls with the steps through the event tree at which the control operates. In the steering example, the first layer of controls applies the ASIL to the steering system and is aligned to the beginning of the tree as it reduces the frequency of the cause. The protective function is aligned to the centre of the event tree as it is needed after the hazard but before the accident. The diagram also shows accident controls on the right. In our example, this could be pedestrian impact protection to reduce the severity of the accident in the event of all other controls failing. Some controls, for example a speed limiter for the autonomous vehicle, act throughout the sequence. A lower speed reduces the probability of losing control during uncommanded steering inputs, but also reduces the severity of impact, and gives the other party a better chance of avoidance. It is at the discretion of the safety engineer analysing the sequence how best to use this in the event tree.

The post-mitigation accident risk is now calculated and compared to the acceptability criteria for acceptance or for the initiation of further controls. The frequencies or probabilities for the integrities can be entered directly into the event tree, and any information from descriptive sources converted by a method such as that shown in Table 1. At this stage, the safety engineer must show a lot of care in using the figures from different standards. In using the ASIL for the steering system, the engineer may need to consider usage in the domain of the standard and apply a de-rating factor to the figures used to account for the different conditions in the intended domain of use. Also, as in the individual standards, the safety engineer must be aware of common mode failures to ensure that the layers are truly independent.

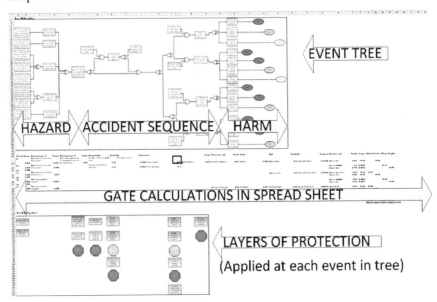

Fig. 11. Accident sequence spreadsheet with layers of protection

This approach is also useful for work in a domain where ALARP is a requirement. The controls are portrayed in a hierarchy of preference (from left to right in Figure 12). The controls can be switched on and off in the spreadsheet to assess the value of each layer of control for a cost-benefit analysis.

5 Conclusion

The use of accident sequence analysis by event tree is a tool that can be used in domains where, due to their novelty or their small market, have not yet attracted standards for their safety. It combines the safety analyses from differing standards where the criteria may not be equivalent by using a common currency of frequency through an event tree. By using the frequency calculated in the event tree with a consequential severity, the risk is assessed. An ALARP or acceptability argument can be then be developed.

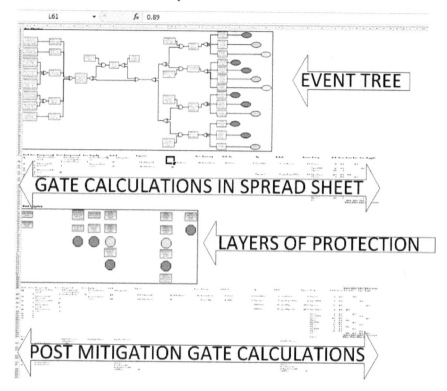

Fig. 12. Final accident sequence spreadsheet

If the argument indicates that the level of safety is not acceptable, safety requirements are applied for risk reduction. The risk reduction can be within the scope of the standard applied to the sub-system to achieve a higher integrity or by providing layers of defence throughout the event tree. It is possible, through layers, to use components designed to standards outside of the product's domain and still be able to assess the effect. In both cases, the risk reduction is modelled on the event tree and the acceptability re-assessed.

References

HMG (1974) Health and Safety at Work Act
HMG (1986a) Provision and Use of Work Equipment Regulations. UK SI 1998 No 2306 plus amendments
HMG (1986b) Road Vehicles (Construction and Use) Regulations. UK SI 1986 No 1078 plus amendments
HMG (1991) Road Traffic Act
HMG (2008) Supply of Machinery (Safety) Regulations. UK SI 2008 No 1597 plus amendments

IEC (2010) IEC 61508 Functional safety of electrical/electronic/programmable electronic safety related systems. International Electrotechnical Commission

ISO (2011) ISO 26262 Road vehicles – functional safety. International Organization for Standardization

MoD (2007) Defence Standard 00-56 Safety management requirements for defence systems. Issue 4

The Strategic Implications of ISO 26262

Donna Champion[1] and Roger Rivett[2]

[1]Loughborough University, Loughborough, UK

[2]Jaguar Land Rover, Gaydon, UK

Abstract   The new functional safety standard for the automotive industry, ISO 26262, emphasises the need for through-life monitoring of system safety for systems and products containing electronic and electrical systems. The information management challenge that this presents for the automotive industry and OEMs in particular, requires a step-change in the way that design and development activities are structured and managed. This paper examines the strategic implications of ISO 26262 for the automotive sector and sets out guidance on the practices and business models that companies should develop to succeed in this new environment. The automotive industry is facing a critical phase and how companies choose to manage their information will be integral to their survival beyond 2020.

1 Introduction

The new automotive functional safety standard: ISO 26262 has been introduced with the aim of setting out best practice for all activities through-life for automotive products with electric, or electronic, safety-related systems. The recent trend in the automotive industry to exploit the use of software for improved performance and functionality means that there is now a need to integrate many hundreds of different software applications and to understand the emerging complex system properties from software and hardware integration on a scale of complexity not previously envisaged. This increased systems complexity and the pressure to deliver products to market in shorter time scales increases the risk of undetected errors and unexpected emergent properties developing once a product is in the field (Sikora et al. 2012). The systems and products being developed, and also the organizational environment where development is taking place, are becoming vastly more complex, and this complexity creates a step change in the level of difficulty in understanding the emerging properties of a system and the potential interactions between systems at both a technical and human level (Bonjour and Micaelli 2010, Ellims et al. 2006).

In the past, the introduction of international standards such as IEC 61508 has resulted in organisational change across the industry. This paper explores the stra-

tegic and managerial challenges that are implicated in the introduction of ISO
26262 (ISO 2011). Most discussions in the automotive industry have focused on
the operational impacts for the engineering process, with some discussion of what
suitable team structures might be needed. These discussions very much reflect the
range of impact of previous safety standards such as IEC 61508. This paper argues
that ISO 26262 will have a much wider impact on automotive OEMs resulting in
the need for significant organisational restructuring.

We first summarise the challenges and impacts that have previously been experienced when new safety related standards have been introduced. We then suggest that future leaders in the automotive industry will need to operate in a similar
way to managers in software companies and set out some of the practices and
business models that companies should consider developing in order to succeed in
this new environment. The automotive industry is facing a critical phase and how
companies choose to manage their information will be integral to their survival
beyond 2020.

2 The managerial challenges in developing functionally safe complex products

Increased systems complexity, along with the pressure to understand integration
issues and manage the associated information, have been some of the main drivers
in the development of a functional safety standard, ISO26262, specifically for the
automotive industry. Traditional approaches to systems design and development
have tended to be based on a component-based view of the systems under development (Boehm and Basili 2001, Champion et al. 2005, Valverde et al. 2011), but
this approach has proved to be inadequate for electrical and electronics systems
controlled by embedded software in complex products. In a component-based
approach, designs are broken down into detailed work units, the aim being to
seamlessly integrate them into a complete product (Beuche et al. 2007; Ellims et
al. 2006). This approach often leads to unforeseen and unexpected relationships
between systems that only become apparent when a design enters the build phase.
Systems that passed verification and validation testing in the design phase can
prove to be difficult to fit together during the build and have unexpected conflicts
with other systems. And issues identified at this stage of the development are notoriously difficult and expensive to fix. For example, unexpected integration issues between software controllers embedded in 'black box' components sourced
globally can lead to expensive changes and reworking of designs further down the
work stream (Valverde et al. 2011). One of the main limitations of the component-
based underpinning of traditional design and development approaches is that such
an approach does not facilitate an integrated and iterative approach to functional
behaviour testing and so can be incompatible with best practice functional safety
life cycle processes (Gil and Tether 2011).

It is recognised across the engineering profession that managing software design and development has unique challenges and leading practice in the avionics and automotive industries has moved towards Model Based Engineering (MBE) design practices. The Object Management Group (OMG 2013) in particular has championed the adoption of model-driven approaches to design in order to improve systems specification and interoperability. The contribution of a Model Driven Architecture (MDA) is that systems can be specified without having to pre-determine how they will be implemented. This means that interoperability between different systems can be achieved by exchanging the metadata and the principles for sharing information between systems. But model based approaches and architectures are still not a complete approach. Models still contain areas of ambiguity and as products, systems and software are now often developed across global supply chains, there is still a need for accompanying textual descriptions and legal contracts. In today's highly complex products, where sensors and control units support multiple systems, it is only once a design is understood from a system and functional perspective that customer features can be safely linked to hardware and software components.

The ISO 26262 functional safety standard defines its reach as being across the entire lifecycle of a product with electrical and electronic systems from conception to disposal, and so by definition, the standard also encompasses all of the organisational processes and structures within an enterprise. Functional safety no longer belongs to specialist teams but impacts on each employee across the automotive supply chain. This means the implementation of ISO 26262 will necessitate a robust, but also more flexible, collaborative approach to knowledge and information sharing across the entire product creation lifecycle. This in turn requires companies to continually improve and facilitate better communication and cross-stream working between different disciplines and experts. In large organizations in particular, this can be a significant challenge.

It is interesting to reflect back on the impact of the implementation of IEC 61508, a general functional safety standard for electrical and electronic systems, not specific to the automotive industry. IEC 61508 was developed as a standard for functional safety for general application across a number of different industries. The IEC define functional safety as being 'the part of the overall safety that depends on a system or equipment operating correctly in response to its inputs'. IEC 61508 sets out the risks and also requirements on how to avoid or detect and control faults in systems with complex electronics. The standard has been enthusiastically and widely adopted and the benefits that have ensued from the publication of IEC 61508 have included better risk analysis and a more requirement driven approach to complex systems design and development. In some industries though, including the automotive industry, the general nature of IEC 61508 has led to some parts of the standard being interpreted differently in different companies and across the supply chain.

3 Learning from the software industry

Most electronic and electrical systems are now programmable and although software design tools and development methods are well embedded in the software industry, such an approach to design and testing is only now gaining acceptance in the automotive industry. The capability to work at the 'information level' of a complex product is still not commonplace in the automotive industry but these skills are becoming more important as customers increasingly expect instant performance upgrades, in a similar way to how their other electronic devices are regularly updated. In the automotive sector, this capability is regarded increasingly as being essential to future survival as autonomous vehicles enter the mainstream, but there is a capability gap and many engineers, project managers and senior managers still do not have the experience or expertise to apply such approaches in their work.

With the publication of ISO26262 what becomes apparent is the lack of guidance for managing communication issues and working practices during complex systems design and development. The only communication issues that have been specifically identified in the academic literature have been associated with prioritization issues and also requirements release activities and most authors in the engineering literature have recommended a 'single-capture process' for requirements management (Boehm 1991, Charette 1989, Egbert and Neve 2001, Keil et al. 1999). In practice, in large manufacturing environments with simultaneous design and development of several product lines, a 'single-capture process' approach to requirements is infeasible. One of the impractical assumptions that is associated with adopting a single-capture requirements process is that it is considered a relatively easy task to assign 'content ownership' of any requirement (Gil and Tether 2011). Identifying content owners for each requirement is, of course, essential, but it is equally important to identify those responsible for communication activities, cross-stream collaboration and feedback mechanisms, and these activities may or may not be undertaken by the 'content owner'. For example, some sensors and electronic control units manage several different systems and so changes in one system can have unpredictable emergent properties across several sub-systems. It is over-simplistic to just decide that the 'sensor owner' has responsibility in such situations, as this person may lack the experience or knowledge necessary to specify all the necessary potential faults. Such activities need to be managed by groups of engineers with sufficient qualifications and experience across a range of systems. Any signing off of such multi-system requirements then needs to be managed by a more senior, suitably qualified and experienced person, often as a collaborative exercise. This hierarchy of management and control in the technical process is rarely considered in the academic literature as it adds an unwelcome layer of complexity.

It is also important to state that project management activities do not address the sorts of technical issues described above. Project managers often have little engineering design experience, and with the increase in complexity in systems and products, such decision points are becoming increasingly frequent. There are of course many 'gateway and evaluation' processes to oversee and manage the design activities across programmes, but these activities are not set up to deal with technical problems in the level of detail and frequency that is becoming required in order to develop safe systems. This increased complexity arises from the vastly increased information set that needs to be considered. One of the implications of the ISO 26262 standard will be that automotive companies will need to adopt practices from IT companies. These skill sets are in very short supply and companies will need to introduce strategies to ensure they keep and grow the capability they need.

4 Organising for ISO 26262

The challenge for those responsible for functional safety within automotive OEMs is how to embed the necessary practices and skills across the organisation. Most OEMs have a need to work towards developing the capability and capacity across the enterprise in order to meet the demands of ISO 26262. There are two common organisational structures for the functional safety process adopted within OEMs.

4.1 Functional safety expertise dispersed in product design teams

The functional safety function can be dispersed across the engineering design teams, with functional safety expertise being embedded within particular specialisms. This approach is often adopted by companies that adopt a programme-centric resource model, with little work being undertaken that cannot be assigned to a specific project. This approach can result in limited interaction across disciplines, across functions and between the engineering and service divisions of an OEM. The lack of communication and of significant cross-functional relationships (as they are not valued) can result in disjointed and inconsistent support for the development of the enterprise-wide approach to functional safety envisaged in the standard. One of the serious drawbacks to this approach is that programme managers can be reluctant to fund work to embed feedback lessons into future design as they will be working to a budget. This can condemn the organisation to repeat failure states and to experience recurring defects. These problems can be mitigated somewhat with the introduction of a fully recognised governance structure for functional safety that is supported by the senior management. Achieving the proper resourcing for training and development to build functional safety capability and resource is better achieved via a central funding mechanism.

4.2. A functional safety team independent of product design teams

An alternative organisational structure for functional safety management across the enterprise is to create a cross-discipline with a management structure that is independent of a specific discipline group. New organisational structures often shift the power balance in an enterprise, most notably amongst the senior team and so this can be an unpopular approach. However, if such a team is created, the lines of responsibility and communication are less ambiguous so this approach can ensure a more co-ordinated and structured approach to functional safety from concept through design, manufacture, service and end of life processes.

Regardless of the structural arrangements for overseeing functional safety across an enterprise, the current scarcity of functional safety skills and experience in the automotive sector can create difficulties. Justification for investment in developing the functional safety capability across the enterprise should focus on the additional benefits that a dedicated functional safety team could achieve. For example, the whole-lifecycle remit of a functional safety team offers the opportunity to co-ordinate and communicate new multi-disciplinary practices across a company. This in turn could be a very effective means of developing an appreciation of the interrelationships of all the information, data sets and inter-dependencies across a product offering the potential for improved feedback into the design process. In order to achieve this virtuous feedback loop, managers should focus on developing flexible, dynamic, multi-disciplinary teams with clear and regular communication events that have senior involvement.

5 Strategies for achieving value from ISO 26262 implementation

The strategic implications for the implementation of ISO 26262 centre on how to encourage, support and develop appropriate networks and collaborative working across the enterprise. A networked organisation necessitates a more distributed view of resource allocation, with functional safety work being undertaken outside specific projects or programmes. This more distributed approach to functional safety work also impacts on which frameworks for performance management are suitable.

Traditional approaches to performance management in the manufacturing sector have centred on rewarding delivery of projects to time and cost targets. It is suggested here that in addition to such approaches it is important to build in support and recognition for collaborative working and networking. Without these practices and behaviours being recognised, innovation and improvement will be prevented, as the workforce tends to 'stay safe' by copying previous approaches to projects. This is a particular danger in companies where there is a reliance on the highly specified 'roadmaps' typical of engineering approaches. Whilst systematic and well documented practices are essential for managing the information associated with product and system development, a different, 'soft systems' approach can facilitate communication, innovation and collaboration across groups.

One framework that has been applied to support the planning, management and reflecting back on collaborative working is the PEArL framework (Champion and Stowell 2003, Champion 2007). PEArL is a mnemonic that encompasses the essential elements for managing multi-disciplinary practices (see Table 1).

Table 1. Elements of the PEArL mnemonic

Element	Description
Participants	Who is involved in an initiative and why those participants were chosen. Why other potential participants were not invited to participate is particularly important to understand as this offers insight into how the problem was initially understood. Participation in a project or initiative also usually fluctuates over time and this changing membership should be recorded and reflected upon.
Engagement	The manner in which people have been engaged in activities is crucial to achieving success. For example, if the group has mixed technical and non-technical membership, have the methods of sharing knowledge been designed so that everyone can participate?
Authority	In projects, authority is often associated with financial control. But intellectual authority is a more important aspect to consider when working for a successful outcome. Ensuring that those with the intellectual authority to undertake a full critique of work and also those with the social, or institutional, authority to instigate change are involved is essential to success.
relationships	This is the most important aspect of the mnemonic. Supporting the development of key relationships across the enterprise should be a prime concern of all senior managers. Innovation and improvement occurs when good communication and mixed disciplinary groups collaborate.
Learning	Ensuring that there are processes in place to embed learning into future interventions is key to success and needs to be planned for at the start of any initiative.

The framework can be applied to any collaborative initiative and is based on systems theory (Champion and Stowell 2003). The elements of the PEArL mnemonic draw attention to the manner in which an initiative is undertaken rather than defining the 'solution' or plan of action. In focusing on the way in which an initiative is undertaken it supports managers in making sure that any initiative has the credibility to succeed. If those with the relevant experience and intellectual authority are seen to be responsible for a project, confidence will build. This may seem obvious but in high pressure manufacturing environments it is rare that consideration is given to such niceties. Too often whoever is available is put on a project, or external consultants with no organisational credibility or 'capital' are given a task. If an initiative is considered strategically important, then it is vital that senior managers are seen to value it and hence put their best team in place to deliver.

The functional safety arena for automotive also presents a unique challenge in building up sufficient human resource. Training needs to be provided by specialists of which there are few, so courses can be at some distance from the location of personnel. Introductory courses can often be arranged on-site, but for those pre-

pared to study at a higher level, dedicated funding and release from activities can
be difficult to secure. Examining how far companies are prepared to support all
levels of training in their organisation reveals their commitment (or not) to the
principles of ISO 26262. Audit trails for functional safety should adopt the holistic
approach of the standard and include an assessment of training and support across
the workforce, including areas traditionally not engaged with functional safety
such as service organizations. Hence strategically smart companies will use ISO
26262 to support the management of change across the enterprise and so achieve
value through better comnunication, more innovation and better understanding of
interrelationships.

References

Beuche D, Birk A, Dreiger H et al (2007) Using requirements management tools in software
    product line engineering: the state of the practice. Software product line conference 84-96.
    IEEE Computer Society. http://ieeexplore.ieee.org/xpl/mostRecentIssue.jsp?punumber=
    4339239. Accessed 23 October 2013
Boehm B (1991) Software risk management: principles and practices. IEEE Softw 8(1):32-41
Boehm B, Basili V (2001) Software defect reduction: Top 10 list. IEEE Computer 21(5):61-72
Bonjour E, Micaelli J (2010) Design core competence diagnosis: a case from the automotive
    industry. IEEE Trans Eng Man 57(2):323-337
Champion D (2007) Managing action research: the PEArL framework. Systemic Practice and
    Action Research 20(6):455-465
Champion D, Stowell FA (2003) Validating action research field studies: PEArL. Systemic Prac-
    tice and Action Research 16(1):21-36
Champion D, Stowell FA, Callaghan A (2005) Client-Led Information system Creation (CLIC):
    navigating the gap. Info Sys Journal 15:213-231
Charette RN (1989) Software risk analysis and management. McGraw-Hill, New York
Egbert C, Neve PD (2001) Surviving global software development. IEEE Softw 18(2):62-69
Ellims M, Bridges J, Ince DC (2006) The economics of unit testing. Empirical Software Engi-
    neering 11:5-31
Gil NA, Tether BS (2011) Project management and design flexibility: analysing a case and con-
    ditions of complementarity. Research Policy 40:415-428
ISO (2011) ISO 26262 International standard for automotive functional safety. http://www.iso
    .org/iso/catalogue_detail?csnumber=43464. Accessed 20 March 2012
Keil M, Cule PE, Lyytinen K et al (1999) A framework for identifying software project man-
    agement risks. Commun ACM 41(11)76-83
OMG (2013) Object Management Group. http://www.omg.org. Accessed 15 November 2013
Sikora E, Tenbergen B, Pohl K (2012) Industry needs and research directions in requirements
    engineering for embedded systems. Requirements Engineering 17:57-78
Valverde R, Toleman M, Cater-Steel A (2011) A method for comparing traditional and compo-
    nent-based models in information systems re-engineering. Info Sys E-Bus Man 9:89-107

Electronic Safety Cases in an Explosives Environment

Ian Barnes[1], George Cleland[2] and Elaine Holden[3]

[1]Defence Ordnance Safety Group, MOD, Bristol, UK

[2]Adelard, London, UK

[3]Defence Munitions, MOD, Gosport, UK

Abstract   This paper describes the simple, cost effective and robust methodology for electronic site safety cases currently being utilised by Defence Munitions (DM) to demonstrate that all its depots have a consolidated risk management approach to their wide ranging activities, which meets the significant regulatory burden applicable to a complex industrial site dealing with high explosives, fuel and chemical hazards, often in surroundings designated as areas of significant environmental interest, such as Sites of Special Scientific Interest. Having been successfully trialled at two sites (DM Kineton and DM Gosport), it is now being rolled out across all DM sites. Although the work described here is in an explosives context, the application of the approach is potentially useful across other complex high risk industrial domains.

1 Introduction

This paper describes a collaborative effort between departments within the Ministry of Defence (MOD) and the Adelard risk management consultancy which details and expands upon recent efforts to introduce a systematic and repeatable electronic safety case methodology into the MOD.

1.1 Background

The Defence Ordnance Safety Group (DOSG) had spent effort in 2008 reviewing a number of safety and risk management approaches, researching which would facilitate improvement of risk management within the MOD. Of those reviewed, the Adelard Assurance and Safety Case Environment (ASCE) (Adelard 2013) was identified as having high potential for use with MOD safety cases. Together,

DOSG and Adelard explored how best the tool could be configured and exploited for Weapons, Ordnance, Munitions and Explosives (WOME) cases. This ultimately led to the development of a generic WOME safety case template and an associated approved code of practice for electronic safety cases applied within the Weapons Operating Centre (Adelard and MOD 2012).

Within the Defence Equipment and Support (DE&S) organisation (annual budget £14 billion) sits the DE&S Weapons Operating Centre (WOC) where currently some 20 Project Teams (PTs), which are responsible for delivering safe and dependable weapons systems and providing in-service support, are producing safety cases using the WOME template which is being systematically rolled out. They are using the approach to produce safety and environmental case submissions in order to obtain a Certificate of Safety for Ordnance, Munitions and Explosives (CSOME), which is a mandatory requirement within the MOD to permit a weapon system to be taken into service.

Given the success of the approach, the participants felt that it would be beneficial to promulgate its benefits to a wider audience, which resulted in this paper on how the approach was developed and deployed in the MOD's DM sites. DM are responsible for receiving, transporting, storing, processing and delivering munitions at a number of locations in the UK and Germany. These are complex industrial sites with potentially high risk hazards.

1.2 Aim

The aim of this paper is to describe the simple, cost effective and robust methodology for electronic site safety cases currently being deployed by DM to demonstrate that all its depots have a consolidated risk management approach to their wide ranging activities. It describes a methodology which meets the significant audit, regulatory and licensing burden applicable to complex industrial sites dealing with high explosives, fuel and chemical hazards, often in surroundings designated as areas of significant environmental interest, such as Sites of Special Scientific Interest. Having been successfully trialled at two sites (DM Kineton and DM Gosport), it is now being rolled out across all DM sites.

At MOD DM Head Office, it was realised that whilst individual munitions, systems and services were all subject to their own safety assessments, there was no all-encompassing site safety case to provide an assurance to the duty holders that each of its munitions sites 'as a whole' was operating in compliance with the plethora of legislation applicable to a high hazard site. Many of the DM sites are subject to the Major Accident Control Regulations (MACR sites); MACR (MOD 2013) is the MOD equivalent to the Control of Major Accident Hazard (COMAH) regulations, and DM Head Office considered it essential that all elements of site safety should be brought together into a single site safety case using a single electronic management environment. They sought advice from DOSG who suggested that the template approach used for WOME cases might provide a simple and effective way of structuring arguments and delivering evidence in support of a safety case, helping to manage the potential size and complexity.

1.3 Participating organisations

This paper has been devised by two key stakeholders (DOSG and Adelard) and a representative of DM (representing the DM user group), all of whom have been involved in the work.

1.3.1 Defence Ordnance Safety Group

The DOSG is a specialist engineering group which is the MOD's focal point for WOME safety. DOSG provide policy, advice and assessment functions on behalf of the Secretary of State for Defence and monitor departmental performance to provide assurance on WOME safety to the Secretary of State through the Defence Ordnance Environment and Safety Board. It is pan MOD, with primary responsibility for matters relating to WOME strategy, safety policy and its implementation, performance measurement and support. DOSG also provide advice and technical support for a range of safety cases including: conventional, complex and nuclear weapons and weapons systems, platform and site cases as well as expertise in risk policy and risk analysis and management.

The work was led by the ST2 section of DOSG which is responsible for ordnance risk assessment, advice and support.

1.3.2 Adelard

Adelard is an independent consultancy, founded in 1987. Since then the company has provided its clients with industry leading techniques and methods, solving difficult problems in the areas of safety, dependability, security and risk management. They have developed and market the ASCE tool which is in use across the MOD, and many other sectors, for the development of safety and other (environmental, security, governance, etc.) cases. While ASCE is the technical basis of the work described in this paper, it is not the focus, which is the approach which has been developed and deployed.

Adelard have been working with DOSG to develop, evaluate and deploy safety and environmental safety case templates over the past five years, with the intention of providing a common approach to provide support for simplified development and maintenance of safety and environmental cases. In particular, the approach supports delivery of these as operational, not just regulatory, documents.

1.3.3 Defence Munitions Gosport, representing Defence Munitions

DM Gosport is one of eight UK and German based munitions sites operated within DM by the DE&S. It is situated in Gosport adjacent to Portsmouth harbour (on the opposite side from Portsmouth), and covers an area of approximately 550 acres. This makes it relatively small in physical size in comparison to some other DM sites such as DM Kineton, which covers 2,500 acres, and has 3 miles of arterial road and 29 miles of railway. The site also houses the Defence Explosive ordnance disposal, Munitions and Search School (DEMSS), comprising the munitions wing and Improvised Explosive Device Disposal (IEDD) wing delivering munitions management training and IEDD training respectively. There is also an extensive military family base at Kineton adjacent to the site.

DM Gosport has a number of explosives facilities which include 2 integrated weapon complexes, which are cruciform concrete structures, with large processing areas extending from a central test equipment house, designed for multi-weapon testing and used for repair and test of complex weapons, 24 processing rooms and 26 explosives storehouses, all of which are subject to an explosives licensing regime operated by Secretary of State for Defence. The weapons systems stored and maintained at DM Gosport include Sea Viper (Aster), Sea Wolf, Sea Skua, and Sea Dart missiles as well as the Sting Ray lightweight torpedo. There is also a small amount of general munitions processing work undertaken in support of issues to ships loading in Portsmouth Harbour and the site provides a comprehensive support service for all large and medium calibre naval weaponry both ashore and on board ship wherever they are in the world, for small arms weapons. It has a jetty which is used to load barges for transport of munitions to ships in Portsmouth Harbour.

All DM sites operate in a reasonably similar manner although the landlocked ones do not have jetties. DM Gosport is a centre of excellence for complex weapons. DM Kineton's operations predominantly involve conventional munitions. These two sites piloted use of the DM template to produce a site-wide safety case and those developing the cases were pleased by the level of information which can be captured and the ease of access the template provides. Both sites have produced comprehensive safety reports from the approach and as a result the trial has been deemed successful and use of the approach to produce a comprehensive site safety case is now mandated by the Defence Munitions Management Board across all DM sites.

The other DM sites are:

- Beith: complex weapons
- Crombie: conventional munitions, jetty
- Glen Douglas: conventional munitions, jetty
- Longtown: conventional munitions
- Plymouth: complex weapons, jetty
- Wulfen (Germany): conventional munitions.

However, in order to produce a suitable and comprehensive safety case methodology, the sites first needed to fully understand the nature of a site safety case and its purpose.

2 Safety cases

Safety cases are structured bodies of information that are crucial in the delivery of today's dependable systems. The safety case should argue convincingly that a particular system or service will meet its safety requirements, and what those safety requirements are. The arguments will be over the adequate identification of safety requirements, and the justification of meeting those requirements around the design, manufacture, deployment, operation and maintenance and (possibly also disposal) of the equipment, plant, service, etc. The safety case comprises safety claims, justifying arguments and the supporting evidence.

Many industries have already adopted a safety case approach, and in other sectors they are used to reduce project risk by justifying the safety arguments and supporting evidence and effectively communicating this and the underlying risk management approach to a range of relevant stakeholders. Even though these bodies of argument and evidence are sometimes not called safety cases, they often have the same characteristics as safety cases. Where structured arguments are used to demonstrate and communicate other high integrity requirements apart from safety, these are sometimes known as assurance cases, dependability cases or compliance cases.

Within the MOD a safety case is defined in Def Stan 00-56 (MOD 2007) as:

'a structured argument, supported by a body of evidence that provides a compelling, comprehensive and valid case that a system is safe for a given application in a given environment'.

However, safety cases are not a single entity or document, but rather an amalgam of safety requirements, the safety argument which makes the case that these requirements are met and the body of evidence that substantiates the argument. This information is developed and maintained throughout the system's (or service's or site's) life. As changes to requirements are implemented and additional or updated supporting information is included the argument structure usually stays relatively stable but content is modified. It can become increasing difficult to gather and maintain all of the requisite information in one location on a computer system as data may come from different sources or stakeholders and may be subject to different configuration/control systems.

Or, as with DM, there may be more than one site within the organisation, all working to the same set of rules, but all operating slightly differently and because of these operational differences, putting a slightly different interpretation on how to comply with the requirements/rules. There may be a substantial outsourcing component to the operation, and there will be considerable dependencies in the interface between the customer (ships etc.), and the supplier (e.g. project teams).

Site safety cases are therefore complex bodies of information consisting of detailed safety and licensing requirements, derived safety requirements, compliance arguments, and links to supporting evidence, probably not under completely coherent configuration control because of the many parties contributing. They consist of several hundred, or even thousands, of documents, stored in all sorts of formats: narrative, spreadsheets, databases, as well as specialist systems like requirements management, hazard log or quantitative risk assessment tool formats. This can be complicated by the requirement to store elements of information in a corporate document management system or within a layered security system.

Safety case reports however, are a fully controlled projection of the safety rationale, usually at key review points in a site's operation. These reports pull information into the report structure from the underlying safety case, often into a detailed report structure required by a regulator or auditor. Traditionally this was a labour intensive, mandraulic process. We will show below how the template approach simplifies this process, provides greater transparency and provenance of information, and simplifies the reporting regime.

2.1 Defence Munitions safety case requirements

Adelard's ASCE tool had been used to develop the WOME template, and it was chosen as the basis for the DM work. It supports the two common argumentation notations: Claims Arguments and Evidence (CAE) (Adelard and MOD 2012a, ISO 2011) and Goal Structuring Notation (GSN) (Adelard and MOD 2012a, GSN 2011). The DM work uses CAE, but the same approach could be used with GSN. The results are also delivered as HTML documents, so these can viewed using a normal web browser, without the requirement for a copy of ASCE. The WOME templates (in both CAE and GSN) and supporting documentation are freely available for download (Adelard and MOD 2012b). The DM site template is also available by application to the authors[1]. This might be useful for those considering developing an industrial site safety case.

While CAE and GSN are graphical tools for argument description, a crucial element of the work described in this paper was the ability to handle narrative background content. This greatly increased the ability to improve information management. It also simplified the reporting regime.

As mentioned above, safety arguments are typically communicated in a safety case report using narrative text with embedded graphics. One of the common problems with narrative safety arguments is that they can be poorly structured, may be ambiguous, and may not make the underpinning argument explicit. The challenge when constructing a safety case is to ensure that all stakeholders in-

---

[1] Contact: info@adelard.com.

volved share the same understanding of the arguments and evidence put forward. Use of the template allows targeting of problems with a proven approach to help deliver a robust safety case by managing information complexity and communicating key arguments to stakeholders. It also simplified the production of various safety case reports.

For example, transforming this safety case for a weapon system to this report (Figure 1) takes less than three minutes using the WOME template approach. Such reports usually have to be produced frequently during a system's life, so the approach can save substantial effort.

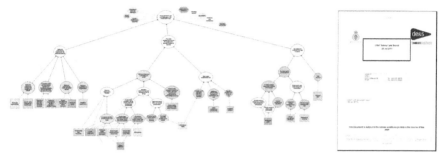

Fig. 1. Report example

3 Consolidated approach

Having decided that it wanted a comprehensive site safety case for each of its munitions sites, DM Head Office decided to adopt a consolidated approach to production of safety cases and that the template approach was to be used DM-wide. Given the wide range of munitions and activities covered by the eight DM sites, one of which is in Germany, this required commitment on behalf of the sites, their management and the personnel nominated to produce the safety cases.

In February 2012, Adelard started working with key DM personnel and DOSG on initial template development. By April 2012, a basic template had been produced (Figure 2), which not only provided the vehicle for production of a structured argument but which also had the capability to link into guidance in various MOD and HSE regulations. This guidance informs the instantiation of the specific site cases.

Figure 2 is not meant to be readable; it just shows the structure of the template.

- The main diagram in the centre is the main template.

  - The elliptical nodes represent the refinement of claims and sub-claims.
  - The rectangular nodes are evidence references.

- The hexagonal nodes represent contextual information.

- The linear structure along the bottom represents the structure of a MACR report for reporting on the status of the content of the site safety case.

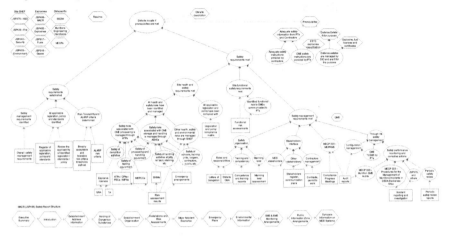

Fig. 2. DM site safety case template

The collection of nodes at the top left contains the text of a number of standards or regulations required for elaboration and development of the template into a full site safety case.

The linear structure at the bottom is a representation of the structure of a MACR report. This report has been produced automatically from the safety case by DM sites in their work in developing their case.

We will not discuss the whole structure, although a copy, as mentioned above, is available on application to the authors. However, the top level safety argument is as shown in Figure 3.

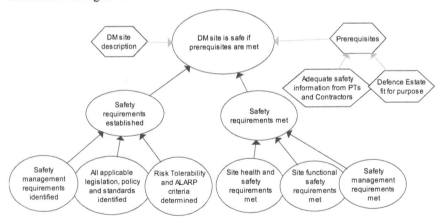

Fig. 3. Top level template structure

We will not elaborate on this further, but it can be seen that the structure, apart from the prerequisites, is very generic and could be applied to many other types of industrial sites. This is something we found on the WOME safety work earlier – that the approach has much wider potential application than in the specific area investigated.

4 Initial trials

In April 2012, DM Gosport and DM Kineton set about creating and populating a site safety case for each of their respective sites by using the initial template. By Sept 2012, this had resulted in the production of two very different safety cases, both of which contained key information for each site's immediate needs. DM Kineton focused on creating a case which would provide a comprehensive MACR safety report for an impending inspection whilst DM Gosport attempted to create a case more closely aligned to the original template (albeit with numerous additional nodes). In order to allow sites to use the template to meet their needs but to still maintain a degree of conformity it was decided that the structure could follow any format providing it contained key nodes and supporting evidence. By targeting key nodes for inclusion in the network, regardless of layout, a consolidated approach to the safety case was secured for all sites.

The approach also has the capability to consolidate case elements from different sites into a single report. For example, in the case of DM, all sites have now produced initial safety cases, all of which follow different formats whilst still containing the core elements necessary to demonstrate a consolidated risk management approach to safety. This includes sharing a set of common information (e.g. references to standards and regulation, licensing requirements). All of this information, if required, could be extracted from individual site cases and integrated into a DM-wide safety case report, to demonstrate to senior management boards, where risk areas exist. For example, it will be straightforward to produce a report demonstrating the current state of explosives licensing across all sites or to identify any areas where confidence in a product or procedure is deemed to be low.

Alternatively, PTs who procure and provision for maintenance of the commodities can reference and share their safety cases, or relevant parts thereof, with the DM sites storing and maintaining their commodities. This allows each DM site storing that munition to link to common munition case material to demonstrate with supporting evidence that munitions are safe to store and process due to the detail in the individual munitions safety cases. The template has the ability to detect change in the linked munitions case. This helps with impact analysis of change.

In view of the versatility of the approach and the perceived success of the trial phase, in September 2012 the DM Management Board approved the use of the approach across all DM sites and instructed that all sites should produce an outline site safety case by April 2013. This was later revised to June 2013 to accommodate unforeseen minor difficulties in rolling out the required software to several MOD sites.

The approach has a versatility which facilitates its use to produce a safety case covering anything from a simple individual item, such an airfield radio, through complex items such as warships, combat aircraft or complex munitions, through to whole site cases for high hazard industrial sites. This concept is equally applicable to non-MOD sites/equipment, e.g. petroleum companies, distilleries, chemical plants (individually or linked via processes), commercial shipping ports and ultimately in the nuclear industry, where it is currently being developed.

5 Graphical displays of safety cases

Although different in the detail of products/services provided, all DM sites share a common requirement to demonstrate through a body of evidence that they are safe in design and operation. The template approach encourages a thought process, through application of the structured argument approach (whether GSN or CAE), which can challenge (in the DM case, has challenged) long held assumptions. It has also identified areas where technology has progressed but documentation and procedures have not kept pace with the associated developments and changes.

One of the significant problems experienced by the trial sites was how to approach constructing a site safety case, even with the benefit of the basic template, retrospectively.

The initial template had very few argument nodes and the sites discovered that there was a plethora of evidence to be reconciled and recorded within the template, but identifying exactly where was proving problematic. However, because of the graphical layout of the template, the introduction of a number of appropriately focused argument nodes helped the creators to identify which pieces of evidence should be attributed to individual claims nodes.

6 Achieving the regulatory obligation

In addition to the normal regulatory requirements, as previously stated, the majority of DM sites are also MACR sites, equivalent to COMAH sites (MOD 2013). As a MACR site, each DM establishment must be able to demonstrate that for all its high hazard risks, there is a major accident prevention plan in place as well as comprehensive emergency arrangements to mitigate the potential effects of any major incident should the prevention plans fail. The level of detail required to demonstrate compliance is considerable as would be expected for high hazard areas. MACR top tier sites are required to develop both a Major Accident Prevention Plan (MAPP) and a Safety Report (SR).

Once completed the MAPP (and, for top tier sites, SR) is the establishment's live documented major accident safety case and operational plan.

The MAPP/SR is a dynamic document which acts as a signpost to other policies, procedures and requirements that in their totality comprise the information underlying the MACR safety case report. Its purpose is to demonstrate that major accident hazards and possible major accident scenarios have been identified and that the necessary measures have been taken to prevent such accidents and to limit the consequences for human health and the environment. It should demonstrate that adequate safety and reliability have been taken into account in the design, construction, operation and maintenance of any installation, storage facility, equipment and infrastructure connected to the operations which are linked to major accident hazards inside the establishment. It demonstrates that internal emergency plans have been drawn up and that appropriate information has been supplied to enable external emergency plans to be drawn up. The approach adopted by the trial sites provides the perfect vehicle for producing MAPPs and SRs, in addition to full blown safety cases.

7 Conclusions

A methodology has been developed which meets the significant regulatory burden applicable to a complex industrial site dealing with high explosives, fuel and chemical hazards. The requirement was to show compliance with an extensive range of standards, regulations and licensing requirements. This has been achieved with the approach documented in this paper. However, the major benefits are that we have created dynamic argumentation structures supported by evidence, that are much easier to maintain, and most important, that not only demonstrate regulatory compliance, but will be used as live operational documents.

The approach uncovered issues which had not previously been identified. These were usually not to do with the practice, which had been ingrained because of a good implicit safety culture, but with lack of documentation of the practice, and audit. This has helped to pinpoint areas in need of rectification.

The ability of the approach to detect change in supporting or embedded information is a crucial element in management of the safety case. This allows you to identify any standards or regulations which you reference that have changed, and work out the impact on your safety case regime. It can help with identifying changes in supporting facility or munition safety cases, again helping with impact analysis. It can also help in a 'negative' way – identifying documents which have not been updated, but should have been, e.g. regular reviews.

The approach will also greatly ease the effort involved with the substantial audit requirement for DM sites. Audits are required on a regular basis. These include (but are not limited to): internal audits; safe system of work audits; MACR inspections; HSE inspections; environmental inspections; and local authority briefings. Each of these audits could take from days to weeks, requiring a great deal of effort for both auditors and the audited. The approach allows us to deliver a 'package' of safety case documentation on a CD or DVD to auditors to review at base, then spend a much smaller amount of time on site examining specific issues.

The approach, while specifically developed for DM sites, has much wider potential application to other complex industrial installations. And not necessarily at great expense, based on or experience in this work. The benefits could be substantial in terms of improved quality and reduced cost.

The initial trials at DM Gosport and DM Kineton were successful, and DM Head Office decided to roll the approach out across all DM sites. That we have been able to develop initial site cases for all the DM sites, within 18 months from the start of the overall project (including development of the template), with relatively modest effort given the complexity of the context, is gratifying.

The approach is now being considered for other application areas including environmental (e.g for environmental management systems and environmental risk assessments) and quality management.

References

Adelard (2013)ASCE – The Assurance and Safety Case Environment. http://www.adelard.com/asce/choosing-asce/index.html. Accessed 5 November 2013

Adelard and MOD (2012a) Weapons operating centre, approved code of practice for electronic safety cases. W/193/10106/1 V1.0. http://www.adelard.com/services/WOMESafetyEnvCase Tmplt/w1939v10_ACoP_Electronic_Safety_Case.pdf. Accessed 5 November 2013

Adelard and MOD (2012b) WOME templates. http://www.adelard.com/services/WOMESafety EnvCaseTmplt/index.html. Accessed 5 November 2013

GSN (2011) GSN community standard. Version 1. http://www.goalstructuringnotation.info/documents/GSN_Standard.pdf. Accessed 5 November 2013

ISO (2011) ISO/IEC 15026-2 Systems and software engineering – systems and software assurance. Part 2: assurance case

MOD (2007) Defence Standard 00-56, Safety management requirements for defence systems. Issue 4. https://www.gov.uk/uk-defence-standardization. Accessed 5 November 2013

MOD (2013) Joint Service Publication 498 – Major accident control regulations

International Engineering Safety Management for the Rail Industry

Paul Cheeseman

Technical Programme Delivery Limited

London, UK

Abstract   This paper introduces the new international Engineering Safety Management (iESM) guidance for the worldwide railway industry been developed by Technical Programme Delivery Ltd and reviewed by an international working group of senior practitioners, supported by MTR Corporation Hong Kong. The aims of the new iESM guidance are to help:

- tackle the pressures from increased complexity of railway systems
- address decreased public and passenger tolerance for avoidable accidents
- focus spending on preventing incidents and smooth the way for acceptance of new technology or novel applications.

The guidance has been written principally for people around the world who use their judgement to take or review decisions that affect railway safety and to help them exercise their judgement in a systematic and informed manner. iESM was launched to enthusiastic support in Hong Kong and Florida in April 2013 and work has continued to develop more detailed guidance application in the areas of independent assessment, human safety and evaluating risk.

The guidance is freely available form www.intesm.org where progressively other useful and relevant information is being made available.

1 Introduction

Formal system safety management has developed significantly during the last 20 years and whilst it has made a major contribution to preventing accidents during a period in which railway systems themselves have become more complex and railways have become more intensively used, there have been a number of problems. Poor practice has seen the production of paper mountains instead of concise information, and safety engineering starting too late after key decisions have been made resulting in safety work and safety cases being blamed for project delays and overspends.

Since 2000 significant development has continued within Europe on the CENELEC family of railway application standards. The Common Safety Method (CSM) and guidance (ERA 2009) has been established in European legislation, CENELEC EN50128 (IEC62279) (CENELEC 2011) was re-issued in 2011 and guidance notes supporting CENELEC EN50129 (IEC62425) on cross acceptance (CENELEC 2007) and assurance (CENELEC 2009) have been issued. Yet some users of these standards still struggle to know how to apply them to a real project.

In parallel, experience in the application of engineering safety management has matured throughout the world and many emerging economies needed guidance in moving their safety management towards good practice. Expertise is no longer UK-centric.

This paper has space only to show some of the highlights of iESM. In summary, the new iESM guidance:

- is advisory, not mandatory
- provides good practice guidance and will continue to reflect emerging good practice
- is applicable in an international market
- moves forward from the former UK rail industry guidance known as 'Yellow Book' which was used extensively around the world, not just in English speaking countries
- supports use of CENELEC standards and CSMs for risk assessment, with practical, cost-effective advice
- is guided by an international working group of practitioners and supporters giving it credibility with the avoidance of bias.

2 iESM Working Group

The aim of the iESM Working Group (iESM WG) is to assist the international railway industry in delivering acceptable levels of safety by promulgating good practice in railway engineering safety management. The iESM WG pursues its aims by:

- acting as design authority for iESM for engineering safety management guidance and any associated supporting materials (e.g. application notes, templates and checklists)
- facilitating the efficient and effective application of iESM for engineering safety management
- promoting and facilitating the exchange of good practice that is found in the world railway community and other relevant industries
- setting up and overseeing support groups as necessary.

The scope of activities excludes certification of people, products or services.

iESM WG activities are performed on a not-for-profit basis by practitioners supported by their employing organisations. The group proceeds by consensus which may sound like a recipe for inaction. In practice the desire to make progress has outweighed any political posturing or technical esotericism. The initial chair is Dr Robert Davis (a former chair of the original UK Rail Yellow Book Steering Group) and meetings have been held approximately quarterly so far in Hong Kong, London and Vancouver. RSSB in UK is supporting this initiative with a view to sharing GB rail experience and practice in the safe management of engineering change and also to identify good practice from these other companies, some of whom are working on extremely ambitious rail programmes.

iESM WG aims to be broadly representative of the international railway community. All members of the iESM WG are:

- recognised as having significant standing within the industry on matters relating to the management of safety
- available and committed to the work of the iESM WG
- able to provide a professional contribution to iESM WG activities based on their skills and expertise.

3 iESM principles and processes

The iESM principles, processes and flows of information between them are shown in Figure 1. The principles are arranged in five groups, three relating to lifecycle activities and two pan-lifecycle:

- definition
- risk analysis
- risk control
- technical support
- team support.

The activities in the central boxes represent the main flow of the iESM process while the activities in the boxes down each side represent supporting activities that are performed throughout the durations of the activities in the darker boxes. The guidance does not provide a complete framework for making decisions about railway work. It is concerned with safety and does not consider non-safety benefits. Even as regards safety, the guidance does not dictate the values which underlie decisions to accept or reject risk. However, it does provide a rational framework for making sure that such decisions stay within the law and reflect the organization's values and those of society at large, and then for demonstrating that this is the case. iESM provides a structured and systematic approach to managing railway system safety and aims to reflect emerging good practice – all in one place.

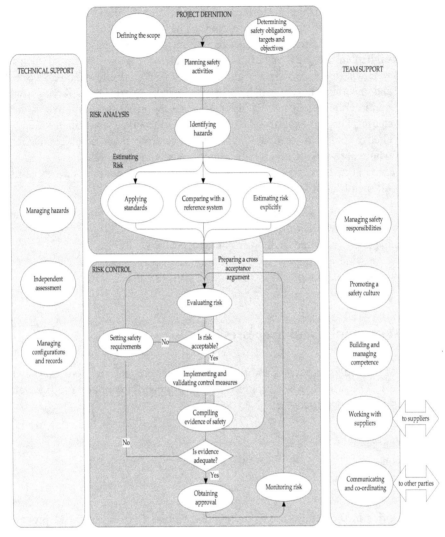

Fig. 1. iESM principles and processes

4.Using the iESM guidance

4.1 Preamble

iESM is not an 'add-on' overhead – it should be an integral part of all engineering activities. For example, the generic ESM process contains activities, such as configuration management, which are essential to deliver safety but are also required for other reasons. There may be activities in the generic process that are regarded as parts of other processes. It may be that the specific organization or project draws the boundaries between activities in different places or gives them different names How they are structured and named makes no difference to their effectiveness. What matters is that they should be done, and done well.

At its core are three main approaches to risk management – compliance with standards, comparison with a reference system and explicit risk estimation. These are the three parallel paths in Figure 1. Importantly these three approaches are integrated into one framework, to make most effective use of time and resources. Typically civil engineers rely on standards to manage risk, whilst those developing more novel signalling systems might adopt a QRA approach and at other times simply repeat what was done at another location. iESM allows for all these approaches. It also overcomes some of the criticism of previous guidance which was seen to be too onerous for low risk projects whilst at the same time providing little help to those for whom standards compliance is inadequate in specific applications. The approaches are illustrated in the following subsections. Note they are applied to hazards not at (sub)system nor project level. The importance of robust and vigorous hazard identification remains.

4.2 Definition

This is not so much the definition of words or terms, but the definition of what is to be done by the project and under what rules of engagement; in particular, the safety success criteria. Knowing these two things will enable a coherent safety plan to be produced to guide the work and in due course provide evidence that the project has followed a systematic process.

Fundamental to this is the need to obtain a clear understanding of the system or product and its boundaries and interfaces (including the non-physical ones). It is also important to make sure that the responsibilities for safety are clear. If there is not sufficient information available to completely define the system or product, then it is important to make explicit assumptions, to be confirmed later.

The other ingredient to safety planning is determining precisely the targets and objectives for safety. This may not be simple but it will be a lot simpler than trying to retrospectively demonstrate compliance of the work done, towards the end of the project. Further it is important to identify who will approve the work and agree with them how the evidence for safety will be presented.

The size and depth of the plan will depend on the complexity and level of risk presented by the project. For simple and low-risk projects a brief plan defining the project personnel and justifying a simple approach may be sufficient although this assumption needs to be explicit and action planned to confirm it.

The safety plan may permit reliance on previous work to demonstrate acceptable risks if the previous work used good practice; it covered all of the project risk; and there is little novelty in development, application or use. It is sensible to integrate the ESM plans with plans for managing other elements of the project, e.g. human factors. The safety plan should be approved or at least agreed by people who will later approve the system or product.

4.3 Compliance with standards

If a hazard is fully addressed by accepted standards that define agreed ways of controlling it, showing compliance with these standards may be enough to control the hazard or to meet legal obligations (or both). For example, the electrical safety of ordinary office equipment is normally shown by meeting electrical standards. iESM uses the word 'standard' to include other forms of authoritative guidance such as rules and codes of practice.

Any standard shall at least satisfy following requirements:

- be widely acknowledged in railway domain. If not the case, the standard will have to be justified.
- be relevant for control of considered hazards in system under assessment
- be publicly available for all who want to use it.

However as the Safety-related Systems Guidance (Hazards Forum 2002) reminds us:

> 'Mere compliance to standards is unlikely to be regarded as evidence that sufficient care has been taken or that best practice was followed. It will be necessary to demonstrate that the standards complied with are relevant and appropriate to the system and the circumstances in which it was to operate.'

This must therefore form part of our safety argument. Compliance with standards can be (almost) sufficient if all of these are true:

- The equipment or process is being used as intended.
- All the risk is covered by the standard(s).
- The standard(s) cover the specific situation.
- Users of the standard have sufficient understanding of current good practice and the world around them.
- There are no obvious or reasonably practicable ways of reducing risk further.

An example of this approach is providing lighting on platforms that complies to the latest standards during an upgrade. This mitigates the hazard of passenger slips, trips and falls. However at one station, situated just beyond a long tunnel section, the modern lighting may be so bright that it may dazzle the train driver. Risk monitoring (an iESM principle) is valuable to monitor the situation to see if other measures need to be taken.

However, compliance to standards has limits and other approaches as described below may be necessary.

4.4 Reference system

If it is possible to show that the project or system is sufficiently similar to a reference system – another system that is known to be safe – and that the risk associated with some hazards of the project or system is no more than that associated with the reference system, then it may be possible to conclude that those hazards are controlled. This can be effective but requires a suitable similar system – and significant amounts of information about it – to form the reference. This is not always available.

This approach has been used in some countries extensively and is similar in concept to the Globalement Au Moins Aussi Bon (GAMAB) as described in CENELEC EN50126 (published as IEC62278) (CENELEC 1999) but applied at the hazard level rather than the system level.

A reference system shall at least satisfy following:

- It has already been proven in-use to have an acceptable safety level and would still qualify for acceptance where change is to be introduced.
- It has similar functions and interfaces as system under assessment.
- It is used under similar operational conditions as system under assessment.
- It is used under similar environmental conditions as system under assessment.

Note also that this is not a 'cross acceptance' process as described in the CENELEC standards and below, but simply a comparison at the level of a hazard. An example might be stepping distances on an older railway where the cost to reduce or eliminate platform gaps would be high and the most effective risk control would be to close the station – clearly an unacceptable outcome. However on a network where passengers are used to the step and other mitigation measures are in place (for example illumination, painted warnings and announcements) this hazard may be managed through reference to a similar station having comparable distances, trains and passenger loadings.

4.5 Explicit risk estimation

This approach will be familiar to those who used 'Yellow Book' and most other QRA approaches. It may be possible to make an explicit estimation of the risk, that is, estimate the frequency with which incidents will occur and the harm done, either as numbers or by selecting from a number of categories. It is useful and can be accurate but it is time consuming and requires significant expertise. It is however, the only way to deal with new risks or very significant risks. Thus, the need for explicit risk estimation could arise:

- when the system under assessment is entirely new and therefore there is some uncertainty
- where there are deviations from a standard or a reference system

- when the chosen design strategy does not allow the usage of standard or similar reference system because, for example, of a wish to produce a more cost effective design that has not been tried before.

One major contribution of this approach is that explicit risk estimation allows modelling of the interactions between the various risks in order to show the combined effects and, if required (it normally is!), the overall risk level. It has also been said that doing the thinking to produce a QRA model is almost as important as the result of the model itself. In this paper we will not repeat the methods described extensively elsewhere.

Novelty and complexity can be thought of as measures of the uncertainty of outcome – the likelihood that the proposed change, once implemented, will or will not behave as predicted. The more novel and the more complex a change or a technology is, the higher the likelihood that it may behave in an unpredicted and possibly undesirable way. Therefore, the more novel and the more complex a change is, the more it is likely to need an explicit risk estimation approach. It is necessary to consider both what is innovative in the railway industry, and what is merely new just for the organisation implementing the change.

4.6 Cross acceptance

There is guidance on using a cross acceptance 'short cut'. This is an approach that has promised savings in time and money but not always been able to deliver on them. Experience shows that when a certificate is issued it often covers more in terms of functionality, interfaces and environment than is actually deployed on the first applications. This means that it sometimes those following the cross acceptance approach that run into difficulties in applying something that is apparently already approved, but not in fact proven.

The iESM guidance helps identify the information that a cross accepter may need to seek from the native environment. It can however offer no help in actually obtaining or validating that information.

4.7 Technical support

Not only is it important to produce safe work, it is necessary to demonstrate that produced safe work. This group contains three activities that provide technical support to the other iESM activities and help provide evidence for the safety argument. They are 'cross functional' in that they require contribution and commitment across the organizations performing the work. These three important supporting acts to iESM are:

- hazard identification

- independent assessment
- configuration management.

The challenge is that these activities cross functional boundaries and are typically performed differently by different departments/functions.

4.8 Team support

This group of principles contains a number of activities that support the iESM activities discussed so far by ensuring that the people involved in these activities are competent and well-organized. Some could be called structured common sense so we will not spend a lot of time explaining them here. The iESM principles here are:

- managing safety responsibilities
- promoting a safety culture
- building and managing competence
- working with suppliers
- communicating and co-ordinating.

One however, has been shown by experience to be very, very important – 'promoting a safety culture'. This underpins most of the iESM activities and requires sustained commitment.

Some railway companies have chosen to build the iESM guidance into their own safety management systems. They have linked it to their competency arrangements as a way of objectively demonstrating that their staff are trained and capable of doing the work required of them. Training and certification are available on behalf of the iESM WG to suit most needs:

- conversion or refreshing from other engineering safety management training with exam
- one day practitioner course with exam
- optional second day practitioner with a practical case study
- hazard identification and management
- independent safety assessment.

All those trained are listed on www.intesm.org. Suppliers too have found it useful when working in an international market so that they can reuse safety evidence more easily.

4.9 Monitoring risk

Experience shows that too often the contract end at commissioning of a new pro-ject creates an often irreparable break in the safety engineering lifecycle. An iESM principle states that all reasonable steps to monitor and improve the management of risk should be taken by identifying, collecting and analyzing data that could be used to improve the management of risk, as long as responsibility for safety re-mains. At some point that responsibility may pass to others and that should be done in a managed way with active agreement between the parties.

5. Real life example

To illustrate some of the iESM principles in action in the context of a real project, here is an example. The author had the role of lead independent assessor for a se-ries of new metro lines being opened in cities across the People's Republic of China. The signalling system supplier and system integrator produced a series of safety arguments to allow commissioning.

Figure 2 shows that a Generic Application Safety Case (GASC) had been pro-duced to demonstrate the safety of the communications based train control system in the generic context of a metro railway. This had been assessed and a certificate obtained from a reputable independent assessment body and formed the basis of a cross acceptance approach. No further assessment of the GASC was needed apart from minor changes that evolved.

Fig. 2. Example application of iESM approach to Chinese metro

Then for the first line, Chengdu Line 1 (CDL1), a Specific Application Safety Case (SASC) was developed based on the core GASC dealing with the hazards and safety requirement for that project.

This was independently assessed and the metro was successfully opened in 2011. Since then it has been extended and functionality added. Subsequent metro lines in Chengdu and other cities have adopted a 'reference system' approach to the management of the majority of their specific application hazards. A few hazards, unique to each application have been addressed in more detail either through compliance with appropriate standards or my risk analysis. These have related mainly to different interfaces and different client operational requirements. This approach has facilitated the rapid roll out of similar systems without the need to rework safety arguments at a deep level nor repeat independent assessment activities.

6. Conclusion

Absolute safety is not achievable in the real world and therefore success relies on two fundamentals, good processes and good people, so that when there is a problem or failure in one, the railway can be sustained by the other. iESM can provide the processes that can be used by suitably trained, experienced and qualified people to support this.

If there is already an ESM process in place, the generic iESM process described here could be used as a benchmark for assessment and improvement. If there is not already an ESM process in place, the generic process should be useful for creating one. For every principle, there is guidance in Volume 2 of the iESM guidance on performing that activity. No one has to use the approach described and it is not the only effective approach, however it has been proven in practice and has the support of some of the leading professionals in the world.

The intention is that iESM provides good practice guidance and will continue to reflect emerging good practice. iESM does not claim that it is always best practice and does not in any way intend to stop going further or doing more. Finally, iESM resources and a list of competent practitioners may be found at www.intesm.org.

Acknowledgements The significant support of the directors of Technical Programme Delivery Ltd in the development of iESM is acknowledged as is the support for the iESM Working Group by MTR Corporation Hong Kong. The members of the iESM WG are thanked for giving their time and expertise freely and effectively towards the usefulness and accuracy of the resulting guidance.

References

CENELEC (1999) EN50126 Railway applications – Communication, signalling and processing systems – The specification and demonstration of RAMS for railway control and protection systems
CENELEC (2007) Railway applications – Communication, signalling and processing systems – Application Guide for EN 50129 Part 1: Cross-acceptance. PD CLC/TR50506-1

CENELEC (2009) Railway applications – Communication, signalling and processing systems – Application Guide for EN 50129 Part 2: Safety assurance. PD CLC/TR 50506-2

CENELEC (2011) EN50128 Railway applications – Communication, signalling and processing systems – Software for railway control and protection systems

ERA (2009) Guide for the application of the Commission Regulation on the adoption of a Common Safety Method on Risk Evaluation and Assessment as referred to in Article 6(3)(a) of the Railway Safety Directive. V1.1

Hazards Forum (2002) Safety-related Systems Guidance for Engineers

Scale, Scope and Control: Safety Integrity Challenges in Railway Control Systems

Alastair Faulkner and Phillip Proctor

Abbeymeade Limited, UK

Lloyds Register Rail, Derby, UK

Abstract   Many of the railway control systems currently in use on the UK rail infrastructure are a patchwork of modern technologies interlaced with remnants of the original Victorian era and therefore many of the current upgrade programmes seek to provide a single control technology for both the infrastructure and the trains. These upgrade programmes have therefore also demanded changes in the technologies that provide train protection systems and train regulation. Perhaps one of the widest ranging changes currently being planned for imminent future implementation is Network Rail's Traffic Management Solution. This system will be highly dependent on commercial computational platforms and data. While these systems are not new, they are all in existence on other railways around the world, the salient safety issues are the scale, scope and nature of the proposed span of control and the means by which a safety argument may need to be constructed to demonstrate safety.

This paper will illustrate the integrity required from the 'controlling element', akin to a signalling control centre, and hence identify the significant challenges for the Traffic Management Solution, its equipment and system acceptance.

1 Introduction

The use of technology to provide 'better', 'faster', and more efficient solutions is not a new phenomenon. In this paper we choose to address the impact of technology through the lens of the UK railway control system. In particular we observe a change in the nature of such systems in scale, scope and complexity, and a growing dependence on the use of data within these systems. Before such systems can be 'set to work' in the context of the regulated UK rail network these systems must gain safety acceptance and approval. However, safety acceptance and approval must also evolve to address these changes in technology. Statutory frameworks have also changed from the Railways and Other Transport Systems (approval of works, plant and equipment) regulations (ROTS 1994) to the Railways and Other Guided transport systems (Safety) regulations (ROGS 2006)[1] and more recently we have seen the introduction and application of the Common Safety Method (CSM) (ERA 2013).

In this paper, we argue that the nature of safety systems is changing. In particular that the sources and nature of evidences used to justify these systems is no longer dominated by process evidence derived from the development environment. These evidences are increasingly partitioned between the product development, the managed configuration, the delivery project and the operational context (its processes and procedures). A further dimension to the acceptance problem is the increased scope of application coupled with the use of configured and configurable systems (and components).

We illustrate this position by consideration of a simple (constrained) system and develop this approach to address adaption of these systems into general purpose solutions adapted to each new instantiation by configuration. This configuration may take a number of forms, although it will be typically dominated through the use of data.

A system created for a specific application, with no possibility of adaption, is only applicable to that specific domain, its operation and use. Its creation is based on the premise that its safety behaviour can be adequately defined through specification, analysis and as such its compliance to that specification (including its safety behaviours) is demonstrable through verification and validation. The tacit assumption is that the client can specify what the operator will do and how he will do it. This position is rarely the case even for systems of all but modest scale, scope and complexity.

A reluctance or even an inability to adequately specify requirements creates pressures to produce systems that can be adapted to foreseeable changes in use driven by economic pressures. In this way the burden of the definition of the system is shifted from the client to the producer. As a consequence the safety management of such systems is presented with additional challenges. These challenges extend the established processes of safety engineering and safety assurance to encompass the construction of safety arguments for configured systems. In this paper we argue that the form and nature of safety acceptance and approval must also adapt to address these new challenges. To illustrate this point we provide a brief overview of the evolution of UK railway command and control systems in the context of the statutory and regulatory frameworks.

2 UK railway control systems: from IECC to the proposed TMS

Network Rail's Traffic Management Solution (TMS) is not the first attempt to implement wide ranging UK infrastructure control systems. In this paper we

---

[1] ROGS replaced the Railways (Safety Case) Regulations 2000, the Railways (Safety Critical Work) Regulations 1994, and ROTS.

choose to start from the Integrated Electronic Control Centres (IECC), recognising Railtrack's 1998 Network Management Centre (NMC) project and the subsequent bid process for the TMS. Other systems have been implemented since the demise of the NMC project circa 2004, but these represent a variety of scales largely akin to the original IECC.

2.1 The IECC

The IECC (Wikipedia 2013a, Mitchell 2003) was developed in conjunction with Solid Sate Interlocking (SSI) (Wikipedia 2013b, Stratton 1988) during the late 1980s by the British Rail Research Division, based in Derby. In its generalised form the IECC consists of a number of operator based VDU based workstations whose initial implementation was based on a 32-bit architecture which employed its own real time operating system BRX (British Rail real time executive) specifi-cally designed to support the networking capacity and process duplication re-quired to deliver very high system availability. The IECC also employed a number of automatic functions based upon the execution of electronic copies of the time-table.

In parallel the implementation of signalling control via SSI was undertaken by three groups: British Rail's Research Division, GEC-General Signal and Westing-house Signals Ltd. The SSI utilises a 2oo3 architecture. The SSI was conceived as a configurable solution for use with geographic interlocking data, relating to the area of railway under control. The initial IECC and SSI used non volatile data descriptions fixed in EPROM, which limited the ability to change data. The IECC workstation and the SSI are closely linked and therefore their data is also linked. The first IECC to go live was at Liverpool Street in Easter 1989 and this was quickly followed by one in York.

At this time the UK Railways were in state ownership. Concern had been mounting over the future of funding, and one option was privatisation. Privatisa-tion took place and Railtrack (Wikipedia 2013c) took control of the railway infra-structure on 1 April 1994. A precursor to privatisation was the enactment of the Railways (Safety Case) Regulations, 1994. As a generalisation the Railtrack Rail-way Safety Case (RTRSC) provided a safety justification for the UK heavy rail network which covered three broad areas: infrastructure control, infrastructure maintenance and train operating companies.

Acceptance and approval was managed through submission to the System Re-view Panel (SRP). Submissions derived their safety risk model from the Appendi-ces of the RTRSC. The safety management process for the IECC also generated hazard and risk logs. Significant safety experience was also gained through the operation of the IECC. Upgrade based upon sets of EPROMS was identified as a significant burden.

During this period the ubiquity of disk based technologies, coupled with an in-creasing use of desk top computing made the use of EPROMS unsustainable, providing the stimulus for change. Evolution of the IECC workstation continued, through the sale of the system to AEA Technology Rail; acceptance and approval is based upon defined scope, limited primarily to individual control areas.

2.2 The NMC

Conceived as a development from the IECC to create a UK wide communications network based signalling solution the NMC concept was for regional control centres with re-configurable workstations and an ability to pass control areas between individual workstations and the regional control centres. Union Switch and Signal (US&S) won the contract for the initial development of the first NMC which was eventually due to be installed at Saltley in Birmingham, and was programmed for implementation as part of the West Coast route modernisation programme. The NMC was to be a customisation of an existing US&S product, modified to accommodate UK signalling practices (a substantial task!). The key feature of the NMC concept was a Remote Interface (RIF), to be placed in the equipment room, and to use network technologies to connect to the NMC(s). The operational concept also required control areas that could be re-assigned between workstations and that the number of control areas managed by an operator would be based upon workload. In peak operating times the operator would handle fewer control areas, at other times they would handle more. A number of metrics were also identified as part of this operational concept which included the number of train movements, track miles and track complexity.

There were several significant acceptance and approval issues associated with the NMC many of which were based upon those propagated from the IECC hazard and risk logs with one of the salient safety analyses (JPT 2001) being derived from the generalised 'controlling element' aspects of the risk model contained in the RTRSC (Railtrack 2001).

The assessment of the 'controlling element' (as shown in Figure 1) identified a SIL2 boundary for information passing across the system boundary with the infrastructure and the control system, with a further higher integrity (SIL4) boundary for the protection system, the interlocking.

From the description provided by this analysis it was demonstrated that the time table (TSDB) provided by Railtrack Information Systems had an influence on the operation of the system. However, the timetable was constructed based upon several constraints (rule book, rules of the route, rules of the plan and the route utilisation strategy). These constraints were also the basis of the operational procedures.

Significant acceptance and approval issues included a recognition that these constraints and their data held in external information systems would no longer be subject to 'grandfather rights', and would require some form of safety justification based upon the changes to existing equipment and systems. The cost impact of such approvals played a significant part in the consideration of the initial 'setting to work' costs of the NMC. Therefore factors affecting NMC acceptance and approval included not only the technology issues of the NMC (system architecture, workstations, their operating systems, the RIF, telecommunications and the operational process and procedures), but also the systems connected through (data) interfaces to the NMC. The NMC was not delivered and the project closed in 2004.

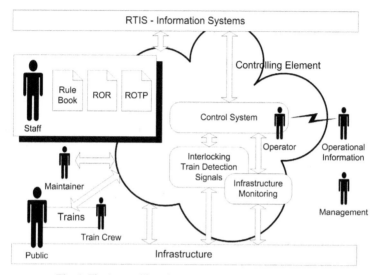

Fig. 1. The 'controlling element' in the UK heavy rail sector

2.3 The TMS

Conceived as a commercial computation platform based solution, heavily dependent on data (indeed a data-centric system) provided from an upgraded (re-implemented) set of Network Rail Information Management (NRIM) systems such as the Integrated Train Planner (which replaced TSDB) and connecting to the existing infrastructure by means of a remote interface, the TMS may introduce several novel supervisory, peer, and subordinate systems, all with increased scale, increased scope and additional and wide ranging dynamic management functionality of allocated control areas, which will above all increase its reliance on data (and its integrity).

In the period between the closure of the NMC and the start of the TMS the statutory regime has changed from ROTS to ROGS. Many of the responsibilities have migrated to RSSB and Railtrack's successor, Network Rail, no longer maintains the overall railway safety case. RSSB maintain the railway risk model and European pressures have created the CSM, with the RSSB risk model being normalised to adapt to the CSM.

TMS is in its formative stages and it would be imprudent to second guess the system description. However it is clear that there will be an increased use of information technology and its associated equipments and systems and this strategy, quite rightly, will attempt to manage many of the obsolescence issues that have dogged the UK railway and made control system upgrades prohibitively expensive.

3 Safety management of data centric systems

The description above illustrates the changing nature of the development and implementation of control systems in the UK railway. They have evolved from being primarily based around the control area and its interlocking (SIL4), to groups of interlocking and implementation issues based upon the regulation of trains across the network, no longer concerned with single signal boxes but workstation based assignments within control areas.

Taking the safety assurance perspective, how should such systems be supported and justified to provide a sufficient and robust safety case? A clear trend is the use of general purpose equipment and systems that are configured to the particular installation with groups of such installations arranged to form the overall system. This provides a safety approval mechanism for a hierarchy of components, subsystems and systems as described in EN 50129 (CENELEC 2003).

The position we choose to highlight in this paper is that the source of the evidence used to support the safety and assurance works is changing. The primary source of evidence would normally be the product, its accreditation and associated safety manual. This position is illustrated by the use of general purpose computational platforms, in particular, as the basis of signalling control systems. Evidences from such platforms falls into seven broad categories; the product; control over its configuration; the 'delivery' projects implementation; data passed across the system interfaces; a data supply chain; the sources of data; and the system hierarchy. These categories are developed below:

3.1 Product based evidence

This group is probably the most commonly recognisable, clearly consisting of hardware, software, people and process. The increasing use of generalised solutions may only specify a broad set of requirements of the hardware and the computational environment (a PC based workstation, and an operating system), all under an appropriate level of configuration control.

The software architecture and the failure behaviours of its constituent applications are likely to be expressed as a series of example configurations. These are typically designed to demonstrate specific feature sets and to facilitate test for verification and validation. The description of people (roles) and process are likely to exist in only the broadest outline, recognising that the final customer and its users will create the operational process and procedures specific to their use.

Product based evidence is therefore likely to be focused on the development environment (its use of techniques and measures), the system architecture, tool supports (T1 to T3 (IEC 61508:2010)), and configuration support.

3.2 Control over configuration (and its evidence)

In this paper we choose to illustrate control over configuration through the use of an identified group – the 'configuration group'; we define their function as the management of known configurations (we describe as patterns) recorded as use cases. This group will also manage the use of these patterns in a set of combinations. Such combinations require simulation to establish metrics for capabilities such as throughput and latency. More crucially they will also record anti-patterns.

It is likely that configuration will be achieved through a number of means. These range from the use of Full Variability (FVL) and Limited Variability Languages (LVL), to the use of data. We clearly see a trend towards the generalised solution, which is becoming increasingly biased towards the configuration and combination of systems. Of particular concern is the omission of barriers to escalation, where errors, faults and failures give rise to hazards and may cause harm (to people, equipment or the environment).

Safety analysis on the use cases provides a basis for HAZID (Hazard Identification), and subsequent cause and consequence analysis leading directly to the identification of safety requirements. It is at this point that we recognise the almost infinite number of system states based upon the definition of use cases, their possible combinations and the possible sets of data they may produce or consume (or both). Interfaces should also contain a means of checking both input and output data, which then raises questions of built-in test and diagnostic coverage (and where to report these issues too).

From the safety acceptance perspective; how much evidence should be produced and what should this evidence be used to justify? If safety accreditation were to be sought, one would expect the accreditation to identify significant limitations on scope, scale and complexity. The safety manual should also contain a (large) section on prohibitions (things not to do with the system).

3.3 Delivery project (and its safety argument)

This is the group tasked with the instantiation of the product, its configuration patterns, and the client requirements for delivery. We expect the delivery project to work with the configuration group to identify the patterns to be used, the combinations of patterns and any gaps. It is the treatment of these gaps that is often problematic, requiring the construction of fragments 'glued' together to adapt to some unforeseen (development and configuration) circumstance.

Issues associated with scope, scale and complexity are expected to dominate. Limitations in the product and its configuration may also require the organisation to adapt to the system rather than the system being adapted to the organisation. In many instances the imposition of the system may also provide a formal definition of an existing operational process. Interfaces to existing systems often require fit-form-function replacement, typically within a brown-field environment. Often 'free text' fields in such interfaces are reused by groups for their own undocumented purposes.

The safety argument should be based on an appropriate set of requirements, system description, its context, its intended use. We now build on the point made for the configuration group where we recognise the almost infinite states of the system (for the configuration group) is compounded in the delivery project by the use of 'glue', and possibly the undocumented behaviours of fit-form-function interfaces.

Delivery projects require even simple safety-related systems to have extensive documentation and effective configuration management, as by definition such systems should be deterministic based upon requirements to manage and mitigate hazards that may cause harm (to people, equipment or the environment). Therefore as systems get bigger in scope, scale and complexity effective safety management demands effective partitioning of the system to create 'barriers to escalation', including features such as built in test and diagnostic coverage.

The safety evidences required from these delivery projects to support the safety justification must therefore follow established safety management good practice. The basic safety questions are still valid: what does the system do; how can the system fail; what impact do those failures have (do they give rise to hazards) and how can they be mitigated.

3.4 Data interfaces

Data presented at the system interfaces may be consumed by the system. Where such data describes behaviour of the system (in whole or in part), it is clear that errors in this data will influence the behaviour of the system. The influence of data on the system should be assessed as part of the safety analysis; logic as well as good practice demands that data should attract an apportionment of the safety integrity requirements.

Data integrity requirements should also address verification and validation of the data at the system interface; and evidences supporting claimed data integrity should address the source of the data and the transportation of the data from its origin, to the system, through the use of a data supply chain.

Established means of data verification and validation already address properties such as range check and plausibility; often these tests also address groups of data and protect from possible corruption through the use of CRC checks. However, evidence from these data interfaces should also establish criteria for reasonableness and filtering. For a hardware component, one of the techniques to demonstrate its integrity is through the use of diagnostic coverage or built-in-test. Once data is attributed integrity requirements, common sense and good practise demand similar properties of the data design. Therefore safety evidences are required to support the data integrity claimed (and delivered).

3.5 Data supply chain

The means by which data is presented at the system interfaces also requires consideration. Data may be collated from several sources, transported across several organisational boundaries during which time it may be processed and fragments of that data presented at the system interface. The data may be used (and reused) by several systems. This data will have a number of properties (timeliness, accuracy, resolution, format, completeness and 'assurance level') (RTCA 1998) and require a data processing model addressing (Faulkner and Storey 2002):

1. origination: whereby values, names or other information are determined and assigned to required data elements for subsequent use
2. transmission: a process where data is moved from one physical location to another
3. data preparation: where a variety of data elements are analysed, translated, complied and/or formatted to produce data configured for use
4. data application integration: a process whereby data, in an application specific configuration and format, is made available to the target application
5. end-use of data: a process for assessing and acting upon the output of an application.

One of the key features of the definition of data integrity requirements is the selection of the system boundary, for the purpose of creating a system safety case. The system boundary should be set at the interface requiring data delivered to the system to be of the required integrity. The correct selection of this boundary then forces the safety argument to address the integrity of the data supply chain and, separately, the integrity of the data origin (Faulkner and Storey 2003).

3.6 Data origination

Data may be produced by a number of means, from simple data entry to complex and diverse automated toolsets. A data source may be created from data already within the data supply chain (consolidate phase) or data may be originated locally as a result of a process such as survey. Data may also originate remotely as data extracted from external information systems.

The integrity of the data origin will be a significant influence upon the integrity required from the supply chain. Low integrity at the data source may render the source unusable, whilst the supply chain should maintain the integrity of all data passed along to the consuming systems (Faulkner 2003).

Safety justification of the suitability of the data origin will therefore also require evidence from assessments, not only that the data is suitable for use, but also that it will continue to be suitable for use.

3.7 Safety system hierarchy

Scale, scope and complexity provide their own challenges, when these are combined with the requirements of a (configurable) control system which makes extensive use of data they create their own set of safety assurance challenges. A number of salient features of data-driven systems are listed below (Faulkner and Storey 2002):

1. Data-driven systems are often complex in comparison with conventional computer-based systems.
2. Data-driven systems often form part of a hierarchy of computers (Faulkner and Nicholson 2014) that exchange real-time data.
3. This complexity, and the interchange of data, makes data-driven systems challenging to design. It may also make it difficult for those charged with configuring the systems to gain a full insight into the original design intent.
4. Current approaches to configuration and validation of specific applications depend on assumptions of modularity and independence of the data.
5. Modularity and independence require well-structured data that has well-defined interfaces to the application software. These are often missing from current data-driven systems.
6. These deficiencies can produce problems for system validation.
7. Data may be drawn from external information systems to be used either as static configuration data or to influence the dynamic behaviour of the system.
8. Data supplied to these systems is through a supply chain, which may introduce errors during transmission or adaptation.

Data may change on a regular basis. The process of data modification and upgrade should also be required to demonstrate that these changes to the data do not affect overall system safety. Therefore this data process also requires a safety case.

4 Other safety systems in rail domains

We have deliberately focused on the UK railway control systems as a means to illustrate the changes in scale, scope and complexity. These changes also require those involved in safety assurance and safety acceptance to recognise the forthcoming challenges and adapt. We note that many of the safety standards in the domain address hardware and software, and to a limited extent configuration (FVL verses LVL); however, little is said of data.

We note that computer systems in general, and those employed in the rail domain in particular, are all pervasive. Perhaps one of the most significant changes in the UK rail environment will be the wholesale deployment of the European Railway Traffic Management System. The integration required between infrastructure control and train operation will place additional pressures on train maintenance and operation. To illustrate the point many modern rolling stock fleets contain train management systems controlling aspects of the train operation from air conditioning through lighting to correct side door operation. These systems will require update and therefore demand effective configuration management and change control. The maintenance of such complexity is moving away from rolling stock operators towards the rolling stock supplier. In addition, a number of the safety related systems are being replaced by computer based systems (for example brake systems were commonly based on a primary pneumatic (brake) train line with computer based systems as a secondary function).

The implementation of computer based technologies is not new. We observe that the UK rail industry is now at a turning point. Such is the number and diversity of the application of computer systems that their safety management is experiencing a 'change of scale'. Indeed the underlying nature of these systems is also changing from fixed specialised equipments and systems to more generalised configured systems. We detect that there is also a progressive and inevitable change away from the more 'traditional' configuration based on FVL and LVL to data configured and therefore data-centric systems.

5 Discussion

Data configured and therefore data-centric systems pose significant challenges for safety engineering, safety assurance and those who would accept and approve such safety systems. Scope, scale and complexity introduce a range of systematic errors previously associated with development of individual components, subsystems, systems and potentially whole domains into the operational domain. Earlier we introduced the concept of a 'change of scale'. We infer that greater discipline is required from all actors in the wider system to enforce and effectively implement the enabling processes (such as change control and configuration management). We observe that other industries have successfully employed such measures, aviation being a salient example. We recognise that such disciplines will require changes in working practices and involve substantial training, accreditation and assurance activities.

A 'change of scale' also implies that components and systems have become bigger, more interconnected and interdependent. Many industries effectively employ strategies to address these issues through recognition of a need to enforce boundaries through modularity. Our primary concern in this paper is the safety management and accreditation of these systems. In such large scale interconnected systems the propagation of errors across the system must be controlled. An increase in the number of any particular system type coupled with a decrease in the variety of these systems will lead to an increased exposure to common cause failures. The 'change of scale' will therefore require acceptance bodies to consider where the barriers to escalation are implemented. This implies that acceptance bodies will need to be cognisant of the 'bigger picture', maintaining a context of the rail industry as a whole. This will only be possible if the systems presented for acceptance are described in terms of a system hierarchy and that their respective influence and impact on the existing installations are adequately identified.

In this paper we do not challenge the established processes for safety engineering, safety assurance or acceptance and approval. HAZID, hazard logs, hazard management and risk models (cause and consequence) are still required. We suggest that a 'change of scale' requires greater discipline from all involved in safety systems, and that these systems should be supported by a systems engineering context (and by implication greater use of its techniques across the wider industrial base).

6 Conclusion

In this paper we have illustrated the integrity required from the 'controlling element', akin to a signalling control centre, and hence identify the significant challenges for the TMS, its equipment and system acceptance. The controlling element is part of a hierarchy requiring greater safety integrity closer to the running lines (SIL4 interlocking, SIL2 signalling control systems, etc). We have also identified issues with the scope, scale and complexity of such systems and their potential impact on the wider rail network. Indeed such issues are not limited to the TMS as similar issues can be found in the fleets of modern rolling stock.

A 'change of scale' demands greater discipline from those involved in safety management, in particular the diligent application of change control and configuration management. An increasing use of interconnected and interdependent systems may also lead to unexpected outcomes. The phrase 'foreseeable misuse' acquires new dimensions where data is produced, consumed (and reused) by data centric systems. It is data reuse that may prove to the greatest area of safety concern.

The safety justification of such systems requires a statement of the system within the overall railway system. The safety justification will also contain arguments (supported by appropriate evidences) addressing product development, configuration patterns, system instantiation (as part of a delivery project), data interfaces, data supply chain, and the data origin. Changes to data also need to be effectively controlled, in order to maintain the required system safety. It is noted that these evidences were once largely derived from the techniques and measures used within the development environment. The use of configured systems requires evidences to support the use of patterns (and sequences of patterns). The use of data centric systems will therefore require that the primary sources of evidence are derived from activities supporting the demonstration that the data integrity requirement are met and that they will continue to be met. The balance of contribution of evidences will therefore move away from the development environment towards the operational domain.

Safety is a system property which is ultimately the responsibility of the duty holder. Is the maintenance of an adequate description of the system hierarchy, its layers and required modularity (to provide appropriate barriers to escalation) also the responsibility of the duty holder?

Is this perhaps the greatest impact of the 'change of scale' in safety management and its ability to manage scope, scale and complexity that arise through the use of data centric systems?

References

CENELEC (2003) EN 50129, Railway applications – safety related electronic systems for signalling

ERA (2013) Common safety methods for risk assessment. European Railway Agency. http://www.era.europa.eu/Core-Activities/Safety/Safety-Management-System/Pages/Risk-Assessment.aspx. Accessed 6 October 2013

Faulkner A (2003) Data-intensive systems: sourcing data of the required integrity, the problem of origination. Proceedings of the Engineering Doctorate Conference, IMC Univ of Warwick

Faulkner A, Nicholson M (2014) An assessment framework for data-centric systems. Safety-critical Systems Symposium

Faulkner A, Storey N (2002) Data: an often-ignored component of safety-related systems. Proceedings of the MoD Equipment Safety Assurance Symposium ESAS02, Bristol, UK

Faulkner A, Storey N (2003) Strategies for the management of data-intensive safety-related systems. Proceedings of the 21st International Safety System Conference, Ottawa, Canada

IEC (2010) IEC 61508-3 Functional safety of electrical/electronic/programmable electronic safety-related systems – Part 3: Software requirements. International Electrotechnical Commission, Geneva

JPT (2001) Railtrack's railway safety case review for applicability to a controlling element such as the NMC. NMC Joint Project Team Document KD57268/Rep/003 (unpublished)

Mitchell IH (2003) Signalling control centres today and tomorrow. IRSE Proceedings

Railtrack (2001) Railtrack Railway Safety Case. Version 24. Volumes 1 and 2

ROGS (2006) The Railways and Other Guided transport systems (Safety) regulations (as amended)

ROTS (1994) The Railways and Other Transport Systems (approval of works, plant and equipment) regulations

RTCA (1998) DO 200A Standards for processing aeronautical data. Radio Technical Commission for Aeronautics. Washington

Stratton DH (1988) Solid state interlocking. 1st Edition. IRSE

Wikipedia (2013a) Integrated Electronic Control Centre. http://en.wikipedia.org/wiki/Integrated_Electronic_Control_Centre. Accessed 6 October 2013

Wikipedia (2013b) Solid State Interlocking. http://en.wikipedia.org/wiki/Solid_State_Interlocking. Accessed 6 October 2013

Wikipedia (2013c) Railtrack. http://en.wikipedia.org/wiki/Railtrack. Accessed 6 October 2013

Safety versus Security in Healthcare IT

Harold Thimbleby

Swansea University

Swansea, UK

Abstract   Safety and security are different but closely related concepts. Security is especially relevant in domains like finance, and safety is especially relevant in domains like healthcare and aviation. We review some of the safety problems besetting healthcare IT systems, and we show that some problems are technically open to improvement. Given that there are almost-free technologies (e.g., as part routine software upgrades) to improve safety, it is important to explore the reasons why healthcare safety does not get the priority that, for instance, security does in finance or safety does in aviation.

1 Introduction

Patient safety is a global priority (Donaldson and Philip 2004), and computers are surely part of the solution to improving healthcare. Yet healthcare has become a computing problem: computer systems under-perform and seem counter-productive. In contrast, in some domains like finance, computers have been enormously successful. Your and my bank accounts can be computerised the same way, but your health records are very different to mine. Nothing as simple as addition can summarise my patient records. Since finance is uniform but healthcare very dependent on the patient and needs of the practitioner (radiotherapist, consultant, pharmacist) some commentators have identified the much greater need for User Centred Design (UCD) in healthcare (Landauer 1996). But those comments were made in the last century, and international standards (such as ISO 14971 (ISO 2012) on the application of risk management to medical devices) are based on them. UCD (at least as interpreted by the ISO standards), or the lack of it, is not at the root of problems.

This paper reviews the context of healthcare safety as it relates to computing systems. We then contrast the state of healthcare with finance; the drivers are interestingly different, and we suggest that the differences between safety and security are insightful.

2 Healthcare error

The World Health Organization (WHO) defines 'never events' as errors that should not occur. An example is 'wrong site surgery' such as operating on the wrong patient or on the wrong part of the right patient. The idea is that never events do not and should not occur.

Yet approximately one in ten hospital patients suffer a preventable error. Obviously no professional makes errors deliberately, so errors must be unnoticed at the time they occur. A *preventable error* is defined as one that would have been avoided had all the known information been correctly interpreted and acted upon in the correct way. For example if you are allergic to a certain drug but nobody knew until your allergic reaction, giving you the drug would be an error only in hindsight, but it was not a simple preventable error. Often preventable errors are defined as being unprofessional, and are potentially criminal, for the nurses or clinicians involved.

Consider the following example. A nurse gives a patient 5 mg of morphine, and they are over-dosed and die. The consultant's prescription the nurse read said .5 mg, and by misreading the decimal point a dose ten times too high was administered. Perhaps the nurse thought the dose was high and asked a colleague to check it. Perhaps the second nurse also thought the prescription said 5 mg. Here the nurse has taken steps to prevent an error; the probability of an error occurring was reduced (though in fact it still occurred).

There are rules (ISMP 2007) for writing drug doses, and 'naked decimal points' (as in the decimal point in .5) are not allowed. So far as the nurse is concerned, they made an *induced error* – a recognised problem, misreading .5 as 5, occurred, and it should have been prevented by writing 0.5 mg or writing 500 mcg (1,000 mcg = 1 mg; note that µg is not used because it can be misread as mg). In other words, the environment the nurse worked in, in this case somebody writing .5, induced the error where 0.5 was misread as 5. So although we might not blame the nurse for the slip, we still blame somebody else, in this case the person who wrote down the prescription for not following standard procedures.

Imagine now that a computer is involved in the event. For example, the nurse read 5 mg off a computer screen rather than off a hand-written prescription. There is now an audit trail that shows the display really did indeed show 5 mg. There is also an audit trail to show the consultant keyed in 5 mg. The computer system is behaving as designed, so now it is clear that the consultant made an error. The consultant should have entered 0.5 mg but they entered 5 mg.

Let us imagine the consultant correctly planned to enter 0.5 mg. Unfortunately they hit • (the decimal point) and they accidentally clicked it twice. They noticed this keying error, and hence having keyed • twice, they pressed DELETE, then 5, then hit SEND. Had they been using Microsoft Office, they would indeed have entered 0.5 at the end of this sequence, but they are using special-purpose software designed for patient records. The user interface has been badly designed and poorly implemented: pressing decimal points more than once is ignored, so pressing DELETE deletes the 'only' decimal point. Hence 0 • • DELETE 5 becomes 05 which is treated as 5. This is the source of the ten times error, but the logs of the consultant's activities show they simply entered 5 mg. The records 'prove' the consultant is to blame. An incautious consultant might incriminate themselves, 'I didn't think I entered 5 mg, but the logs say I did, so yes, I must admit I made the mistake.' The logs do not show what the system did, nor how it turned (in this case) a *correctly corrected* error into an actual error leading to patient harm.

We agree an error has occurred; moreover, the error led to a patient receiving a ten times overdose of morphine, and this (in the story) leads to death. A computer system is part of the story, but it has been certified for medical use *and it did not malfunction*. It did was it was designed to do. Therefore (it seems) the error *must* have been caused by the operators: here, the consultant. However, as we described the sequence of events, such reasoning would be flawed.

The culture in healthcare is that professionals are perfect, and they have been professionally trained. The computer systems are perfect too, and they have been certified. The computer systems worked as designed; therefore the nurse (or other professional) must have betrayed us. It is not unusual to find the media vitriolically reporting stories of 'witches' – angels who have gone bad.

Healthcare chooses to focus on error rather than patient harm. Some errors are unprofessional and are so-called never events. Yet many errors do not lead to harm, and even never events can be mitigated – for example, a surgeon making an incision in the wrong place need not escalate that error into removing the wrong kidney if the error is noticed and intercepted. Indeed, there is a movement to promote resilience, reducing the impact of error: in 'Safety I' the focus is on the errors, and often blaming the people making identifiable errors; in contrast in the more enlightened 'Safety II' the point is that 99.9% or more of the time there is no harm – so focus on making that 99.9% a larger proportion of the time. Instead of blaming bad things, support and encourage good things (Eurocontrol 2013).

As we showed above, if the focus is on blaming bad things, we have to be very sure we are blaming the right bad things – in our example, suspending or sacking the consultant misleadingly seems to solve the problem (the system has got rid of a 'culprit'), but in fact the system that induces the problem has remained unexamined and likely to induce further errors. Worse, the culture of identifying individual failures encourages users to keep quiet about any problems they encounter – which is a twofold problem. The organization cannot learn how to improve and take advantage of learning from these workarounds; secondly, if new computer systems are designed, they will be designed as if these workarounds do not exist (because nobody knows about them), and therefore they will perpetuate and perhaps exacerbate the error-inducing behaviours. More clinicians will be terminated on the high altar of software.

3 Healthcare versus finance

It is interesting to contrast the healthcare profession's approach to patient safety with the financial industry's approach to loss. The WHO says some events are never events; they do not and should not occur. There is no prioritising. In finance, one expects some loss, and the idea is to minimise it to acceptable levels – acknowledging that there may be vanishing returns in doing so. In particular, it is recognised that reducing loss is a cost, and there is a trade-off: ultimately there are vanishing returns from reducing loss.

Finance distinguishes between loss from external problems and loss from internal problems, such as fraud. There is no reason to ignore external loss (though one might not want to tell shareholders). In contrast, in healthcare 'fraud' is very rare, and there is no such thing as *external* loss – all preventable harm is presumed caused by staff. In other words, when patient harm occurs, somebody within the organisation is in principle responsible.

Patients in hospitals are ill – if they weren't they should have been discharged already. So it is unsurprising that patients catch infections and perhaps get worse and die through nobody's fault. It is then a short step to disguise some preventable errors as the inevitable consequence of a patient's illness: 'I'm sorry your father died. He was very ill and in his weak state caught an infection that killed him.' A longer story might have been: 'I'm sorry your father died. We forgot to change his central line, so he caught an infection from it, from which he died' (Pronovost 2010). So, most of the time the healthcare organization underestimates the rate of preventable error, because much harm is being disguised as inevitable.

When patient harm occurs that must have an explanation (e.g., because somebody has complained), it then appears that it is exceptional. Normally there are no 'errors' and so now there is an investigation uncovering errors, these must be exceptionally unprofessional. Perhaps an example then needs to be made out of the carer who made 'the mistake'.

4 Safety versus security

Safety and security are very similar concepts. Making a mountain climber safe means making them secure; conversely, making them secure makes them safe. A financier might talk about safe investments, making very little distinction between secure and safe. It is more helpful to make these words refer to clearly distinct concepts. Thus, *safety* is about achieving well-being, health and physical wholeness of people (or possibly animals or the natural environment more broadly); and *security* is virtual wholeness – only the right people have access to the information. Money rather blurs this distinction: because it is fungible it can be made either virtual or physical and still work just as well. Moreover, somebody who has very little money (e.g., who loses their money through a security breach) starts to be at risk of starvation or other safety problems. It is not surprising the words have vague definitions retaining overlaps in various domains. Here, however, we are particularly interested in the use of these words for computer system design, and computers are increasingly making the distinctions hard: a door lock that provides physical security (with metal keys) can be implemented by a computer using virtual security (passwords and smart cards), and the lock may be used to ensure that people *securely* behind the locked door are protected from intruders and are therefore *safer*.

In a hospital, safety is primarily focussed on patient safety (staff safety is not much different in a hospital from any other workplace, apart from increased risk of illness). Security is about ensuring only authorised users have access to patient records; security in a hospital does relate to normal operations, and clinicians will therefore often take short cuts such as sharing passwords. In contrast, in a bank, the primary concern is security. The bank does not want to lose money to unauthorised people. Of course, staff safety is a major concern, but this is usually achieved through physical protections (such as door locks and thick glass screens) rather than by normal computer system operations.

5 Defining usability, security and safety for system designers

We can make some contrasts between the usability/security/safety concepts clearer by a narrower set of definitions based around the engineering decisions we have to make when designing computer systems. A philosophical or etymological debate is all very well, but how do we design more effective systems? As engineers, we want to improve the world.

- *Usability* is about making systems easy to use for everyone.
- *Security* is about making systems easy to use for designated people and very hard (if not impossible) for everyone else. It is about designing systems to be hard to use for the wrong people; we do not want the wrong people to do bad things with the systems. There are bad people, and we do not want them to easily access or use our systems.
- *Safety* is about stopping the right people doing bad things. Good people make slips and errors; in a safe system those errors should not escalate to untoward incidents, harm or other safety issues.

These simple and nicely contrasting definitions raise immediate tensions. A secure system may not be very usable. In turn this will encourage its users to find workarounds to make their daily use of the system more 'user friendly'. Thus a hospital system may end up with everyone sharing the same password, as this is much easier than remembering individual passwords and logging in and out repeatedly. But making it usable for the right people has also made it usable for the wrong people (e.g., intruders), and thus undermines security.

The definitions seem to take it for granted what 'good' and 'bad' mean. But these are more subtle concepts. Good users do not intend their activities ever to be bad, but those actions may turn out to have bad consequences. So, safety is about designing for good people who may inadvertently set in motion things that end up going bad. Often users are dedicated to getting their jobs done, and because the computer systems they use are not well designed, the users prioritise doing their jobs well regardless of obstacles the computers throw at them (Blythe et al. 2013). Their managers might think that their workarounds are 'bad' because they are not standard operating procedures, but often managers have no idea about what really goes on! So: although in the definitions the meanings of 'bad' and 'good' seem self-evident, in reality thinking that a good person does bad things is a short step away from scape-goating that well-intentioned person. What is really meant is that a good person does great things, but the system as a whole is broken and badly-designed, so a well-intentioned action leads irretrievably to a bad outcome. We gave an example of this above: a consultant corrects a typo, the wrong dose ends up being administered. 'A good person did a bad thing' clearly captures too little of the reality of the problem.

The number of users is an important consideration when designing systems. In the limiting case, the programmer is the only user, and they know how to use any program they develop. Hence programmers are very experienced at building user interfaces that are special cases. When systems are used by many users, usability problems often arise because the majority of their users are unlike programmers, and have no deep knowledge of the implementation. Furthermore, when systems are used by many users, some of them are more likely to be bad, so security becomes increasingly important.

The problem is that most programmers develop their experience and skills in the limiting case, and hence unconsciously under-play managing the issues that unavoidably arise in real systems. Good UCD practice requires experimental assessment of proposed designs, iterative development, with the actual users of the system.

A subtle consideration is the proportion of computers to users. In a typical financial application, the ratio is about 1:1. A user logs on to the secure system, and stays using it. In a hospital, the ratio is perhaps 1:20. Now users frequently have to log in and log out because the computer is shared. Since this is tedious and interferes with the task these users are performing (i.e., patient care), a common workaround is to log in one user, and then share their credentials for the remainder of the shift. Since passwords are often complex (so intruders cannot work them out) it is common for the passwords to be displayed prominently; while this helps the good users know the password, it has the side-effect of showing the password to potential bad users. Such workarounds make logging in easier and save logging in and out repeatedly, and improve the safety patient care. Ironically, the more extreme the computer:user ratio, the higher the overhead of logging in and out in proportion to the cost of doing tasks, and also, with more users, the higher the probability that there is a bad user wanting to gain access to the system. But security is not top of a carer's agenda.

A series of people using medical systems without logging in and out can cause unfortunate problems. For example, most ECG monitors allow the sensitivity to be changed. If sensitivity is reduced by one operator, and the next operator is taking the ECG from a patient with Left Ventricular Hypertrophy (LVH), a symptom of which is higher voltages, this problem will be very hard to notice. I don't know of any ECG monitors that bother to have logging in and out protocols and reset their settings in-between, because they are 'just' devices.

Whether workarounds in healthcare compromise security in a significant way is a matter for careful assessment. What is clear is that without proper UCD no designer would know – you have to watch the systems in use, not look at their logs. The fact that they appear to be being used successfully does not mean that the operating practices have not become risky, compromising both safety and security.

6 Expectations and culture

We have defined security as stopping bad people doing bad things. An engineer might use this definition to help think about passwords and so forth. But there is a more interesting angle: we *expect* bad people to do bad things. So when bad things happen, this is to be expected. We expect robbers to try to rob!

In contrast, safety is about stopping good people doing bad things. Again, an engineer might use this definition to think about confirmation dialog boxes, undo features, and so forth. But there is a more interesting angle: we do not expect good people to do bad things. It is more like a betrayal when they do. We do not expect nurses to kill patients.

Perhaps this is why financial systems are designed to protect against security breaches, but healthcare systems are not designed to protect against human error? Designers do not expect good people to be bad. Unfortunately, 'to err is human' – everybody makes errors eventually. This does not mean they are bad, but it does mean that the systems they use should be designed so that they are protected from their predictable errors.

However, the safety/security 'divide' cannot be the whole story: civil aviation safety is improving, but healthcare safety is not.

The US Institute of Medicine has made the memorable comparison that preventable deaths in US hospitals is as bad as a jumbo jet crashing and killing all passengers every week.

When an aircraft crashes the accident is visible, even, depressingly, photogenic. The consequences become publicly visible. From the airline's point of view, they have lost a very expensive piece of equipment – the airframe – and from their and the manufacturer's point of view potentially lost a lot of credibility and future market share. There is therefore high motivation to *correctly* seek out the causes of the incident so that there can be learning and similar incidents avoided in the future. For example, if the pilot was asleep, was that caused by inappropriate flying schedules? Certainly, blaming the pilot (so-called 'pilot error') is a misdirection from the full story.

In contrast, in healthcare, the deaths (and other harms) occur one at a time and usually in private. Often the patient was seriously ill to start with, so their death may not be surprising – whereas death from an aircraft accident is surprising. It is easy to think of many simple reasons why a sick patient dies rather than seek the real causes (cf. the comments about central line infections above). The patient's ill-health can often be blamed; whereas, except in cases of terrorism, it is not legitimate to blame the passengers for an aircraft accident.

When an aircraft crashes it is self-evident that the system failed to do what it is designed to do, namely to get an aircraft fly (and land) safely. When a patient dies, often the medical device involved (such as the linear accelerator that generated the radiation overdose) had been certified as compliant to relevant standards. It therefore seems logical that any error must have been due to the user if it was not the device. Some examples of this type of thinking are given in Thimbleby (2013) – unfortunately it often leads to inappropriate and indeed unproductive reprimands.

However, that a device is compliant does not mean it could not be better; and if it could be better, perhaps the incident in question might have been prevented by better design rather than being caused by operator error? We will give a concrete example of this possibility below: we show that a compliant system can be made safer; it follows that the relevant standards are not perfect. Some errors are induced by poor design.

So if there are many possible reasons why a patient died it is tempting to find the cheapest answers – namely fate or nurse error – and thus avoid seeking improvements in the system. In contrast, in aviation, the least costly option in the long run is to fix any failures in the system – blaming pilot error might be easy, but it won't stop the next pilot making the same error. Moreover, if a second crash occurs for the same system reasons (e.g., a failure in the airframe design or in the airline's operating procedures), when this becomes common knowledge the manufacturer or carrier will be even worse off. The profile of air accidents forces investigations to seek the truth; the personal nature of healthcare incidents encourages delay, deny and scapegoat.

7 Example – reducing the probability of out by ten errors

There may be cultural reasons for differences, but if some of the unsolved problems are not solvable then there are also engineering problems. If so, one would then have to seek solutions to improving healthcare in, for instance, better training or incentives. We now show that quite simple engineering interventions can make systems safer. One wonders why these ideas are not more widely used.

Let us assume the nurse notices an error with probability q; in our simple model we assume the error is either noticed immediately or not at all.

Example. The nurse should enter 5. With probability p they will press a random key other than 5 and if so, with probability q, they will press CLEAR or take other appropriate action (correctly using the particular user interface being modelled) to recover from that noticed error.

If the nurse notices an error, they will correct it, and it will not lead to harm. Unnoticed errors are problematic, since when they occur nothing in the system intercepts them. One might use training to increase q; one might design operating procedures that increase q – for example, having two nurses perform a calculation allows them to check each other, thus ideally increasing q to $1 - (1 - q)^2$ *except* that nurses are not independent, so the probabilities do not multiply up so nicely. For example, with a q of 0.5 each nurse we might hope the probability of noticing errors would improved to 0.75 by using a pair of nurses as 'buddies' to check each other. Unfortunately, if one nurse misses an error, the other nurse is likely to miss it too (many of the reasons the first nurse missed it will still apply to the second nurse, so the probabilities are not independent). Worse, human psychology means that if we think a pair of nurses is safer, we may take greater risks; or perhaps the second nurse does not actually check the first nurse's actions, but just feels the first nurse must have got it right. Some hospitals therefore require critical calculations to be done by a *single* nurse: since they have nobody else to rely on, hopefully this increases their attention to the details of the task and hence their q. This somewhat digressive discussion will motivate an alternative approach to improving q below.

Dose Error Reduction Systems (DERS) have been introduced for exactly this reason. A DERS knows the drug a patient is prescribed, and then limits the ranges of dosage to within safe values; effectively, it notices out-of-range errors and intercepts them. DERS have been shown to reduce patient harm.

The probability that the user makes a keying error is p, which is around 1% – that is, about 1 in 100 hundred keystrokes of an attentive nurse is in error.

With these assumptions, it is possible to simulate nurses entering data, making slips, and possibly intercepting those slips; similar methods have been discussed elsewhere (Thimbleby and Cairns 2010, Cauchi et al. 2013). One can then consider alternate designs and select those that let through fewer errors. One can also explore trade-offs; for example, it may be preferable to reduce significant errors preferentially, or if reducing unnoticed errors means significantly increasing the time it takes to enter data, in some cases (like resuscitation) where time is of the essence, some error latitude may be acceptable. The user interfaces analysed in this paper behave identically if the user makes no errors, and, in particular, the sequence of keystrokes required to enter a number correctly is identical in all cases.

A standard definition of significant errors for numerical data is an out by ten error. An out by ten error occurs when a number entered is ten times out (too high or too low) from the intended value. For almost all medication, an out by ten error results in significant patient harm (possibly including unnecessary pain and longer stays in hospital, etc.).

A Monte Carlo model assumes a user makes key slip errors with probability p, notices these errors with probability q, and corrects them (again potentially making further keystroke errors with probability p). We generate key sequences for numbers, and compare the intended and final values for several designs. Figure 1 shows typical results. The graph shows that the probability of out by ten errors decreases with increasing q for every design considered, but more interestingly it shows that designs differ significantly in how dependable they are. Furthermore, the safety ranking of the design assessments are independent of q. (In fact, but not shown here, the rankings are also independent of p or whether we measure 'out by 10' or 'out by k' for any $k > 1$.)

Three contrasting designs are chosen:

1. The user interface of the common HP EasyCalc 100 handheld calculator (introduced in 2009). This device has a DELETE key that is faulty: it deletes only digits and ignores decimal points (so that, e.g., 1 2 • DELETE is treated as 1).
2. A user interface with a correction key that works correctly.
3. A proposed user interface that enforces the Institute of Safer Medication Practices guidelines for writing drug doses (ISMP 2007), as discussed above.

The status of these three designs can be contrasted:

1. This is a general purpose calculator and as such may be found in hospitals for routine calculations, such as drug dosage.
2. Many user interfaces of this type have been certified for medical use.
3. No known system in use adheres to the ISMP guidelines.

For simplicity we do not consider here other design choices; for example, many user interfaces (like the HP EasyCalc 100) ignore multiple decimal point key presses. On these, pressing 0 • • 5 has the same effect as pressing 0 • 5, and pressing 0 • 5 • would also be treated as 0 • 5, as if the second decimal point is ignored. The ISMP user interface however would treat any number with more than one decimal point as an error. Moreover, the ISMP interface blocks the user until they correct the error; that is, for the limited class of error that ISMP recognizes, q is effectively 1; thus, in the ISMP design, q is therefore measuring the user's ability to detect non-ISMP errors. Evidently ISMP errors account for about half of all input errors and, as these results show, it is surprising that enforcing ISMP guidelines is not routine in healthcare user interfaces. Put another way, if the system can detect a class of error, the user does not need to be trained and vigilant to detect those errors.

We note that the ISMP guidelines say:

'They [writing numbers in the specified error-prone ways] should NEVER [original emphasis] be used when communicating medical information. This includes internal communications, telephone/verbal prescriptions, computer-generated labels, labels for drug storage bins, medication administration records, as well as pharmacy and prescriber computer order entry screens.'

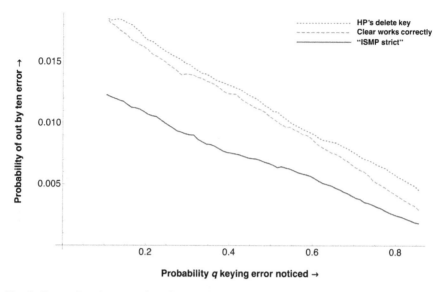

Fig. 1. Comparing three user interface designs for safety. The lower the line in the graph, the lower the probability of serious error, hence the better. The graph shows that a commercially-available but buggy user interface is least safe (of the three designs compared) and that a normal user interface is about twice as bad as an innovative user interface that implements the ISMP guidelines as part of its design rather than relying on user training for conformance to the guidelines. (The lines are based on Monte Carlo simulations of user behaviour, randomly entering typical drug doses, and therefore the plots are not smooth.)

Although ISMP do not explicitly mention medical devices like infusion pumps or linear accelerators, the intention is clearly there. Moreover, the number format guidelines we implemented in the 'ISMP strict' user interface are also recognised by the US Joint Commission National Patient Safety Goals, which specify that these error-prone abbreviations must be listed in organizational do-not-use lists.

Despite these high profile recommendations, designers have failed to make the obvious connection to user interface design! As our analysis shows, applying the recommendations would, unsurprisingly, improve safety. Figure 2 shows the effective increase in q for a single user; the worse the user was at detecting errors, the better the improvement.

Notably, the 'ISMP strict' user interface differs from the other two only in its programming: the keyboard and screen design are not changed (they are not even part of the analytic model). Any medical device or system relying on firmware or software could be improved next time the software is updated ... for virtually no cost, since the firmware of these things is being updated all the time to introduce new features and fix bugs.

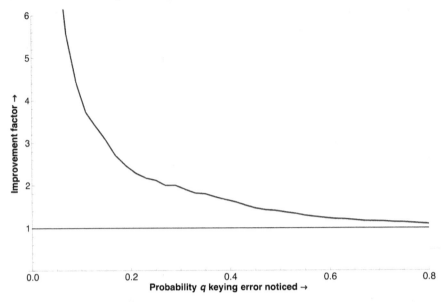

Fig. 2. Effective improvement in error detection. Effectively, the ISMP style user interface makes nurses less error-prone, and the worse the nurse, the more impressive the factor of improvement. Obviously, for a very good nurse error detection probability (q tending to 1) the improvement factor must diminish to 1 – and it never makes it worse. Specifically, the graph compares the out by ten error rate of a normal user interface (not the buggy Hewlett Packard interface also shown in Figure 1) and the improved ISMP style of user interface. (The graph above plots $s^{-1}(ismp(q))/q$ where $s(q)$ is the probability of an out by ten error for a standard user interface, and $ismp(q)$ is the probability of an out by ten error for the proposed ISMP style user interface. The graph is derived from the Figure 1 Monte Carlo simulations and therefore is not completely smooth.)

8 Conclusions

Healthcare is recognized as unsafe, and despite increasing computing interventions its safety record is not improving as well as other areas, such as civilian aviation. In fact, because computers are ubiquitous, from implants to patient record systems, healthcare is coming to be seen as a major IT problem – arguably, improving computer systems will improve healthcare outcomes better than by conventional (pharmaceutical, medical, social, etc.) interventions.

This paper explored cultural reasons why there is a lower priority to fix healthcare safety than to fix the security of financial systems or the safety of aviation systems. However, a key point is that this state of affairs need not be accepted. We showed it is straightforward to make some illustrative aspects of healthcare safer by simple engineering interventions. Essentially, the graph in Figure 1 shows that better engineered systems are safer, as one would expect. It also shows that a large improvement in dependability can be achieved by enforcing already-known recommendations to improve safety; the relative improvement is shown in Figure 2: the worse the problem the more the engineering approach helps. Essentially, the conventional approach is to treat ISMP guidance as *human* guidance; here we have shown that the ISMP guidance can be engineered into the *system* so the system can help the user notice more errors, specifically those mistakes the ISMP guidance (based on evidence) forbids.

A strong point of the present paper is that it shows that improvements in healthcare can be achieved by better engineering, and this requires no training or improved human factors awareness or even, in many cases, any changes in standard operating procedures. In other words, improving computer systems is very cost-effective and of lasting value.

The final question is how do we make improvements start to happen?

Arguably the bizarre behaviour of the Hewlett Packard calculator happened because nobody prioritised assessing it rigorously for dependability; the calculator is not a market failure, however, and apparently, no users are aware of its design problems either. The techniques used to compare designs (illustrated in the Figures) are examples of engineering assessments of safety that could be developed into rigorous safety procedures to inform design, procurement or consumer ratings. Once measured, we then need to make the safety assessments of systems visible at the point of sale and point of use. Doing so will generate economic pressure (and public pressure) to improve the engineering (Thimbleby 2013).

Acknowledgments   The work reported in this paper was partly funded by EPSRC Grant EP/G059063/1. Ross Anderson made insightful comments for which the author is grateful.

References

Blythe J, Koppel R, Smith SW (2013) Circumvention of security: Good users do bad things. IEEE Security & Privacy 11(5):80–83

Cauchi A, Curzon P, Gimblett A et al (2012) Safer '5-key' number entry user interfaces using differential formal analysis. In: Proceedings BCS Conference on HCI, Vol XXVI pp 29–38. Oxford University Press

Donaldson L, Philip P (2004) Patient safety – a global priority. Bulletin of the World Health Organization 82(12):892–893

Eurocontrol (2013) From Safety I to Safety II: a white paper. European Organisation for the Safety of Air Navigation. http://www.eurocontrol.int/sites/default/files/content/documents/nm/safety/safety_whitepaper_sept_2013-web.pdf. Accessed 7 November 2013

ISMP (2007) ISMP's list of error-prone abbreviations, symbols, and dose designations. Institute for Safe Medication Practices. http://www.ismp.org/Tools/errorproneabbreviations.pdf. Accessed 7 November 2013

ISO (2012) ISO14971 Medical devices – Application of risk management to medical devices

Landauer, TK (1996) The trouble with computers: usefulness, usability and productivity. MIT Press

Pronovost P (2010) Safe patients, smart hospitals: how one doctor's checklist can help us change health care from the inside out. Hudson Street Press

Thimbleby H (2013) Improving safety in medical devices and systems. In: Proceedings IEEE International Conference on Healthcare Informatics (IEEE ICHI), pp1–13

Thimbleby H, Cairns P (2010) Reducing number entry errors: solving a widespread, serious problem. Journal Royal Society Interface 7(51):1429–1439

Safety and Human Factors: Two Sides of the Same Coin

Andy Lowrey[1] and Branka Subotić[2]

[1]NATS Directorate of Safety, Fareham, UK

[2]NATS Global Consultancy, London, UK

Abstract   In an integrated change management project, human factors and functional safety cannot be considered separately. Both must work closely together to
provide appropriate and comprehensive assurance for the introduction of complex
changes to safety critical industries. This paper presents case studies of two different projects where safety and human factors were joined up in a coherent set of
activities across all project phases. The first project looks at the UK airspace design changes to air traffic management in preparation for the London 2012 Olympics. The second examines the introduction of an advanced set of controller tools
(iFACTS), introduced at the Swanwick London Area Control Centre in 2011.
Both case studies represent examples of effective integration of safety and human
factors assurance activities.

1 The UK's leading air traffic service provider

NATS is the UK's largest air traffic management provider, maintaining the or-
derly, efficient and, above all, safe passage of aircraft through UK airspace and
beyond. NATS handled over 2.2 million flights in FY 2011/12.

NATS service starts from 30 degrees longitude west over the Atlantic Ocean,
expands into the UK en-route control and terminal control. The London terminal
control airspace represents one of the most complex airspaces in the world, handling traffic coming into and out of five London airports. These include Gatwick,
the busiest single runway in the world, and Heathrow, the busiest dual runway
airport in the world. Our service further includes provision of Air Traffic Control
(ATC) at fifteen of the UK's largest airports as well as ten Spanish airports.

Safety in NATS is managed and delivered through a number of different roles.
In addition to safety functions dedicated to the delivery of projects, a separate department, the NATS Directorate of Safety, is responsible for providing independent assurance to the Director of Safety. This department consists of safety specialists from different facets of organisation, bringing engineering and operational

experience. Around half of the staff in the Directorate of Safety are Human Factors (HF) specialists with a diverse set of skills. These include ergonomics, occupational psychology, cognitive psychology, operational safety, software development, and systems engineering. The key to the Directorate's ability to provide oversight of all safety risks and activities in the company is this diversity of specialisms, including both safety and human performance.

In NATS as a whole, as in the Directorate, safety is recognised as being more than a narrow focus on equipment reliability. Consequently, HF and safety specialists work closely together to manage safety of all operational changes as well as steady state operations.

2 Complete identification of risk in air traffic management

The management of safety in safety-critical industries is well defined and documented. Although less ubiquitous, the HF specialists in many companies are becoming an important part of project engineering and day to day operations. However, in many organisations, HF and safety are functionally separated, with safety focusing on equipment reliability and assurance arguments for technical change, while HF focuses on human reliability, ergonomics, Human Machine Interface (HMI) design or occupational psychology. In the past, this was certainly the case within NATS. This distinction and separation of the two areas constrained the NATS' ability to achieve a holistic risk profiling and assessment within its operation.

In spite of decades of HF development and evolution, the discipline is still not fully embedded in the operational environments of all safety-critical industries. The nuclear industry can be seen as a leader in the integration of safety and HF. The picture in the aviation industry, however, is more variable. Apart from aircraft manufacturers and equipment suppliers, where HF departments can be quite large, the HF specialists in European air traffic service providers, airports, and airlines are scarce. Furthermore, in companies where the HF specialists are embedded, they are usually separate from the safety department in the organisational design and structure.

In ATC today, technology is being used much more to provide decision support and flag up potential hazards to an air traffic controller. However, the controller retains the ultimate executive control and responsibility for maintaining separation between aircraft (Wickens et al. 1998).

Understanding that, within NATS, the controller is the key element in maintaining safety. NATS recognises that the measurement and management of human performance is essential in managing operational risk and the study and management of human performance started as a subset of research and development. As a result, the study and management of human performance became integrated fully into the NATS Safety Management System (SMS), and logically, moved more central in the corporate organisational structure. This integration has evolved over more than a decade. Merging human performance and safety, both in the company structure and SMS, has identified activities that have provided most benefit. The following sections provide a brief overview of some of these activities, where problems were encountered and overcome more efficiently.

2.1 Safety and human performance – presenting an integrated assurance argument

In the safety-critical industries, very few changes do not impact all three areas: people, procedures and equipment. Consequently, any assurance argument that wishes to truly understand the potential risk attached to a change programme must consider all of these areas together.

Rather than addressing equipment reliability, human performance and procedural design in isolation, NATS developed a single integrated assurance case, based upon claims, arguments and evidence covering all impacted areas. This brings particular value to the understanding of safety. The isolated focus on a single area (for example operating procedures) limits the ability of the organisation to identify risks and provide holistic assurance that occurs across the boundaries and interfaces of the human-technical system. The integrated human performance and safety approach prevents specialists from working in 'silos', with limited required interaction, and truly enables a 'total system' approach when it comes to safety of operation.

The integrated safety argument became a norm within NATS making an overarching claim that the total change is acceptably safe. This top claim is then decomposed to provide logically linked strands. For example, the top level arguments surrounding procedural design might be that the system functional boundaries are known, that the division of activity between the equipment and the human are known, and that the procedures are consequently usable and correct. Evidence for these three areas necessarily comes from multiple sources:

- engineers, sharing their understanding of the equipment design and limitations
- the HF specialist, applying the key principles of cognitive psychology and human information processing to inform the procedure design
- the operational procedure specialists, that the procedure is fit for purpose and appropriate for operational staff.

In most change programmes within NATS, the assurance argument is assembled and managed by safety engineers throughout the life of the project, closely collaborating with HF specialists. This allows the presentation of a single integrated safety 'snapshot' at each significant point in the project lifecycle, which covers all equipment, organisational and human performance planning, assurance evidence and outstanding risks. This approach delivers a number of benefits, including the ability to present a holistic argument about risk management and identify risks across specialism boundaries (for example software safety and HMI design).

2.2 The building blocks of safety – requirement management

The timely derivation of a complete and coherent set of requirements is instrumental to any project. For every change, the NATS project team works on identifying a complete set of requirements. This has always proved challenging , as the specification of requirements at the start of a project is always going to be hampered by an imperfect understanding of the change, its impacts, and the activities and emergent properties encountered as the project progresses towards implementation. For example, large NATS projects rely on hundreds of verification and validation requirements, which will only be addressed and assessed for correctness many months or years after they are devised.

In any project, a complete set of requirements informs what system validation evidence needs to be collected and what material, tests and documentation needs to be published for the verification evidence to be collected. Therefore, it is essential to gather requirements from all stakeholders, including HF specialists who brings expertise around the project human performance goals. However, it is hard for HF specialists to have an input early enough in the project life cycle if they are not invited. The reason for this is usually that HF is not treated with similar 'weight' as other traditional technical domains (such as system engineering or software development) or the programme management does not understand the scope of human performance impact that the change may have.

As a result, the HF specialists are sometimes brought into the later stages of the project life-cycle to fix an emerging or unforeseen problem, but when consequent remedial design changes are costly and require considerable evidence to support their funding. Figure 1 highlights the cost saving achieved by incorporating HF as early as possible in the design ('proactive human factors') as opposed to 'reactive' or 'no human factors' involvement during the project life cycle.

Within NATS, the ubiquitous nature of the access to, and review of, requirements means that human performance requirements are given equal weight alongside technical safety requirements, and are articulated early in the change lifecycle. Although it is still difficulty to draft good requirements at an early stage, this timely collaborative approach has been shown to negate potential problems. This approach delivers a number of benefits, such as:

- Early sight and review of requirements minimises surprises later in the project.
- Inclusion of HF and safety requirements in the same depository ensures appropriate rigor and attention to both areas.

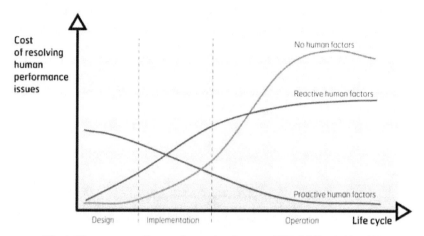

Fig. 1. The true cost of human factors involvement (EUROCONTROL 1999)

2.3 Did we build the right product? – the importance of system validation

Over time, NATS has developed a mature system validation methodology. This system validation evidence forms a key aspect of safety and human factors assurance arguments. In the world of the project manager or unit general manager, it helps to answer three questions:

- Does the system do what it was hoped to do?
- Can the users deliver the benefits of the change?
- Is the project ready to go live with the change?

The NATS system validation methodology is structured into six steps, as shown in Figure 2. Taking these steps in turn:

1. The first step aims to identify a complete set of requirements that must be validated. This activity involves close collaboration between safety and HF specialists as well as technical experts across the business.
2. Each requirement is then captured in a range of scenarios. Some requirements will require a specific event to be simulated for validation evidence to be captured (for example an unexpected airspace infringement) whilst others will be generic, and able to be captured in each and every scenario.
3. Once a comprehensive set of requirements and scenarios are defined, it becomes necessary to map each requirement with relevant measures in this step. In general, these are a mix of subjective, behavioural and objective measures.
4. Once the relevant measures are selected, it is necessary to define a target range for each measure of interest. This allows the project team to clearly understand and articulate the criteria for system validation of each requirement. This is

usually based upon the baseline captured using the current system/procedure/
operation, and fine-tuned using expert judgement.

5. Next, the design of all measures of interest selected in Step 3 is completed.
   Some of the measures are widely used elsewhere and readily available (for example in the measurement of cognitive workload), whilst others must be tailored specifically for the task under consideration.
6. Finally, Step 6 is conducting the validation exercise itself.

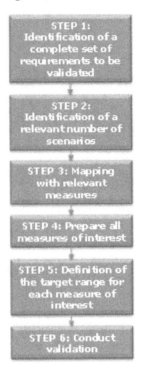

Fig. 2. Steps in system validation methodology

NATS philosophy emphasises a phased implementation of large change projects.
This phased implementation of a change is preceded by phased system validation.
Following successful system validation, publication of all project documentation
and gaining internal and external acceptance, Limited Operational Service (LOS)
trials take place in the live operational environment under strictly controlled operational conditions.

There are a number of benefits of focusing on human performance in the system validation process:

- The technical system is not examined in isolation, but instead the users' ability
  to safely use the system and deliver the expected benefit is empirically measured.

- A set of clearly articulated performance goals appropriate for each stage of system validation is produced. This gives a clear, common understanding of success or failure to all parties; be they the project team senior management, or the regulator.
- The decision to 'go live' is evidence-based, with a clear set of mandatory actions to be completed.

2.4 When is enough enough? – measuring training effectiveness

Training of operational staff within the scope of major change projects is very costly. Large scale changes that impact operational tasks not only require a significant training programme but also complex rostering to ensure that the operations room runs smoothly and that service provision is unaffected throughout the duration of training.

As a result, NATS has increasingly focused on ensuring that the delivery of training is lean and effective, and that the training plan delivers fully trained operational staff in a manner that is seamless to the point of service delivery. This focus led to the development of a NATS training effectiveness methodology that, as with system validation, directly informs the safety arguments.

The training effectiveness methodology is based on understanding and differentiation between the new/changed skills and core skills for the operational staff (Figure 3). The assessment is based on a mix of subjective and objective classes of measures. Subjective measures rely on operational staff to rate their level of skill acquisition and overall task performance[1] at different stages of training. Objective measures rely on tests, questionnaires and practical assessment conducted by on-the-job training instructors[2]. The final result is based on an equal contribution of both classes of measures as well as comments by the trainee and the instructor. These training effectiveness results inform the final sign-off; formal acceptance by the trained air traffic controller and the instructor that the air traffic controller is ready to use the changed system in the live operational environment.

As with the measurement of human performance within the system validation activity, this explicit form of assessing the transfer of skills and knowledge has delivered a number of benefits:

- It moves away from a 'box ticking mentality' by simply stating that the training has been delivered.
- It considers whether the trainee is confident in their ability to perform the tasks by using the changed system.

---

[1] Measurement of the overall task performance is only feasible during real-time simulations.

[2] This type of assessment is often utilised in the air traffic control environment for the operational staff.

- The evidence that skills have been transferred or learned form a key part of the safety case argument. Again, this is an example of a human performance argument being key to an integrated change argument.
- The training phase can be concluded once skills are shown to have been acquired to the required level by the trainee through measurement. This reduces the risk of over-training and under-training. The trainees are signed off as soon as they achieve the required level of knowledge and skills. This can happen at three different stages: before the end of planned training, at the point of delivery of planned training, or after the end of planned training, when trainees requires more training time. This enables the most cost effective approach to training and a focused set of training sessions to build the required knowledge or skill.

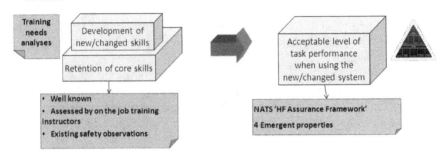

Fig. 3. NATS training effectiveness high-level methodology

2.5 A shared understanding – collaboration between regulator and service provider

All technical and organisational changes within NATS are overseen by a regulatory body, the Safety and Airspace Regulation Group (SARG), part of the UK's Civil Aviation Authority (CAA). The SARG have identified human performance as a thread that runs through all of their key areas of focus in UK aviation safety (UK CAA 2013).

SARG inspectors work closely with NATS across all areas of the operation, particularly where change is proposed. Increasingly, there is an expectation by the regulator that human performance assurance will be provided alongside the technical aspects. Indeed, although the technical correctness argument still remains key, the regulator also concentrates on the argument that all change is user-focused, user-informed, that human performance remains acceptable, and that the user is confident operating the changed system in a live environment.

This changing focus is in part due to the understanding within NATS around the need to integrate human performance and safety, and the development of processes that facilitate this. As projects implement change, they have been able to provide an enhanced and coordinated picture of risk arising from that change. A dynamic has increasingly emerged where this integrated assurance picture is seen as valuable by the regulator, and so NATS projects become structured to provide this information as a matter of course. This has had benefits to both NATS and the regulator.

- The regulator can be confident of receiving an ever more accurate risk footprint in the current operation.
- NATS understands what assurance evidence is important to the regulator, and so can plan to provide it in a timely and effective manner.

3 Case studies of two key projects

3.1 The London 2012 Olympics

When London was announced as the venue for the 2012 Olympics, NATS started a project to ensure that air traffic management over the UK was resilient enough for the expected challenges. Like many projects focusing on air traffic management, the London Olympics were expected to impact the airspace design over Southern England (Figure 4), but also rely on the management of human performance. This led to an assurance structure in which HF specialists worked alongside safety specialists to provide the necessary hazard identification, analysis and evidence gathering to ensure that risk remained within the quantified tolerable range.

At the start of the project, a number of high-level risks were identified. These included:

- the expectation of a sudden, unquantified increase in scheduled and VIP air traffic over the London Terminal Control Area
- the need to accommodate the increased military traffic and security constraints without causing capacity constraints and hazards to civil air traffic
- the need to deliver a high-visibility project, with a delivery date that could not slip.

These high-level risks informed the initial hazard identification work. Rather than use a risk classification scheme focusing on equipment reliability, the project instead used one developed within NATS for the assessment of procedural changes. This was thought to provide a better view of risks that arose from user and organisational causes, rather than those emerging from equipment failures. Safety and human performance specialists workshopped groups of stakeholder experts including controllers, military, air transport and general aviation pilots to identify any potential hazards that might arise from the proposed concept of operations.

When the causal factors for all hazards were analysed as a set, it became clear that the softer areas of the project, such as team working, predominated (Figure 5).

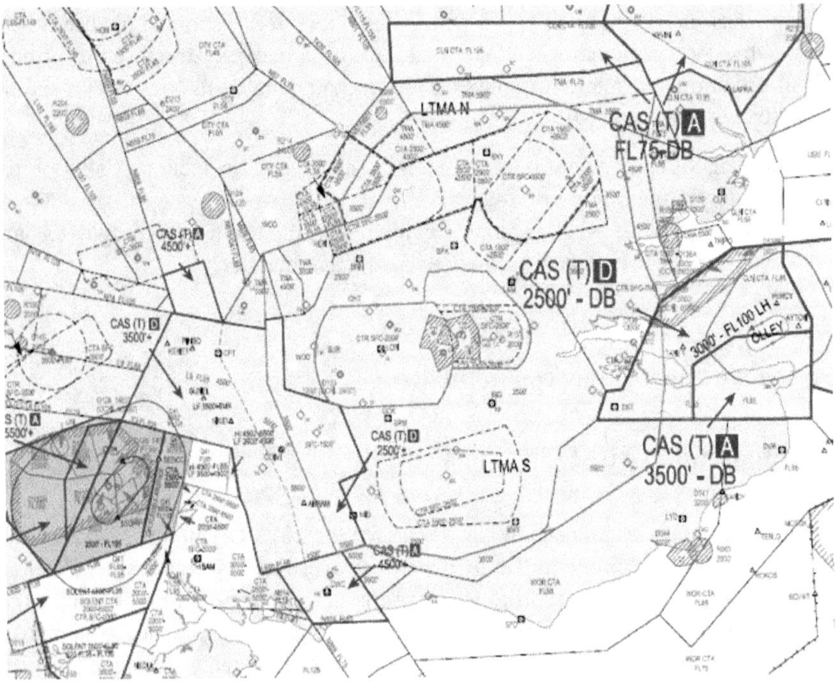

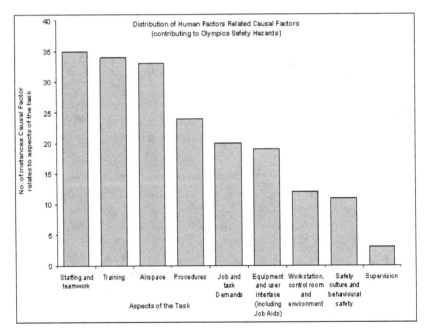

Fig. 4. Airspace sectorisation over Southern England

Fig. 5. Analyses of causal factors indicate importance of staffing & teamwork and training
(Thompson 2011)

To address potential issues surrounding controller workload, NATS assessed the expected changing traffic patterns over the Olympics and Paralympics period. For example, it was predicted that around 150 heads of state and over 70,000 members of the 'Olympic family' would arrive in time for the opening ceremony.

Through simulation activities that increased in complexity and fidelity, evidence was gathered to validate the airspace design, the maintenance of acceptable human performance, and the ability to fulfil the business objectives of managing the expected air traffic. As the design of the simulations was linked to safety requirements derived from the hazard analysis, the system validation evidence gathered became a key part of the safety cases produced to show that the project was progressing towards an acceptably safe outcome.

The initial hazard analysis had predicted one risk, that the traffic-flow management techniques may be only partially effective in preventing excessive controller workload. This was examined though the validation and simulation processes, with sufficient assurance evidence provided to allow a decision that sufficient safeguarding mitigations were in place to move forward. This assessment proved correct, and in live operation, the predicted mitigations were indeed effective, and traffic-flow management was maintained successfully throughout the Olympics period without significant adverse effects on controller human performance.

As highlighted in the initial hazard analysis, the task of training and briefing staff for the Olympics period was complex and time-consuming. Over 400 air traffic controllers received training on the new procedures and airspace structure. As the training applied to changes that were only to be effective during the games period, NATS was aware of the risk of training too early and both risking a fading of skills prior to use, or of the potential for mode confusion when working on existing airspace structures, having been trained for the upcoming temporary changes. Human factors specialists were involved throughout the training programme, using the training effectiveness methodology to show exactly when skills were successfully achieved, and where gaps still remained.

Key safety lessons that arose from the successful project were largely around the people and communication aspects of the change. In order to present a credible safety argument that recognised and addressed all areas of potential risk, the project required interaction and understanding of multiple stakeholders, many of them outside of NATS. Figure 6 summarises the four main areas of the assurance argument structure, and illustrates key inputs to each.

3.2 iFACTS

The project known as interim Future Area Control Tools Support (iFACTS) was born out of NATS research. The iFACTS system uses the current position of the aircraft, the flight plan and complex mathematics to predict the likely future position of all the aircraft in a sector. These positions are then compared for up to 18 minutes into the future and any potential conflicts are highlighted to the controller.

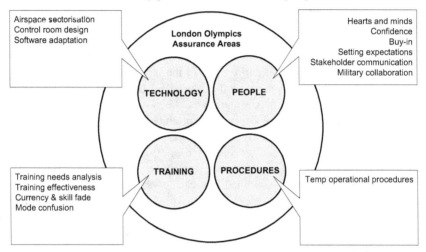

Fig. 6. Aspects of the integrated Olympics assurance argument

iFACTS provides the controller with an advanced set of support tools in order to reduce workload and so increase the amount of traffic he/she can comfortably handle. These tools, based on Trajectory Prediction (TP) and Medium Term Conflict Detection (MTCD), provide decision making support and facilitate the early detection of conflicts in and around the sector of airspace.

iFACTS, which completed transition into service in November 2011 in the London Area Control Centre (LACC), achieved three key objectives:

- Introduced tools support to the controllers to allow them to safely control traffic at higher volumes as the traffic increase in the future.
- Removed paper flight strips with suitable fallback modes and procedures in place (Figure 7). This is the most noticeable change from the past system and the requirement to enter all tactical clearances into the system via keyboard and mouse.
- Reduced a number and severity of safety significant events by introducing MTCD.

The introduction of iFACTS into LACC impacted the 'total system': technical equipment, physical environment (introduction of the third screen on the controller workstation), and also led to significant changes to operational tasks (namely those of tactical and planner controller, assistant, local area supervisor, and system control engineer), staffing arrangements, procedures and training. The recognition that the success of the project relied significantly on ensuring safe human performance as well as equipment change led to an assurance structure in which HF specialists worked alongside safety specialists over a ten year period to provide the necessary hazard analysis, evidence gathering, and building of the safety argument.

Fig. 7. The last paper strip used in LACC – British Airways flight BAW491

Throughout the project's prolonged duration, a number of high-level challenges were identified. These included:

- The in house design of the system meant that not all functionality was available at all times and significant effort had to be placed on minimising the impact of day to day air traffic control service.
- Incremental implementation of the system over five distinct phases, each requiring independent safety and human factors assurance whilst seamlessly providing the uninterrupted services over 200,000 square miles of airspace above England and Wales including the complex airspace of London.
- The need to provide uninterrupted service to military air traffic and accommodate seamless coordination between civil and military air traffic throughout the duration of the project.
- A range of hazard analyses had to be conducted (and some repeated due to the prolonged duration of the project) for every controller tool available within iFACTS and every controller task changed with the introduction of this system (including steady state and fallbacks).
- In the later stages of the project, mitigation of the risk of controllers switching between different modes of controlling: with paper strips (no automation) and with iFACTS (introducing automation).
- Replacement of each controller workstation to enable installation of the third iFACTS display and ensure compliance with the relevant standards and legislation.
- Training a team of more than 300 controllers and supporting staff to the required level of knowledge and skill whilst seamlessly providing the uninterrupted services.

These high level risks informed the initial hazard identification work. Rather than run separate hazard identification workshops for equipment, procedures and human performance hazards, the project ran joint safety and human factors hazard identification workshops. Safety and HF specialists worked with groups of stakeholders including air traffic controllers, engineers, local area supervisors, assistants, military, and the UK regulator.

The NATS system validation, training effectiveness and mode switching methodologies were designed originally for the iFACTS project and fine-tuned over the course of the project. The approach to system validation was incremental, increasing in terms of complexity and fidelity over the course of iFACTS implementation. The system validation continued until a transfer to Interim and Full Operational Service (iFOS and FOS). At each stage of system validation, data was gathered from simulated as well as live operational environment and compared to test the validity of the validation methodology. Figure 8 shows that the transfer of findings from the final stages of system validation (N26) to live operations (iFOS and FOS) was excellent. The shaded area represents the target range for each measure.

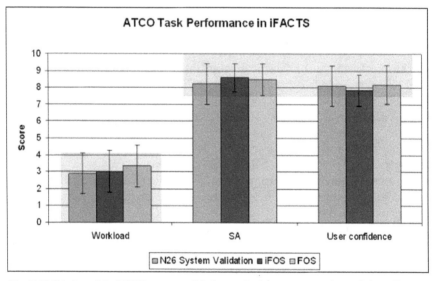

Fig. 8. Validation of the NATS system validation methodology – comparison of air traffic controller performance in real-time simulation and live operational environments

The integration of safety and human performance within NATS projects provided a clearer and more complete picture of the potential risks arising from the iFACTS implementation. The successful delivery of the biggest operational change in the NATS' history was largely an outcome of this collaborative approach. The key inputs to the iFACTS assurance argument are shown in Figure 9, and may usefully be compared against the Olympics inputs shown in Figure 6.

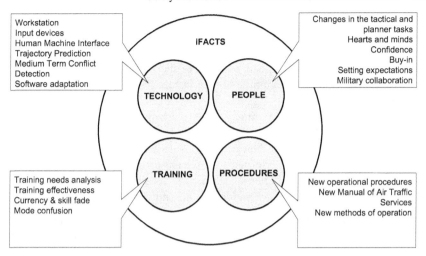

Fig. 9. Aspects of the integrated iFACTS assurance argument

4 Working together to identify and manage a richer risk picture

The iFACTS and London Olympics projects differed greatly in their aims, scope and method of delivery. Whereas iFACTS was a project based around an advanced set of technological tools, the Olympics project focused more on temporary organisational and airspace management changes. Although different, the safety assurance work and deliverables for both projects were centred on integrated safety engineering and human performance argument and supporting evidence.

It can be argued that if a purely engineering approach to safety had been applied, the identification and management of risks in both projects would not have been as complete as they were. Experience from these two example projects, as well as the other projects delivered within NATS, has highlighted the importance and benefits of integrated safety and human performance risk identification and management as the only way forward for NATS.

A culture of integration. It was noted earlier that the application of human performance assurance techniques early in a project may have incurred initial cost, but brings tremendous safety benefits (Figure 1). Within NATS, human performance assurance is considered an integral part of the safety assurance process and is mandated within its safety management system and project governance. Consequently, the HF specialists are sought for support and involvement very early in the project lifecycle. This integration benefits the more traditional safety engineering processes and activities, as it provides visibility and consistency on the 'softer' aspects of any change. It also provides confidence that the safety assurance addresses all affected areas.

The integration within the safety management system is not intended to be overly prescriptive. Rather it allows a proportionate approach, based upon the size of the project or change, and the anticipated risk associated with it. At an early stage in the project, an assessment is made of the potential risk, and planning is carried out to decide on the required human factors resource and most appropriate assurance activities.

Finally, the culture of integrating safety with human performance provides NATS management with a clearer and more complete picture of risks within the operation and effectiveness of their mitigations. In a company where management and maintenance of human performance is seen as a key enabler of safe operation, this integration has become a norm. HF interventions are no longer seen as 'gold plating', but as essential changes required to minimise delays and costs.

Applicable to organisations other than NATS. The NATS best practices and know-how are nowadays offered commercially through the NATS Global Consultancy in the areas of airspace design, procedure design, capacity studies, high intensity runway operations, safety and human factors assurance, simulation, environmental analyses, and training (ATC, safety, and human factors). The NATS Global Consultancy consists of the highly skilled team of consultants responsible for delivery of ATC-related projects in Africa, the Americas, Asia, Australia/ Oceania, and Europe. This is the main vehicle for NATS to collaborate with other aviation organisations, share its experience and practices, and implement practical, workable, and innovative solutions.

Final words. For NATS, the future represents a roadmap of technological, airspace and organisation changes that will enable the company to remain at the forefront of the European and wider international aviation community. As a result, status quo is not an option and continuous improvement is a must, especially in the light of difficult economic times affecting all airlines. The integration between safety and human performance is a norm today within NATS, but far from perfect. This integration will have to evolve even further and tap into better predictive methods for risk identification and management, free from the boundaries imposed by NATS, the United Kingdom, as well as Europe to inform a total safety solution for the future of truly international aviation.

Acknowledgments   The authors would like to express thanks to Paul Repper and Dave Thompson for their assistance on the Olympics case study.

References

EUROCONTROL (1999) Human factors module: A business case for human factors investment. Report No. HUM.ET1.ST13.4000-REP-02
Thompson D (2011) Olympics Human Factors Assurance Report. NATS
UK CAA (2013) Safety first: A strategy for human factors in civil aviation. http:/www.caa.co.uk /docs/2594/HF%20Strategy%20Consultationv3.pdf. Accessed 14 October 2014
Wickens CD, Mavor AS, Parasuraman R, McGee JP (eds) (1998). The future of air traffic control: human operators and automation. Panel on human factors in air traffic control automation, National Research Council

Safety Maturity Model

Karthikeyan Nagarajan[1] and Anil Kumar Davuluri[2]

[1]Cognizant Technology Solutions, Chennai, India

[2]Cognizant Technology Solutions, London, UK

Abstract The industry has learnt a lot about 'safety culture' through safety incidents. The need to create a method to establish safety culture is gaining a lot of importance. The industry as on date lacks a standard model to determine the value of safety associated with safety culture. The proposed Safety Maturity Model (SaMM) will assist organizations engaged in developing safety applications (products and associated services) in defining empirical measurements to measure the safety maturity and safety capability index. This would in turn enable organizations to identify the actions required to improve safety culture and capability. The model is based on industry safety and security standards and CMMI. SaMM assesses the current state and proposes methods to continuously improve the safety culture and reduce the residual safety risk of the organization. SaMM proposes four maturity levels – performing, managing, predicting and optimizing. Each level will have focus areas and associated conditions of satisfaction. SaMM proposes measurements around each level which can be used to measure the capability index and safety maturity. SaMM will potentially increase the confidence in using the safety products among the users and will potentially reduce the product recalls for the Original Equipment Manufacturers (OEMs) and improve the safety culture.

1 Introduction

The proposed safety maturity model will assist organizations engaged in developing safety applications (products and its associated services) to establish their current level of safety maturity and safety capability index, and identify the actions required to improve their safety culture, capability and predictability.

The proposed safety maturity model is set to have four iterative stages. Organizations will progress sequentially though the four stages, by building their strengths and removing the weaknesses of the previous stage. It is therefore not advisable for an organization to skip a stage.

The target industries for applying the safety maturity model are (inclusive but not limited to):

- industrial automation
- railway
- aviation
- road transport
- medical devices (including pharma)
- nuclear
- machinery
- amusement parks
- maritime.

The proposed model will potentially increase the confidence in using the safety products among the users and will potentially reduce the product recalls for the OEMs and improve the safety culture.

The term 'safety culture' came into use after being mentioned in the summary report by the International Nuclear Safety Advisory Group (INSAG) as one of the causes for the Chernobyl nuclear power accident in Ukraine (Wikipedia 2013b). The IAEA (International Atomic Energy Agency) report introduced the concept to explain the organizational errors and the risks that caused the disaster. Since then, 'poor safety culture' has been identified as one of the major causes for a number of high profile accidents such as:

- the fire at King's Cross underground station (Fennell 1998)
- the sinking of the Herald of Free Enterprise passenger ferry
- the passenger train crash at Clapham Junction (Hidden 1989)
- the disasters of the space shuttles Challenger and Columbia (Smith and Wadsworth 2009)
- the Überlingen mid-air collision accident
- the BP oil refinery accident.

2 Safety culture and safety management system

The most important driving factors for any organization involved in the development of safety system are:

- people
- process
- technology.

Safety standard provides the adequate requirements to satisfy the needs for the above listed criteria. However, for any organization to be successful in the safety development, the safety management system and the safety culture play a major role. The safety management system and the safety culture of an organization will complement each other and will form a strong delivery capability for the organizations involved in the safety systems development. The technical/process requirements for a defined SIL/ASIL or equivalent level will be captured as the part of the safety management system. The safety management system will aid in satisfying the need for the safety standards and will help the organization to deliver outputs as deemed by the safety standards. The safety culture is often considered as the soft part requirement for the safety system development. Many of the organizations fail to develop and deliver the safety system because of the culture. The safety standards also are not very explicit in defining the culture part of the requirement. IEC 61508 (IEC 2010), which is considered as the mother publication, addresses the requirements of safety culture very implicitly and the interpretations among the users becomes very subjective. ISO 26262 (ISO 2012) covers the requirements more explicitly. Figure 1 explains the need for the safety culture.

Fig. 1. Need for safety culture

The major vision for the safety culture of the organization is to provide governance and oversight to the way safety measures are carried out in the day-to-day activities. The major levers to achieve this are:

• commitment
• prioritization
• think safety
• accountability.

In a day-to-day activity safety should be given the highest priority. There should never be any issues with safety at any level in the organization.

Cost, scope and schedule resulting in better quality are considered as the major constraints (see Figure 2). Any organizations involved in safety development, safety should be considered as the vertex of the pyramid governing the cost, schedule and scope and hence provide quality by considering quality as an integral and inherent parameter of safety. Quality can be an integral parameter of safety considering the definition of safety as 'safety is freedom from unacceptable risk of physical injury or of damage to the health of people, either directly or indirectly as a result of damage to property or to the environment'.

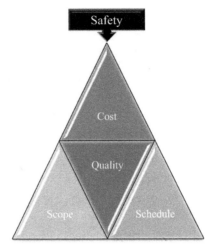

Fig. 2. Constraints

3 Cost of safety and product recalls

Many organizations have robust safety management systems that meet the safety standards and are also certified by independent safety assessors or organizations. In spite of all this, the environment, humans, and the infrastructure equipment are exposed to hazard. Why does the hazard remain despite all these safety measure? The answer to all this lies in the culture of the safety organizations.

The term culture is often misunderstood and is very hard to quantify. Safety management and culture complement each other, so it is very important to understand the importance of 'culture'. The major concepts that have to be understood and studied are:

- cost of safety
- impact of product recalls.

Today's quality systems and procedures have established many metrics to improve the robustness of execution and predictability, which take into consideration project management constraints such as:

- cost of quality
- cost of poor quality
- productivity
- defect density.

Cost of safety is a post-development activity and there is no proven way to calculate it when a product or application is developed. So we cannot develop a model which can predict or determine the cost of safety. The following are reasons why cost of safety cannot be calculated during development:

1. Company CFOs cannot calculate the cost avoidance of events that had not happened. Costs in financial reports can be added only after the incidents occur. Due to these reasons, we cannot calculate the value of operating inherently safe.
2. Safety needs to be considered as part of the economic calculus, which includes environmental stewardship and company sustainability.
3. It is not just about the safety systems. Inherent safety includes good early warning system, security, operations, training, company goals, and the culture of the organization.

3.1 Examples of cost of safety

A classic example for the cost of safety is the accident that occurred at the BP oil refinery in Texas City, Texas on 23 March 2005 (Wikipedia 2013c). This disaster is considered to have occurred due to the lack of safety culture. Fifteen people were reported dead, more than 170 people were injured, the refinery's premises were destroyed (as shown in Figure 3) and the atmosphere was polluted with flammable vapour cloud, explosions, and fire. Apart from the loss of life, there were huge legal, statutory, and insurance costs to be met by the organization. The production loss incurred was close to USD 1.5 billion. The insurance and legal cost accounted for about USD 2 billion. The fines and statuary cost accounted for USD 0.5 billion. These costs do not include the cost of rebuilding the infrastructure or the impact on the environment. This is an example of the huge loss incurred when there is a safety disaster.

Fig 3. BP oil refinery tragedy

Another example, for the cost, organization has to incur due to failure in safety, is the Bhopal gas tragedy in 1984. Now, thirty years after the accident, chemical residue of this disaster remains in the environment affecting newborn babies with brain damage and malformations.

Product recalls also contribute to the cost of safety. There are alarming examples of product recalls around the world. The product recalls are associated with the products which have a robust safety management system.

3.2 Examples of product recalls in the automobile industry (Koopman 2012)

- General Motors had to recall 3.5 million vehicles because of an anti-lock braking software defect in the year 1999.
- Ford Windstar, Crown Victoria, Mercury Grand and Lincoln recalled their vehicles in 2001 because of a software defect that caused airbags to deploy on their own and seatbelts to tighten.
- Mercedes lost USD 30 million after they recalled 680,000 cars due to defects in brake-assist-by-wire system. In 2003, this defect was fixed by applying a software patch.
- Famous Toyota recall in the years 2005-2012.

3.3 Examples of product recalls in medical devices (Morsicato and Shoemaker 2007)

- 6 March 2007: AEDs recalled self-test software that may allow a self-test to clear a previously detected low battery condition.
- 6 June 2006: Ventilators recalled older generation software with incorrect oxygen cell calibration (without compressed air supply) that can also disable all the alarms.
- 6 March 2006: A Class I recall of a dialysis device. This device was used for continuous solute and/or fluid removal in patients with acute renal failure. If the care giver overrides the device's 'incorrect weight change detected' alarm it may result in excessive fluid loss.
- 15 March 2005: An infusion pump was recalled by its manufacturer because it powered off and had to be restarted if it received data at the serial port.

3.4 Samples of aviation mishaps (Wikipedia 2013a)

- In 2010, Aero Caribbean Flight 883, an ATR-72-200, crashed in Sancti Spíritus, Cuba, killing all 68 on board in the joint worst ever accident involving the ATR 72.
- In 2010, Air India Express Flight 812, a Boeing 737-800, crashed at Mangalore International Airport after overshooting the runway with 160 passengers and six crew members on board. A total of 158 people are killed with just eight survivors; this is the worst ever crash involving the 737-800.
- In 2009, Air France Flight 447, an Airbus A330-200 flying from Rio de Janeiro, Brazil to Paris, France, crashed in the Atlantic Ocean, killing all 228 occupants, including 12 crew members; bodies and aircraft debris were not recovered until several days later; the aircraft itself was not found until 2011. The crash is the first fatal accident of the A330 and the worst-ever disaster involving the A330.

4 The solution

To derive the predictability of the organizations and to continuously improve the safety capability and the culture, the safety management system needs to be integrated with the safety culture. An integrated model can be used to benchmark the organizations involved in the safety product and the associated application development. This robust model can use an empirical output to determine the maturity of the organization involved in the safety development.

The proposed Safety Maturity Model (SaMM) is similar to the Integrated Capability Maturity Model of SEI, but will focus on the organizations developing the safety critical/related products and applications. The SaMM will have the following maturity levels:

Performing. Performing is the basic level of any organization involved in the safety products or application. Products comply with the safety management system and comply with the standards requirements. There is no guaranteed predictability between product releases and different applications.

Managing. Consistency is brought in with regards to various safety product lines and applications. Functional safety management is conceived at the organization level and deployed.

Predictive. Organizations can predict the dangerous undetected faults and will have well defined methodology of handling the dangerous undetected faults and predict the safety faults in the products deployed and have a systematic way of handling the same. The intention is to convert the dangerous faults to safe faults.

Optimizing. Organization have the capability of eradicating the dangerous undetected faults using analytics and prediction models.

Every level defined in the SaMM model will have focus areas and each focus area
will have a defined condition of satisfaction associated with it. Each level of the
framework provides the measurement to calculate the maturity and capability index of the organization using the following parameters:

- matrix for the levels
- focus area
- defined condition of satisfaction.

The framework shown in Figure 4 measures the capability index by a scale of ten.

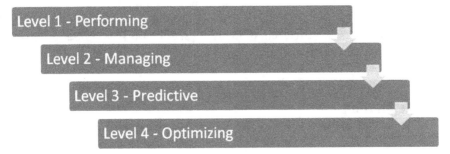

Fig 4. Levels of maturity

4.1 The objectives of the SaMM model

- to provide a framework for developing safety products and safety related applications with a defined maturity level
- to help safety development organizations to assess the current state and continuously improve the safety culture and safety development capabilities and
  mature
- to reduce the cost of safety and the frequency of product recalls
- to reduce the residual safety risk as the maturity of the organization increases,
  with the aim of converting the dangerous undetected faults to safe detected
  faults.

The concept of As Low As Reasonably Practicable (ALARP) displayed in Figure 5, as defined by CEN 50126 (Cenelec 2012), has been used as a reference. The
objective is to reduce the risk into its lowest possible levels which are also practicable. The third and the fourth levels of the SaMM models will help assess the
operation in the broadly acceptable zones.

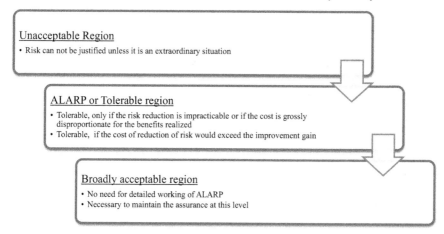

Fig 5. Concept of ALARP

The cost benefit analysis is performed for the risks associated and the organization willingness to eradicate the risk as deemed has to be demonstrated.

5 The model

The safety maturity model will have maturity levels, focus areas and condition of satisfaction for each level for a given maturity level. As discussed earlier the following are the maturity levels for the SaMM:

- performing
- managing
- predicting
- optimizing.

The following seven Focus Areas (FA) have been identified for the model along with the condition of satisfaction.

- safety competency management system
- safety engineering
- safety development process
- functional safety management
- senior management commitment
- fault control
- fault avoidance.

Each FA has to comply with multiple Conditions of Satisfaction (CoS). There are 23 conditions in each level, resulting in 92 conditions in the overall model. Table 1 provides a quick summary of the CoS for each focus area and maturity level. A graphical representation of Table 1 is given in Figure 6.

Table 1. Distribution of conditions of satisfaction across levels and focus areas

Focus area	Levels				
	Performing	Managing	Predictive	Optimizing	Total
Safety competency management system	2	2	3	4	11
Safety engineering	8	8	8	5	29
Safety development process	8	7	3	1	19
Functional safety management	2	2	1	2	7
Senior management commitment	3	3	4	5	15
Fault controls			2	2	4
Fault avoidance		1	2	4	7
Total	23	23	23	23	92

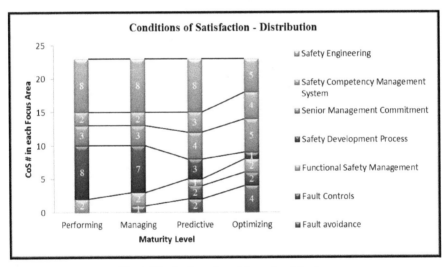

Fig. 6. Distribution of conditions of satisfaction

Each condition of satisfaction is measured by the following two parameters:

- adequacy
- effectiveness.

The score for each CoS will be the average of the two parameters. The assessment for each CoS will result in one of the following:

- Fully Followed (FF) will get a score of 10.
- Partially Followed (PF) will get a score of 5.
- Not Followed (NF) will get a score of 0.
- Not Applicable (NA) with justification will be excluded from the calculation.

If the adequacy is zero then effectiveness will always be zero. Figure 7 depicts the scoring table for a perfect organization, that is, an organization that fully satisfies all the 92 conditions.

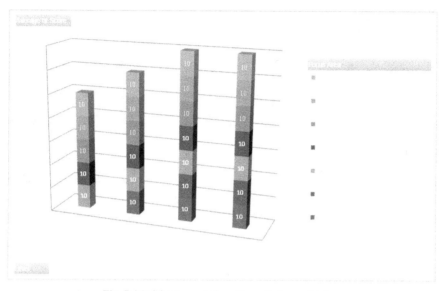

Fig. 7. Model representation of a perfect organization

Every CoS is rated and an average is calculated based on the four assessment values described above. Figure 8 shows the calculations performed by using Microsoft Excel.

6 Focus areas

The safety maturity model of an organization comprises the following seven focus areas, which are described below.

- safety competency management system
- safety engineering
- safety development process
- functional safety management
- senior management commitment
- fault control
- fault avoidance.

	A	B	C	D	E	H	I
1	Focus Area	Practice	Description	Adequacy	Effectiveness	Score	Level
2	Safety Competency Management System	1	Establish a Safety Competency Framework	FF	FF	10	Performing
4	Safety Competency Management System	3	Establish a rewards and recognition program - Appreciates Functional Safety achievement and Penalizes that jeopardizes Safety	FF	FF	10	Managing
16	Safety Engineering	15	Establish security engineering	FF	FF	10	Performing
17	Safety Engineering	16	practice of Safety plan	FF	FF	10	Performing
49	Safety Development Process	48	Security Engineering Process	FF	FF	10	Performing
51	Safety Development Process	50	Product / Application Development Process	PF	PF	5	Managing
52	Safety Development Process	51	Compliance to Industry standards	FF	FF	10	Managing
65	Functional Safety Management	64	Awareness and environment	FF	PF	7.5	Predictive
70	Senior Management Commitment	69	Organization structure	FF	FF	10	Performing
84	Fault Controls	83	Corrective actions for SIL downgrades	FF	FF	10	Predictive
85	Fault Controls	84	control the faults before going to field	FF	FF	10	Optimizing
91	Fault Avoidance	90	Self disclosure	NF	NF	0	Optimizing
93	Fault Avoidance	92	Probabilistic RAMS Analysis	FF	FF	10	Optimizing

Fig. 8. Screen short of a sample model

6.1 Safety competency management system

The following areas pertaining to safety competency management system will be defined:

Establish a safety competency framework. A detailed framework to be established at the organization level to satisfy the needs for safety competency as required by safety standards.

Establish a safety competency policy. An organization level policy to be rolled out for safety development, contribution to safety community and to practice safety culture.

Establish a rewards and recognition program – appreciates functional safety achievement and penalizes what jeopardizes safety. Rewards and recognition program to be instituted to award personnel and also to penalize individuals and units that jeopardize safety.

Establish continuous competency assessment and improvement. A competency framework to be established that facilitates the continuous assessment of personnel or unit involved in safety development. It will also facilitate the improvement of the competency of personnel and hence the unit.

Establish continuous learning and training. An organization-wide infrastructure and environment to be established for continuous learning and training.

Define and follow roles and responsibilities. Roles and the associated responsibilities for all activities to be defined and a mechanism to be established to map competent individuals to the defined roles.

Establish that intellectual diversity is sought valued and integrated in all processes. Organization to define and institute methodology to optimize the intellectual capital and continue to improve it.

Establish a community culture. Organization to establish a free and open community to share and learn about safety and the related technical advancement.

Account for decisions related to functional safety. Organization to establish an environment where the individuals in the organization take and stand by the accountability for any decisions taken, which affects functional safety.

Establish a self-disclosure discipline. Organization to establish an environment which promotes self-disclosure for incidents and issues, and awards appropriately.

Maintain an expertise and experience mapping. Organization to have a defined mapping for the experience and the expertise for the intellect capital available. This will help to associate roles as demanded by the safety standard and the safety project requirements.

6.2 Safety engineering

The following aspects will be performed to ensure safety engineering:

Establish a safety policy. A safety policy to be defined to establish its commitment in using superior tools and methodologies for safety engineering.

Establish safety requirements. A well-defined process and infrastructure to be formed to establish and validate safety requirements subjectively and objectively.

Establish a system and component FMEA. FMEA to be performed at the component and system level. FMEA will effectively be used to derive the diagnostics requirement to improve availability and aid in verification and validation.

Establish security engineering. Security engineering practices to be defined and followed per industry standards as security breach and issues are the early signs for the safety hazards.

Practice of safety plan. A safety plan to be created to achieve specific goals for the development effort and the evidence to be published for the work performed according to the safety plan.

Definition of safety concept. A safety goal and concept to be developed for each development activity. A safety concept sets the goal for a specific project or group of activities.

Creation and compliance of safety case. A safety case to be created and complied for all the activities against the safety plan. A safety case will also aid the independent safety assessing bodies to evaluate the safety for the product/application before deploying in the field.

Perform design reviews. Design reviews to be performed at specific instances of the project to ensure that the safety requirements are designed adequately and all the alternate courses for design are analyzed.

Compliance to techniques as defined in standards. The development for a specific application will follow the techniques defined by the safety standards for the specific industry and defined SIL/ASIL/qualification levels of the product/application developed.

Perform hazard analysis. Preliminary hazard analysis and the system hazard analysis to be performed to deduce the safety requirements.

SIL calculation. Established methodologies to be followed as defined by the safety standards to calculate the capability of the product to satisfy the need to perform the intended functionality at the desired SIL level.

SIL assessment. The extent of risk to be reduced will provide an assessment to develop a product/application at a desired SIL level.

Independent verification and validation. The verification and validation function to be independent of the delivery team at the financial, technical and managerial levels.

Safety and security reviews. Periodic peer reviews and inspection of the safety and security aspects of the project to be conducted.

Security compliance with standards. Compliance with reference to security engineering per the defined standards to be ensured.

Risk evaluations for reliability, availability, maintainability and safety. Maintaining a risk register and evaluating the risks reported during development which affects the reliability, availability, maintainability and safety of the application/product being developed.

Establishing safety assurance function. Independent safety assurance function to ensure that the safety at the desired level is achieved.

Perform safety audits. Safety audits to be performed by the safety assurance function against the requirements of safety standards for a given industry.

Degree of independence. Level of independence required for various functions such as safety assurance, verification and validation as required by the criticality of the application developed.

Independent safety assessment and certification. Independent external safety assessment and certification to be carried out for all the products/applications before the field installations.

Perform threat and vulnerability analysis. Threat and the vulnerability of the application/product to be analyzed and appropriate decisions to be taken.

Safety standards certified COTS. Usage of COTS is permitted and to reduce the risk due to COTS, safety standards certified COTS will be used.

Environmental test – heat and pressure. The product/application to be subjected to environmental tests such as heat and pressure, depending on the application.

Institutionalized infrastructure, tools and techniques. Tools and techniques will be institutionalized across the organization to ensure repeatability of results across projects.

Perform safety analysis. Safety analysis will be carried out at every level of development and as documented by the safety plan.

Dynamic risk assessment and SIL deduction. Risk assessment and the resultant effect of SIL have to be studied for any change that affects the safety goal and concept.

Environmental test – shock, vibration, EMI, and EMC. The product/application to be subject to the environmental tests like shock, vibration, EMI and EMC, depending on the application.

Perform root cause analysis – corrective and preventive actions for incidents reported after installation. Mechanism to perform corrective actions and the preventive actions for the incidents affecting the safety and integrity of the product post installation to be carried out.

6.3 Safety development process

The following processes pertaining to safety development will be implemented:

Establish organization policy. An organization policy to be established with regards to the safety development process and the complying strategy.

Establish quality policy. As part of the quality management system, an organization-wide quality policy to be defined and practiced.

Establish quality management system. A well-defined quality management system complying with standards such as ISO 9001 to be established.

Establish documentation management. A well-defined process for managing the documents generated as a part of the project to be established.

Establish software engineering process. The software engineering process to be defined and adhered for any development.

Establish hardware engineering process. The hardware engineering process to be defined and adhered for any development.

Establish system engineering process. The system engineering process to be defined and adhered for any development.

Establish security engineering process. The security engineering process to be defined and adhered for any development.

Ensure CMMi L3 compliance. The safety development process compliant with the requirements of CMMi L3 requirements to be ensured.

Establish product/application development process. The product/application development process to be defined and adhered to for any development.

Ensure compliance to industry standards. The developed safety development process to be ensured with the compliance to required industry standards and will be practiced for applications/products specific to a given industry.

Establish configuration management. The safety development process to define the requirements for configuration management at every level and will be adhered to for every product/application development.

Establish SIL calculation process. A detailed process for calculating SIL levels to be defined and followed.

Establish quality, safety and product assurance. The safety development process to define the functions and activities including the interface requirements and degree of independence for the quality, safety and product assurance functions.

Practice risk evaluations for reliability, availability, maintainability and safety. Established process for the RAMS risk evaluations to be defined and followed.

Establish organization structure. The organization structure defining various units' functions and interactions to be defined and followed.

Establish safety audits. The safety development process to define the process for performing the safety audits including authority and corrective actions to be established.

COTS and other tools qualification. A well-defined process to qualify COTS and any other internal developed tools, if the tool/COTS is not certified to any safety standard.

Continuous improvement. The organization's focus for continuous improvement to be established and followed.

6.4 Functional safety management

The following policies and processes pertaining to functional safety management will be carried out:

Follow organization policy. The organization policy to explicitly state the organization's commitment to functional safety management.

Follow safety policy. The safety policy to state the need of the functional safety management system.

Establish safety issue notification process. A well-defined process to be established and practiced to notify users regarding a potential safety issue in the installed product/application.

Establish change management. A robust methodology for change management to be established and followed. Any change affecting the safety of installed product will be given the due importance.

Create awareness and environment. An environment and the required awareness regarding the functional safety management and its importance to be created.

Roles and responsibilities. The roles and responsibilities from the functional management perspective to be defined.

Contribution to safety standards development. As an organization contribution to the development of safety standards or participation and contribution to the safety community to be ensured.

6.5 Senior management commitment

Motivate communication. The senior management encourages open communication and participates in communicating any information related to safety.

Practice organization policy. The organization policy to explicitly state the senior management commitment to develop safety products/application.

Establish organization structure. The organization and reporting structure to enable senior management participation in reviews and decision making regarding safety.

Create environment. The senior management to ensure that the environment is conducive to performing safety development.

Think safety. The senior management to promote the 'think safety' environment.

Promote safety culture. The senior management to promote safety culture and encourage open communication with rewards and recognition.

Commitment to safety. The senior management to show interest and commitment for safety development.

Degree of independence. The senior management to ensure the required degree of independence is made available for units to perform their intended functions.

Promote open communication with customers. The senior management to promote open communications for customers regarding safety related issues and work towards improving safety with the customers always.

Enforce safety as highest priority. Safety assumes the highest priority in the organization. The senior management to take proactive measures to maintain the priority.

Rewards and recognition for safety and maintaining the culture. The senior management to institute R&R programs for maintaining the safety culture.

Encourage open communication. The senior management to maintain open communication with all units and individuals within the organization.

Accountability of decisions related to functional safety. The senior management to take accountability for decisions taken on behalf of the organization.

Promote self-disclosure. The senior management to appreciate and reward individuals/units practicing self-disclosure.

Practice proactive attitude. The senior management to practice proactive attitude in disclosing the safety issues with the customers.

6.6 Fault controls

Enforce corrective action. Corrective mechanism to be put forth to correct and control all the faults in the laboratory environment.

Ensure corrective actions for SIL downgrades. Safety issues and risks which could potentially downgrade the SIL for the function to be corrected using the corrective action mechanism.

Control the faults before going to field. The fault control mechanism using statistical techniques or fault control methodologies to control the latent safety faults. The process will convert the dangerous faults to safety faults.

Predict the cost of safety. The statistical mechanism to predict the cost of safety due to safety faults in the field.

6.7 Fault avoidance

Perform independent verification and validation. An independent verification and validation to be performed to avoid faults happening in the field.

Take preventive actions. Lessons learnt and corrective actions taken from organization database to be used as preventive actions to prevent the occurrence of common faults in the field.

Ensure degree of independence. A specific degree of independence to be ensured depending on the criticality to prevent the fault from happening in the field.

Use fault prediction and optimizing models. Fault prediction models using statistical techniques to be used to predict faults and eliminate the same before installing in the field.

Ensure self-disclosure. Open disclosure about inherent faults and workaround solutions with the customer will ensure the faults to be avoided in the field.

Preventive actions for SIL downgrades. Any potential SIL downgrade due to faults to be prevented from occurring in the field.

Probabilistic RAMS analysis. Reliability, Availability, Maintainability and Safety to be analyzed together using probability techniques as their parameters are interdependent.

7 Conclusion

The paper discusses the need for a safety maturity model which accelerates the safety culture improvement of the product development organization. The paper provides a detailed description of the safety maturity model, which provides a framework that assesses the organizations involved in safety development (product and application). The multi focus model is proposed using the combination of adequacy and effectiveness, thereby ensuring safety culture and safety management system. The measurement can be made for various combinations of maturity levels and focus areas to arrive at the capability index. The proposed model consists of four maturity levels, seven focus areas and ninety two conditions of satisfaction. Based on the outcome on a score of ten, improvements can be planned for each focus area.

References

Cenelec (2012) CEN 50126 Railway applications – the specification and demonstration of Reliability, Availability Maintainability and Safety (RAMS).
Fennell D (1988) Investigation into the King's Cross Underground Fire. Department of Transport
Hidden A (1989) Investigation into the Clapham Junction railway accident. London

IEC (2010) IEC 61508 Functional safety of electrical/electronic/programmable electronic safety-related systems, Parts 1-7. Edition 2

ISO (2012) ISO 26262 Road vehicles – functional safety, Parts 1-10

Koopman P (2012) Critical systems engineering.http://www.ece.cmu.edu/~ece649/lectures/20_sweng_crit_sys.pdf. Accessed 16 Oct 2013.

Morsicato R, Shoemaker B (2007) Test-first practices in regulated, safety-critical environments. http://agile2007.agilealliance.org/downloads/handouts/Morsicato_769.pdf. Accessed 16 Oct 2013

Smith AP, Wadsworth EJK (2009) Safety culture, advice and performance. Cardiff University Research Report. http://www.iosh.co.uk/idoc.ashx?docid=c979d7a4-fc21-425a-9c2b-acaa1fc1aaff&version=-1. Accessed 30 Oct 2013

Wikipedia (2013a) Aviation accidents and incidents in the 21st century. Wikipedia, the free encyclopedia. http://en.wikipedia.org/wiki/Category:21st-century_aviation_accidents_and_incidents. Accessed 16 Oct 2013

Wikipedia (2013b) Safety culture. Wikipedia, the free encyclopedia. http://en.wikipedia.org/wiki/Safety_culture. Accessed 30 Oct 2013

Wikipedia (2013c) Texas City Refinery explosion. Wikipedia, the free encyclopedia. http://en.wikipedia.org/wiki/Texas_City_Refinery_explosion. Accessed 16 Oct 2013

Aircraft System Safety Assessment – the Challenge for Future Design and Certification

Pippa Moore

UK Civil Aviation Authority

Gatwick Airport, UK

Abstract   Within the aviation regulatory system the current system safety assessment requirements have been around for 30 years or so and have made significant improvements in overall systems integrity, reliability and safety. However, these requirements are underpinned by some simple assumptions on system design whose continued use may no longer be regarded as appropriate given the highly integrated and complex systems in modern aircraft and the ever more integrated total aviation system that is currently being developed. This paper discusses some potential implications of this and questions what should we be considering for the future.

1 Introduction

The world-wide accident rate is one of the primary means of measuring aviation safety. It has remained relatively constant for a number of years, despite increases in the number of aircraft in service, the number flights being made by operators and the complexity of new aircraft types. Given the level to which these increases in each could stress current aviation infrastructures and the oversight processes used by aviation regulators, managing to maintain a basically stable worldwide accident rate is an impressive achievement by everyone involved in aviation. This is no doubt due to a combination of the evolution of the standards imposed by the regulations, the ever increasing technical capability and reliability of modern aircraft and the assessment processes that underpin these within both the design organisations and the certification authority teams.

If we are confident that the current approaches and ever more complex technical solutions can continue to provide the appropriate balance to compensate for further increases in the number of in-service aircraft and flight operations we should continue to see the current worldwide accident rate at least being maintained – or even improved upon. If we are not so sure of this – or the balance cannot be maintained – one possible outcome is more aircraft accidents. And, in an

© UK Civil Aviation Authority 2014. Published by the Safety-Critical Systems Club. All Rights Reserved

era that has the capability for almost immediate and global media reporting of incidents and accidents the commensurate impact on public perceptions of aviation safety may not be as positive as we would wish for.

Should we not therefore at least consider the implications of a possible increase in accidents and look to where improvements could be made before potential negative reactions from the flying public, the media, politicians or other influential organisations reaches a level that could be damaging to the industry.

The rest of this paper looks at the safety assurance process behind the technical advances that have enabled us to achieve what we have today. It reviews how the civil aviation world currently defines the safety targets that underpin the accepted accident rate, suggests why we should consider revising the approach to safety and offers some options for possible improvements to the overall safety assessment process for aircraft and associated systems.

2 How does the civil aviation world set and maintain its required safety levels?

The civil aviation industry uses three processes to set and maintain its required safety levels: certification processes, continued airworthiness processes and continuing airworthiness processes. The certification processes are used to ensure that an aircraft type, as designed, can be demonstrated to be able to meet the appropriate safety target prior to entering into service. Continued airworthiness refers to the monitoring, reporting and corrective action processes that are put in place for in-service aircraft to assure they maintain this safety standard.

The third process is the continuing airworthiness process; this refers to the ongoing preventative and corrective maintenance and management of the aircraft to confirm correct functioning and to achieve reliable and cost effective operation.

2.1 Aircraft certification processes

Within the civil aviation world, the aircraft certification process is designed to establish a desired level of integrity for an aircraft and demonstrate that that level of integrity can been achieved. In this case, integrity can be taken to include reliability, availability, capability, etc. If the desired level of integrity is consistently met the aircraft and aircraft systems provide an acceptable level of safety for passengers on board and, by inference from continued safe flight, also to persons on the ground.

The certification process has three basic elements:

- the requirements or certification specifications which refine the high level design criteria to be met

- the design organisation aspects which cover the capability and competence for the design of individual parts, systems or complete aircraft
- the production organisation aspects which cover the capability and competence for the manufacture of individual parts, systems or complete aircraft in accordance with the approved design. As this paper is associated with a design/certification topic, it does not go into further detail on the production organisation aspect.

The design organisation is charged with demonstrating to the certification authority that the proposed design is compliant with the certification requirements/certification specifications. There is a set of certification requirements for each category of aircraft – EASA Certification Specification 25 (CS-25) (EASA 2013) for large fixed wing aircraft, CS-29 for large rotorcraft (EASA 2012), etc. – and these also provide guidance material on the intent of the requirement and methods of showing compliance that have been found to be acceptable. Each of these requirement sets includes the system safety requirements, which are often referred to by the applicable paragraph number of 1309.

The requirement given in 1309 defines that the probability of a failure is inversely proportional to the severity of its effect at aircraft level, i.e. high criticality systems are required to have an extremely low probability of failure. These certification requirements were established many years ago and their background, development and intent are described in (Lloyd and Tye 1982), which refers to data for the preceding 30 years along with additional material on fault/failure assessment methodologies and probabilistic risk assessment/analysis techniques. Many of the techniques referenced in this book have since been included in the guidance material for requirement 1309.

In simple terms, the required minimum integrity, or the target level of safety, for an aircraft is based on some simple assumptions whose aim is to define the acceptable fatal accident rate commensurate with the aircraft type. For large, fixed wing, passenger transport aircraft this rate is less than 1 accident in 10 million flight hours (10^{-7} per flight hour). The accident rates for other types of aircraft (small fixed wing aircraft, rotorcraft, etc.) are similarly defined – with all being originally set based on the published worldwide accident rates for those classes of aircraft.

In order to do this and also give further guidance on how to achieve this within a design process some further assumptions were made based on a view of aircraft system complexity at that time, i.e. the number of systems an aircraft typically had and how many critical functional failure modes each of these systemS could likely have. This then enabled target levels of safety to be set for individual failures.

The assumptions for large fixed wing aircraft are as follows:

- An aircraft is considered to have 10 systems.
- Each system is considered to have 10 critical functional failures/failure modes.

Thus, in order to meet the minimum required level of safety a system whose failure or loss could result in an accident is, based on the previously outlined assumptions, required to have a probability of failure of 10^{-9} per flight hour or less.

The certification process therefore uses a fixed probability target for system failure as a Target Level Of Safety (TLOS) which can enable the aircraft system developers to design and demonstrate that their individual system contribution will not undermine the overall level of integrity of the aircraft.

In essence, the process requires that the following steps are followed:

1. An initial set of aircraft level threats/hazards related to functional failures are identified.
2. The severity of the consequence of each of these is determined.
3. The tolerable likelihood is assigned.
4. The systems that could contribute to each of these aircraft level functional failure is defined.
5. The minimum system integrity level is established based on the system's contribution to the overriding aircraft level functional failure.
6. Compliance with at least the minimum required system integrity is demonstrated through assessment and analysis.

2.2 Continued airworthiness processes

The continued airworthiness processes are intended to provide a closed loop monitor and corrective action cycle for aircraft in service to assure that the intended level of safety is maintained. The process encompasses activity within the certification work, for example the development of the maintenance schedules and instructions on how to perform this activity, as well as the monitoring of in-service aircraft and when necessary the definition and promulgation of corrective action instructions.

The development of maintenance schedules uses outputs of the aircraft design and safety assessment processes as an input to determine what maintenance activities are required and how frequently they should be performed to maintain an appropriate level of aircraft integrity. This is commonly undertaken within the forum of a maintenance review board with participation of operators and uses structured methodologies such as MSG-3 analysis[1]. Hence if decisions made here affect the assumptions or analysis of the safety assessment this should be fed back into the assessment.

The monitoring and reporting processes cover a range of aviation-related issues from the ways in which aircraft are operated to maintenance oversight/manage-

---

[1] MSG-3 (the MSG stands for Maintenance Steering Group but the abbreviation is universally used) is a process for determining the initial scheduled maintenance requirements for new aircraft and/or engines.

ment and system reliability and are designed for two purposes: firstly to allow aircraft operators and maintenance-related organisations to identify issues/problems with aircraft, and if necessary obtain alternate or additional instructions before these become a potential safety risk. Secondly, the collection and analysis of in-service information enables the responsible design organisation to be satisfied that the overall level of safety is being achieved, and if necessary, to determine and promulgate corrective actions.

Clearly, if these programmes are run correctly, they have the potential to save these organisations money – it is usually cheaper in terms of both money and time to fix a minor problem before it becomes a serious problem.

2.3 Continuing airworthiness processes

The continuing airworthiness processes are intended to assure that the aircraft are managed and maintained and that these actions are performed correctly in accordance with the design organisation instructions so that assumptions and considerations in the safety assessment remain valid. Thus, it also includes the need for effective communication between the operator and maintenance organisations and the design organisations so that necessary information is shared.

Also, if and when any modifications are made to an aircraft once it has entered service, the continuing airworthiness process supports their appropriate embodiment and incorporates changes to the maintenance requirements.

3 Why should the aviation industry change?

The first question that is usually raised in response to a suggestion that the aviation industry could or should change the way it manages safety is 'Surely we are already constantly reacting to safety issues so why should we consider doing even more?'

This is a valid question that is worthy of an answer. The industry as a whole is almost constantly looking to improve for both safety and financial reasons. The industry's response to the UK Civil Aviation Authority's Significant Seven programme (CAA 2011) is proof of this. The industry has worked hard to co-operate with this drive and continues to do so. As a result, there have been some considerable improvements in safety, both within the UK and within some of the aviation organisations elsewhere in the world. This alone would be proof positive of the aviation world's continued commitment to safety but, as many readers of this paper will already know, the industry is also supporting other safety improvement programmes, for instance Safety Management Systems (SMS) and Fatigue Risk Management Systems (FRMS).

So why does the industry need to consider doing more? The answer is fairly simple; the safety initiatives that we are all working on support the processes that we currently use and therefore help us assure that in-service aircraft continue to meet the safety standards defined under the certification process as applicable at original type certification. Although there are safety gains to be made from the lessons learned in service, the basic processes and standards are based on a set of assumptions and safety targets (see Section 2.1) that were made over 30 years ago. In addition to the increasing number of aircraft that are airborne at any one point in time, aircraft and aircraft systems are now far more complex than anything that was ever envisaged at the time these assumptions were made and the trend of increasing complexity is unlikely to be reversed.

Evidence of the increasing complexity of aircraft and aircraft systems, and the effect that this can have on safety, can be seen in recent aircraft development projects which suffered very public project slips and post entry-into-service failures. The effect on the public's perception of the relative safety of these aircraft was predictable and significant effort was required from the relevant organisations to mitigate this.

Human beings are involved in every stage of an aircraft's life and it may seem trite, but it is a basic truth that human error is often a side effect of complexity. It is also true that, in general, although aircraft and aircraft systems are getting progressively more complex, the initially budgeted time for their development is rarely proportionate to their complexity. In addition to the link between human error and complexity, it is also well known that the need to perform complex tasks under pressure of any kind is likely to increase the probability of human error.

The increased likelihood of human error does not just apply to the development of aircraft and aircraft systems. More complex systems can result in longer and more complicated operating and maintenance instructions, which can, in turn, drive other types of human error. This fact is well known by the industry and system designers are often under pressure to reduce the workload of flight, cabin and maintenance crews. They are frequently asked to achieve this by effectively 'hiding' the complex tasks behind a series of user interfaces. In principle, this seems like a good idea but, in practice, the additional complexities associated with doing this can cause significant difficulties and expense. There have been a number of high profile accidents and incidents in recent years where flight crews have lost situational awareness because the information they were provided was confusing or because the information they needed to see was effectively hidden many pages down in the aircraft reporting interfaces. There have also been high profile accidents or incidents where maintenance crews have made a mistake driven by a combination of confusing instructions and the maintenance tools doing unexpected things. It is also becoming common that maintenance crews are unable to find the root cause of an aircraft problem because the information they were provided with was incomplete or unclear. It is worth noting that airlines can incur significant expenses as a result of a series of 'no fault found' reports, including leasing other aircraft and paying compensation to passengers.

If the aircraft certification and continued airworthiness processes continue to be based on a set of assumptions that no longer adequately reflect the aircraft and systems they are being applied to, it is probable that a time will come when the additional processes the industry has put in place are no longer sufficient to mitigate the risks that are inherent in the development, maintenance and management of highly complex systems.

4 What can be done?

By considering how changes to only the safety assessment requirements could be made we can begin to see the potential for greater understanding of behaviour of increasingly complex systems, the ability to provide better and more useful information to aid situation awareness and enable flight and maintenance crews to act as best appropriate. This could also be expected to improve confidence in the design analyses and give rise to better methods of assuring that future aircraft not only meet the intended safety targets but continue to do so throughout their operational life.

There are two possible ways of changing the approach taken to aviation safety: working within the current general requirements or going beyond the current requirement set.

4.1 Working within the current general requirements

There are a number of possible options for improving aviation safety whilst working within the current requirement set. The following is a shortlist of some of the potential activities related to the safety assessment process.

Option 1. Review and amend the current TLOS values.

Option 2. Revise the current classification criteria to better address current levels of system complexity.

Option 3. Revise the current certification approach (without fundamental changes to TLOS) to better address current levels of system complexity.

Option 4. Revise the certification approach and formalise methodologies to better show compliance with current (and future) TLOS.

Option 5. Revise the certification approach and formalise methodologies to better show whole life compliance with current (and future) TLOS.

Option 6. Review and amend the current requirements regarding warning and cautions/human factors/performance.

4.1.1 Option 1. Review and amend the current TLOS values

One option for improving safety would be to revisit the statistical data upon which the current TLOS values were set and, where necessary, update/consolidate the worldwide accident data sets for the various recognized classes of aircraft, e.g. large fixed wing, small fixed wing, large rotorcraft, small rotorcraft, etc. Using this as a basis, the aviation world could begin to debate and develop new and more demanding safety targets.

This could result in a fundamental change to the almost globally harmonized TLOS figures, requiring a significant level of support internationally. Clearly, this would require the basic principles of regulatory need and burden upon industry to be re-addressed, and considerable evaluation would be required before concluding whether this is a valid way forward. However, as with all new or evolved requirement sets, unless an immediate threat to safety is identified, the applicability of any new TLOS requirements would be limited to new type certification activities undertaken after the updated requirements were agreed. As such, although this would have the potential to require significant change to the development, operation and management of aircraft, it would be a change that would wash in slowly over a number of decades.

4.1.2 Option 2. Revise the current classification criteria to better address current levels of system complexity

As explained in Section 2.1 above, the current TLOS figures were derived from assumptions regarding the level of complexity and potential numbers of failure conditions associated with the various classes of aircraft. Modern aircraft have, as also discussed, reached a level of complexity and integration such that many, if not all, now contain many more systems (or system functions) than was originally envisaged and, due to increased levels of system integration and use of distributed or networked elements, the complexity of potential 'inter-system' failure modes has increased significantly.

In order to maintain the current the current aircraft TLOS of 10^{-7} per flight hour, the set of development and certification processes used by the aviation industry could be re-evaluated to determine whether the process continues to fully account for the potentially increased number of critical failure conditions and, where appropriate, identify gaps that the increased levels of complexity and airspace usage have exposed. One method to address this would be to simply research/review the typical modern aircraft, establish an updated ratio of systems and system failure mechanisms and reassign the TLOS figures over a wider number of systems and system failure mechanisms.

It should be noted that, as this approach does not fundamentally adjust the intended aircraft TLOS figures, the overall safety improvement that could be achieved would still be constrained by the 10^{-7} per flight hour objective. It is also true that implementation of this would necessitate amendments to the guidance material that supports requirement 1309 and to the processes that industry uses to evaluate safety. As such it would require significant discussion among the various elements of the aviation world to ensure that the final result is proportionate and does not place an undue burden on the industry.

Once again, unless an immediate threat to safety is identified, a change such as this would only be applied to new certification projects and, as a result, both the impact and the effect of this change would wash in over a period of several decades.

4.1.3   Option   3.   Revise   the   current   certification   approach   (without fundamental changes to TLOS) to better address current levels of system complexity

An alternative approach could be to ensure that there is a much clearer demonstration that the basic intent of requirement 1309 has been achieved. In this approach, whilst the aircraft TLOS and individual failure condition TLOS figures would remain as currently defined, if an aircraft design resulted in more systems or more critical failure conditions than assumed in the basic requirement (10 x 10 = 100), the onus would be placed on the aircraft design organisation to demonstrate that the overall aircraft accident rate of 10^{-7} per flight hour was still achieved.

This would place a responsibility on the aircraft design organisation to trade levels of integrity across the various systems and may result in a need for them to define their own, more stringent, system integrity requirements in order to meet the overall aircraft safety requirements. Although this approach is new to the civil aviation industry, it is not an unusual approach and it is used across a number of different safety critical industries, including some military aviation projects.

As this approach does not fundamentally adjust the intended TLOS figures and the overall safety improvement achievable is constrained by the 10^{-7} per flight hour objective, focusing and balancing the overall complexity of an aircraft and its systems at the aircraft level could result in significant safety benefits in terms of ensuring that aircraft and system complexity do not degrade compliance with the intent of requirement 1309.

As with Options 1 and 2, unless an immediate threat to aviation safety is identified, this process would only be applied to new certification projects. However, as this option represents a changed approach to compliance demonstration, it would be possible to apply this to any project should an applicant wish to do so simply by agreeing a new set of compliance procedures with the relevant regulator. The implication of this is that, although the total benefits of this approach would wash in over a number of decades, should the industry wish to do so, this change could be implemented sooner than Options 1 and 2.

4.1.4 Option 4. Revise the certification approach and formalize methodologies to better show compliance with current (and future) TLOS

As discussed, modern aircraft have become ever more complex and systems more integrated – or even formed from distributed multi-functional elements – so the definition of the 'system' has become more difficult as has the resolution of the consequence of each failure, because each failure potentially affects multiple functions.

Unfortunately, the evolution in system architecture has not been replicated within the certification processes – expertise remains fixed by technical system discipline (hydraulic-mechanical systems, electrical systems, avionics systems, etc.) rather than the functional capability and thus the implications of failures that affect multiple interfaces can be difficult to manage.

Despite the difficulties of managing the increased complexity of aircraft and systems, there are already methodologies that have been developed to address these issues. The development processes used for software and complex hardware are good examples. For both software and complex hardware, the scale and volume of the individual events are beyond the ability of individuals or even teams to investigate. Thus, the process and procedures to evaluate these systems have been developed to gain the necessary confidence by using multi-layer assessments based on audits, automated tool assessments, etc. Given the success of the processes used for software and complex hardware (particularly with respect to safety critical systems) it seems sensible to review these processes and technologies to determine how effectively they could be applied to, or adapted for use in, the development of aircraft and system level safety assessments. It may be worth determining whether they could be extended or adapted to provide supporting mechanisms to demonstrate the robustness/completeness of safety assessments. It is worth noting that it is possible that these methodologies/technologies could also be applied to other aspects of the aviation industry and that, if correctly applied, they could support a total aviation system assessment.

Additional review and/or research may also be needed to understand the most appropriate organisation and procedural structures for future certification teams to ensure appropriate regulatory overview of certification processes as applied to the systems architectures of modern aircraft.

The initial work regarding this option is mainly founded on research and, as such, this option does not fundamentally change the TLOS figures. This implies that the main safety gain that can be achieved, unless tied in with other actions, would be a more rigorous demonstration of compliance. However, as and when the methodologies mature and become viable, they could be applied as a means of compliance and process/procedural elements for the certification teams, rather than regulatory requirements. This means that the benefits associated with their use could be obtained sooner than other options discussed in this paper. However, the full benefit of these approaches would be realized if they were applied at the aircraft level, hence this approach would be limited to new type certification activities.

4.1.5 Option 5. Revise the certification approach and formalise methodologies to better show whole life compliance with current (and future) TLOS

This approach would follow on from Option 4 and would involve the development of the analysis methods, tool sets, etc. to a point whereby a fully integrated aircraft level failure analysis is built as part of the certification process. Following this approach provides the potential for real time closed loop continuous airworthiness assurance systems where:

- The implications of all in-service failure information can be assessed against the assumed/certification model, and with reliability threshold setting, corrective actions can be instigated proactively, rather than retrospectively, either to the certification model or the aircraft.
- Similarly, actual event descriptions can be verified against the assumed indications, warnings and system behaviours and the models and/or operating procedures/advice corrected if necessary.
- Full and detailed troubleshooting guides could be developed to cover the cross system effects to better support both flight and maintenance crews.

This option is a development of the capability offered under Option 4 and hence is also based on research and not directly related to potential safety gains. However, as with Option 4, once the methodologies mature and become viable, they could be applied as a means of compliance and process/procedural elements for the certification teams, rather than regulatory requirements. This means that the benefits associated with their use can be obtained sooner than other options discussed in this paper. However, as with Option 4, the full benefit of these approaches would only be realized if they were applied at the aircraft level and this approach would be limited to new type certification activities unless applicants wished to work with regulators to implement these measures sooner.

Once again, this approach need not be limited to aircraft safety assessments. In developing the capability to integrate system/functional assessment up to an aircraft level there should also be the possibility to perform similar assessment across the many areas of the aviation system – potentially to represent a total system – and support a total system SMS.

4.1.6 Option 6. Review and amend the current requirements regarding warning and cautions/human factors/performance

This option follows on from Option 3. Whilst the number of accidents that are solely attributable to systems failures have clearly been reduced through the efforts of the aircraft/system development teams, certification teams and improved levels of integrity, human factors (including flight, cabin and maintenance crew performance and the various human machine interfaces in the aviation world) is still an area where additional work could result in further aviation safety benefits. Recent changes in some of the certification specifications (e.g. 25.1302 – 'Installed systems and equipment for use by the flight crew') have introduced new requirements that are intended to deliver some of these benefits. However, the full potential of these new requirements is only likely to be realized when the whole design approach considers the implications for the humans involved in the aviation world, both under normal and abnormal (failure) scenarios within a full and comprehensive analysis.

The increasing complexity of systems could be considered to have evolved to a point whereby the current system based requirements for flight deck warning and cautions fail to ensure that flight crews are presented with the most appropriate/useful information in support of their management of the situation. An example of this would be the multiple system failure warnings and cautions generated by failure of a power supply, which would require the crew to determine the root cause from amongst the total information of associated system failure warnings and cautions from the loss of power. Similar issues exist for maintenance crews who are, on occasion, required to determine the root cause of a problem from sets of information that are increasingly remote from their understanding of the actual aircraft. These are problems that the industry already recognizes but there are also more complex human factors that are driven by unrealistic development timescales. One of the most common outcomes of attempting to provide high levels of complex functionality in too short a time is that either some of the expected functionality cannot be provided or that the originally planned interactions between various aviation systems (e.g. the interactions between Air Traffic Management (ATM) systems and aircraft systems that is proposed to support the Single European Skies initiative) are not achieved on time. Once this has occurred, the gap in procedures or safety has to be filled and if aviation systems cannot fill this gap, human beings will have to do so. The need to fill this gap can push the individuals concerned to behave in a manner that may not have been predicted by the original safety assessments.

The continuing human factors issues that are driven by the current processes indicate that it may be beneficial to instigate further work and/or investigation to determine the advantages and disadvantages of developing requirements to ensure human crew performance is aided by identifying fundamental faults/failures and the most effective corrective actions.

There may also be benefit in developing situational awareness tools that use information on the gradual degradation of technical/system/aircraft capability to help flight crews choose a point of intervention rather than having to deal with a situation when the systems reach their limits.

Providing maintenance engineers with useful human factors information such as error traps within the maintenance instructions and the use of multi-media maintenance data could also address human performance issues in the aircraft maintenance environment.

4.2 Beyond current requirements

Although working within the current regulatory framework will bring some potentially significant safety benefits, it is possible that changing the current regulatory framework to address the future environments would enable even greater benefits. However, considering this option without reference to a specific set of questions may not produce a useful result and so the following questions may provide a good starting point for further discussion:

- Is a fixed probability model, as is currently used, the most appropriate way forward or would the ALARP methodologies utilised by MoD and other industries provide a sensible baseline for a modified, risk based oversight process?
- Looking wider than the aircraft, would standardized design requirements offer potential safety benefits for the ATM systems and other parts of the global aviation system?

4.2.1 Is a fixed probability model the most appropriate way forward?

The current regulatory framework is based on fixed probabilities and, once compliance with these probability-based requirements has been shown, the pressure on an organisation to improve their systems beyond the standard defined is significantly reduced. This process has worked well up to now but, as previously discussed, the increasing levels of air traffic could result in an increased number of accidents, even if the current probability requirements are met.

The ALARP process has provided valuable support within some industries as a means of focusing discussions regarding the point at which the likelihood of threats and hazards affecting safety can be stated to be 'As Low As Reasonably Practicable'.

This is a good thing to consider carefully within any project – there is no sense in making changes that have very little effect and, equally, it may be wise to continue to improve system reliability to further reduce risk even if a probability based requirement has been met. However, industry wide use of the ALARP process would bring its own set of challenges; for instance agreeing a standard interpretation of what is 'as low as reasonably practicable'.

Despite the challenges posed by use of the ALARP principle across a diverse industry such as aviation, there are a number of potential safety benefits associated with evaluating whether the likelihood of an aircraft level incident/accident really is as low as reasonably practical, rather than simply complying with probability based requirements. As such, it is worth investigating the potential benefits and associated costs of moving from a fixed probability based framework to a framework which potentially requires a more proactive approach to reducing and managing risk. Once again, in general certification terms, this approach, if adopted, would only be applied to new projects and the effects of it would wash in over a number of years.

4.2.2 Would standardized design requirements offer safety benefits for ATM systems or other parts of the global aviation system?

ATM and other systems currently tend to utilize bespoke solutions based on Commercial Off The Shelf (COTS) products. Whilst this may offer a flexible approach and use of cost effective applications, it can also suffer from problems of integration and require extensive testing to provide assurance of functional and safety capability.

Standardizing the design requirements for ATM/other systems, or COTS based systems in general, could have a number of benefits. For example, providing clear development mechanisms equivalent to the software assurance levels that underpin aircraft integrity could reduce the lengthy, costly and difficult assessments of the functionality and robustness of COTS products, which, in turn, would have the potential to result in increased confidence in the overall system.

The development of a set of standardized design requirements (or minimum specifications) could also offer a number of benefits including:

- supporting procurement processes by enabling standardisation of products being bought
- assuring a basic level of product robustness
- facilitating a wider harmonisation of regulatory oversight.

Extending the use of standardized design requirements into maintenance and other areas of system management, e.g. maintenance of ATM systems, could also bring additional benefits, for instance maximizing the availability of systems and minimizing the need to use backup systems. This, in turn, would have the potential to provide further robustness in the overall system.

4.3 Other possibilities and considerations

In addition to the airworthiness and ATM topics already addressed in this paper, there are a number of other sources of improvement that can be classified under a banner of 'the total aviation system'. Some of these potential improvements are likely to be forced on the industry by issues such as cyber security which may end up driving a need to re-evaluate how we manage aviation safety as an overall whole rather looking at each sector part (aircraft, ATM, airline management, etc.) separately. Other potential aviation wide improvements have been suggested by the work done in separate sectors of the industry. For instance, the unmanned aviation world has had to reconsider the interface between aircraft control systems, remote pilots and ATM and, in doing so, has had to re-evaluate how safety assessments need to be performed and how to manage the 'blurring' of edges between the various aviation domains.

If the aviation industry concludes that re-evaluating the overall regulatory framework is the best way to manage the hazards inherent with increasing numbers of more complex aircraft, then the development of a total safety model with clear targets for each sector that takes account of the lessons learnt in each sector and can be flowed down through all the relevant processes/products could provide significant benefits. Clearly this would need to be consistently applied to gain the maximum benefit and it may be worth considering supporting system such as a total system SMS approach to ensure that the various aspects of the overall system are properly managed and assumptions/dependencies across the sectors (all interfacing with each other) are fully recognized by each user.

5 Conclusions

The increasing numbers of aircraft being flown and the level of complexity associated with new aircraft and ATM systems mean that, unless proactive measures are taken, the number of aircraft accidents is potentially likely to rise and it is possible that this number will rise sufficiently to damage the public perception of aviation safety.

If proactive measures are to be taken, the industry as a whole needs to determine the best approach to mitigating future threats. There are some improvements that could be made within the current regulatory processes, for instance a further examination of human factors issues, but from a systems point of view, the industry may well be approaching a point of minimum returns for any design changes related to safety. As such, significant improvements in terms of system safety are more likely to be gained from a more radical review of how the industry currently evaluates and manages its system development processes.

As discussed, there are medium to long term options that would allow the industry to continue to work within current regulatory frameworks whilst reviewing how and whether target levels of safety have been met. These would require significant change but this could be implemented over a number of years to minimize the impact on current projects as far as possible. However, if the industry concludes that a more radical rethink is required, there may well be benefits in working together to review the current regulatory framework in terms of its ability to drive risk down to an appropriate level and manage cross boundary issues such as the link between aircraft and ATM systems.

References

CAA (2011) CAA 'Significant Seven' task force reports. Civil Aviation Authority. http://www .caa.co.uk/docs/33/2011_03.pdf. Accessed 18 November 2013

EASA (2012) Certification specifications for large rotorcraft. CS-29 amendment 3. European Aviation Safety Agency

EASA (2013) Certification specifications and acceptable means of compliance for large aeroplanes. CS-25 amendment 13. European Aviation Safety Agency

Lloyd E, Tye W (1982) Systematic safety: safety assessment of aircraft systems. Civil Aviation Authority

Development and Certification of a Safety-Critical Avionics Touch Screen Display using Open Standards

Paul Parkinson[1], David Randall[2] and David Speed[3]

[1]Wind River, Swindon, UK

[2]Presagis, Montreal, Canada

[3]AgustaWestland, Yeovil, UK

Abstract   In this paper the requirements of the upgrade of a cockpit avionics display for a military rotary-wing platform will be presented. The use of open standards-based architectures including ARINC 653 and ARINC 661 with COTS hardware platforms to meet these requirements will be considered. Experience gained by the use of these technologies on a European military helicopter programme will be presented, including the benefits of modular and incremental safety certification and positive impact in reducing operational and through-life costs.

1 Introduction

Avionics cockpit displays have traditionally been developed as Line Replaceable Units (LRUs) which perform a single dedicated function, and have been deployed in many civil and military aircraft as part of federated avionics architecture. However, by the mid-1970s, the number of cockpit instruments continued to grow, improving pilot situational awareness and navigation, but also competed for cockpit space and pilot attention.

The pioneering research undertaken by NASA's Langley 737 flying laboratory (Wallace 1994) into displays which were able to process the raw aircraft system and flight data into an integrated picture of the flight situation resulted in a technology demonstrator of integrated electronic (digital) displays, known as a *glass cockpit*. As the technology used in electronic displays has matured, there has been a significant increase in their deployment in civil and military aircraft over the last decade, enabling the replacement of multiple analogue dials and gauges with digital counterparts. These modern digital displays are comprised of integrated systems which have been designed to meet the requirements of performing the equivalent functions of their analogue predecessors. This is typically implemented using *Multi-Function Displays* (MFDs), comprised of a glass display surrounded by fixed function mechanical buttons which enables the appropriate display to be selected and shown on the screen. Typical helicopter cockpits using analogue displays and multi-function digital displays are shown in Figure 1.

Fig. 1. Helicopter cockpits: (left) analogue displays and (right) MFDs[1]

Whilst the deployment of MFDs has been successful, systems which have been developed using proprietary monolithic software architecture may not provide sufficient flexibility to enable the implementation of additional functionality to meet new operational requirements. In addition, it may not be possible to perform re-certification at reasonable cost. Industry research into upgrades of military aircraft avionics systems has demonstrated that for safety certification of monolithic federated architectures:

> The cost of change is not proportional to the size of the change, but proportional to the size of the system. (Holton 2007)

In this paper, the suitability of an open standards-based approach combined with an open architecture hardware platform for the development of an extensible safety-critical avionics display will be considered. The experiences of AgustaWestland, an Anglo-Italian helicopter company owned by Italy's Finmeccanica, on using this approach on a military helicopter upgrade programme will also be presented.

2 Operational requirements

The military helicopter had previously used avionics display control units within the cockpit and cabin of the aircraft. This used a text-based Human Machine Interface (HMI) to control multiple avionics systems, as shown in Figure 2. The number of options which could be displayed concurrently was limited, due to the space used by text-based menus and the limited physical size of the display. This limitation resulted in a hierarchical menu system of significant depth which took a long

---

[1] Images: © AgustaWestland

time for the aircrew to navigate. Thus, a goal of the upgrade programme was to optimize the usability of the avionics display control unit by exploiting available technologies. There was also a requirement to reduce the impact of obsolescence and the through-life costs of the helicopter avionics display systems. This encompassed development costs, testing and safety certification, operational use through minimizing spares, and reducing future upgrade and certification costs.

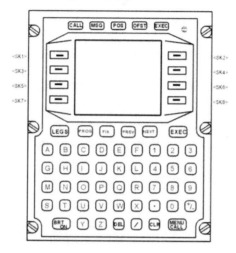

Fig. 2. Military helicopter MFD prior to upgrade[2]

3 System architecture

3.1 Open systems architecture

For the new avionics display control units, it was decided that the ergonomics of the HMI would be dramatically improved through the use of touch screen liquid-crystal displays, as these would enable a physically larger display screen than existing LRUs, and would dispose of the need for mechanical buttons surrounding the glass, which otherwise would limit the size of the glass area. In addition, the combined use of text and graphics would also enable much shallower menu hierarchies to be implemented, enabling faster navigation by the aircrew and therefore providing faster response times.

The AgustaWestland programme evaluated the potential benefits and drawbacks of the use of proprietary hardware and software architecture versus Commercial-Off-The-Shelf (COTS) hardware and *open* software architectures. The purpose of this was to determine which approach would provide the best contribu-

---

[2] Image: © AgustaWestland

tion to through-life cost reduction whilst also meeting the requirements for RTCA DO-178B/EUROCAE ED-12B safety certification (DO-178B 1992, ED-12B 1992).

3.2 Extensible hardware platform architecture

The Barco MFD-2108 touch screen display uses a PowerPC 755 processor for hosting ARINC 653 applications, and also employs two dedicated ARM processors for I/O offload. The MFD-2108 was selected as the hardware platform for the military helicopter's new Touch Screen Unit (TSU) based on a number of selection criteria, including the following:

1. The COTS hardware design enabled the cost of its development to be amortized over multiple programmes on a commercial basis.
2. Barco's Modular Open System Architecture for real-time avionics (MOSArt) provided an extensible framework which enabled AgustaWestland to customize the display system to meet the specific requirements of the upgrade programme.
3. MOSArt is based on the ARINC 653 industry *open* standard, which enabled the display system to be customized to meet the specific requirements of the programme, whilst providing an abstraction layer from the underlying hardware to isolate the software from underlying hardware architecture, reducing the impact of hardware obsolescence. The use of an open standard also enabled the use of third party software written to the standard to be rapidly integrated into a common platform.

3.3 ARINC 653 software architecture

The ARINC 653 avionics software architecture (ARINC 2003) is an industry open standard which defines the requirements for hosting multiple applications concurrently on the same processor. This standard is often used to consolidate multiple federated applications running on separate dedicated hardware platforms onto a single common processing platform. ARINC 653 defines two key concepts to enable the successful deployment of multiple applications running concurrently within an Integrated Modular Avionics (IMA) system – *spatial partitioning* and *temporal partitioning*, also known as time and space partitioning.

Spatial partitioning defines the memory and resource isolation requirements for multiple applications running concurrently on the same computing platform, also known as a module. In this model, applications running in an IMA partition must not be able to deprive each other of shared application resources or those required by the system. This is usually achieved through the use of different virtual memory contexts enforced by the processor's memory management unit. These contexts are referred to as *partitions* in the ARINC 653 standard.

Temporal partitioning defines the processor utilization isolation requirements for multiple applications running concurrently on the same computing platform. This ensures that one application may not utilize the processor for longer than intended to the detriment of the other applications. ARINC 653 addresses the problem by defining an implementation that uses partition-based scheduling where a partition is scheduled for a timeslot of defined width, and other partitions may be allocated timeslots of similar or differing durations.

Barco's MOSArt platform is integrated with Wind River's ARINC 653-compliant VxWorks 653 Real-Time Operating System (RTOS) (Parkinson and Kinnan 2007), which means that it is able to provide these spatial and temporal partitioning capabilities. During the design phase, the decision was taken to exploit ARINC 653's spatial partitioning within the helicopter TSU. Rather than use VxWorks 653 to host multiple independent applications running on the same processor, spatial partitioning was used to decompose the TSU application into modular components running in separate ARINC 653 partitions. This minimized the impact of change to TSU requirements.

The basic system design is described by the following software architecture:

The ARINC661 Cockpit Display System (CDS) partition contains the graphics display stack provided by Presagis to generate all the graphical output for the display.

The master User Application (UA) partition contains functionality to control the unit and is likely to change as a result of changes in requirements, and therefore the impact of change on the other software is minimized.

The physical interface handler partition contains functionality responsible for the communication with other avionics systems via dual-redundant networks. The unit relies on other aircraft systems to provide the data for display as it has no knowledge of what data is being displayed.

The health and system management partition contains functionality to manage the built-in test functionality.

The resulting software architecture (shown in Figure 3) has achieved a balance between minimizing design complexity and minimizing the impact of change to TSU requirements in terms of the burden of retesting and re-qualification for flight.

3.4 ARINC 661 display software architecture

The ARINC 661 specification (ARINC 2010) defines a distributed architecture that facilitates the creation and maintenance of standardized, interactive avionics displays. ARINC 661 was selected as an open industry standard on the basis of providing a suitable architecture, and having growing industry support enabling the programme to leverage investment in the development of ARINC 661 COTS tool support for previous major avionics programmes, in particular the Airbus A380 and Boeing 787 aircraft. The ARINC 661 objectives were also well aligned with the upgrade programme's operational requirements discussed earlier:

- Minimize costs for new display capabilities.
- Minimize costs for changes to new display capabilities.
- Minimize costs for the management of hardware obsolescence.
- Support means of developing standard HMI.

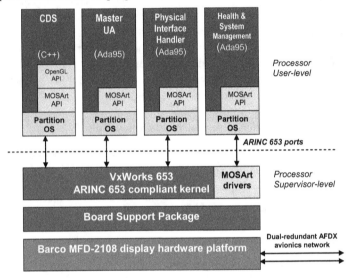

Fig. 3. TSU software architecture

The CDS is responsible for displaying *widgets* to the end user by using a library of all the widgets defined by the ARINC 661 specification. At start-up, the CDS loads and displays widgets based on one or more binary file(s) called Definition File(s) (DFs). Each DF contains one or more *layers*, which are hierarchical listings of all of the widgets that need to be loaded, once or multiple times, along with their initial properties, such as position, colour and visibility.

The UA is responsible for providing data to update the contents of the CDS based on real-time flight data and to react to user interactions with the display. The UA can be connected to one or more layers that are loaded in the CDS. The UA encapsulates the logic processing and behaviour of what is displayed by the CDS.

ARINC 661 defines a bi-directional runtime protocol that is used by the CDS and the UA to exchange data and events. The definition of this protocol is made possible by a set of standard widgets and the architecture put in place by the standard. Layers and widgets are referenced using the IDs that were assigned in the layer definition.

ARINC 661 effectively provides a client server model between the UA and CDS applications which enabled them to be mapped into separate ARINC 653 partitions (as shown in Figure 4). ARINC 661 runtime protocol messages are sent between the two partitions using ARINC 653 APplication EXecutive (APEX) communication ports. This mapping provided additional benefits for the TSU programme in terms of enabling UAs and CDSs of different levels of safety-criticality to be hosted on the same platform, and each component only needing to be tested to its required DO-178B/ED-12B design assurance level. This means that on a single display, layers of differing safety-criticality levels could be displayed in the same window. This contrasted with a monolithic software architecture which would have required all user application software to be tested to the level of the most critical component (system high), and would have incurred undesirable additional testing and certification costs. For further details of implementation and use of ARINC 661, refer to (Lefebvre 2006).

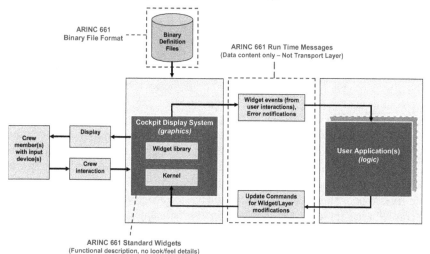

Fig. 4. ARINC 661 display software architecture

Further, since ARINC 661 specifies that the DFs, containing the layer and widget definitions and hierarchies, are outside the coded components of the CDS and UA, modifications to the layout of one or more layers could be implemented without re-certification of the CDS or UA.

4 Development process methodology

4.1 DO-297 role-based development

The ability of the ARINC 653 software architecture to support IMA applications was discussed in an earlier section, but the challenges associated with the integration of IMA hardware, the ARINC 653 APEX, or RTOS kernel, and multiple ARINC 653 applications also must be considered. It is particularly important to consider how an ARINC 653 system can be architected so that incremental changes to a system component in the future can be undertaken in isolation without impacting the rest of the system, so that only the scope of the component which has changed needs to undergo retesting and re-certification. This goal is known as incremental certification.

The RTCA DO-297/EUROCAE ED-124 standard (DO-297 2005, ED-124 2007) provides guidance on the development and certification of IMA systems, and advocates a *role-based development approach*. This guidance involves the assignment of distinct roles and responsibilities for individual stakeholders, these are: certification authority, certification applicant, platform supplier, system integrator and application supplier.

This role-based development approach was used for the development of the TSU, with the platform supplier (Barco) creating the base platform and defining the system configuration. The application suppliers created the separate applications which run in the ARINC 653 partitions; which had their own application configuration data which was kept separate from the underlying platform configuration data. The third DO-297 party, the system integrator, also had configuration data that defined the overall configuration of the system components. In the case of the upgrade programme, AgustaWestland development teams undertook multiple roles (application supplier, system integrator and certification applicant), but this role-based approach has also been successfully applied by multiple independent organizations on global avionics programmes.

The configuration of the IMA system components was defined using a modular XML-based approach. Each application partition was defined independently in XML, enabling the applications to be developed separately from each other, as shown in Figure 5. The XML-based system configuration also enabled validation in an automated manner as part of the build process by using a DO-178B qualified XML compiler. This approach automated the complex process of validation of system configuration data of individual components, and how each component interacted in the overall system. This included validation that:

1. ARINC 653 inter-partition channels are correctly defined.
2. For each channel defined there is a sender and a receiver.
3. The port attribute definitions were mutually consistent.

This validated configuration data was then read in binary format by the ARINC 653 kernel during the system initialization process.

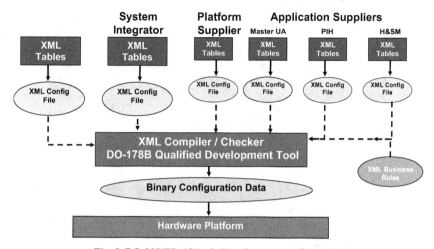

Fig. 5. DO-297/ED-124 role-based system configuration

4.2 Display modelling

In order to enable rapid prototyping of the HMI layout and menu hierarchies the TSU HMI was developed using the ARINC 661 display modelling approach. The Presagis VAPS XT-178 ARINC 661 DO-178 qualifiable HMI tool suite was used to create displays comprised of one or more ARINC 661 layers containing ARINC 661 widgets. The state and behaviour of layers/widgets is defined and processed by the UA. The widget library provided with the delivered TSU is effectively a database of widget definitions provided for use with the TSU.

This HMI visualization capability in the development phase enabled the software development team to collaborate closely with colleagues who were responsible for the ergonomic design, and to perform design iterations without having to create multiple iterations of a full TSU design prototype. This simulation-based approach enabled the HMI design process to be undertaken more quickly. This approach was also further exploited by using a desk-based layer modelling process with a training and simulation environment using touch-sensitive glass panels. This environment was used to perform mission simulation and gain early customer feedback, enabling the display layers to be refined and tuned to exact customer needs before being ported to the real TSU display hardware.

In the resulting design for the TSU top-level display (shown in Figure 6), the top row of the display contains a persistent layer containing critical system messages, and button widgets to enable the aircrew to step backwards from the most recent selection and return to the top-level display. The circular button widgets below the top row enable the aircrew to select the menus for the corresponding helicopter subsystems, and the cross button widgets allow the aircrew to enter input selections and parameters. (The buttons are coloured blue and red respectively on the cockpit display to enable them to be clearly distinguished from each other). ARINC 661 also enabled graphics showing the layout of the helicopter to be used, enabling the crew to easily identify cargo bays and their loads.

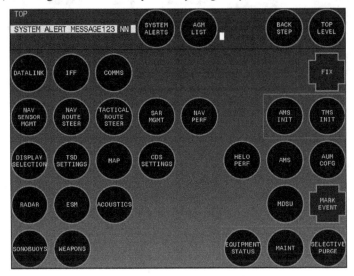

Fig. 6. TSU top-level display[3]

4.3 Application development workflow

The ARINC 661-based development of the CDS was augmented with model-based design of the master UA, physical interface handler, and health and system management applications using Unified Modelling Language (UML 2006). This was developed using Atego Artisan Studio, and resulted in models for 38 use cases for TSU operation, which included the behaviour of the applications and their interaction with the CDS. This approach enabled the application behaviour to be modelled in detail prior to implementation.

Autocode generation was performed from the UML environment to create application frameworks in Ada95. In addition, XML definitions for ARINC 653 inter-partition communication ports were generated. These formats were directly importable into the Wind River Workbench development environment for VxWorks 653, enabling the development flow from design phase to implementation phase to be automated, thus avoiding the risk of errors being introduced manually during the transition between phases.

The implementation phase involved coding the application behaviour of the master UA, physical interface handler, and health and system management applications using Ada95. The Ada programming language was selected due to its

---

[3] Image: © AgustaWestland

strong language typing features to ease the certification process. The Ada language uses a runtime support library (in a similar way to the C programming language), and this is also subject to DO-178B certification. So a decision was taken to use a minimum Ada runtime profile that would support the requirements of the user applications. The AdaCore Zero Footprint Profile (ZFP), which is included in the GNAT Pro High Integrity Edition, was selected to provide a good technical match to balance TSU application requirements with certification demands. The Ada applications were compiled using AdaCore's ZFP, with the Ada application main entry point being called directly from the ARINC 653 application initialization routine in each partition.

Implementation was undertaken using the Wind River Workbench development environment integrated with AdaCore GNAT Pro High Integrity Edition, which enabled the Ada applications to be compiled within ARINC 653 partitions, and these to be combined with the ARINC 661 CDS and MOSArt application programming interface to build a complete VxWorks 653 system. This environment was used to run and debug the VxWorks 653 system running on the Barco hardware platform prior to testing and certification phase.

4.4 Testing, integration and certification

In order to meet the requirements of DO-178B/ED-12B objectives for requirements-based testing and code coverage testing, a three stage testing process was undertaken using Vector Software's DO-178B qualified VectorCAST testing suite:

1. host-based unit testing of each of the ARINC 653 partitions separately
2. integration testing of the combined system with all ARINC 653 partitions
3. system testing of the deployment configuration and final binaries on the target hardware.

The decision taken in the design phase to decompose the TSU application into modular components within ARINC 653 partitions also provided additional benefits in the testing phase, enabling unit testing of the CDS, master UA and other applications to occur independently. This approach will also provide additional benefits in relation to reducing certification costs associated with potential future system upgrades to meet new operational requirements.

These efficiencies were achieved by using independent payload streams rather than a traditional monolithic system image load for the platform. This design and build separation enables TSU application to be updated in the future without rebuilding and retesting the other system binaries. The payload stream was created by the DO-178B qualified tool, VerIMAx (which was developed by Wind River's certification partner Verocel). This tool also checked that the XML definitions and XML files were mutually consistent; and the ARINC 653 Partition OS also performed an additional runtime check during initialization to verify that the XML version number matched the expected configuration version. This approach ensured that incompatible versions of images within the payload stream could not be used in a deployed system.

5 Assumptions

The development of the TSU was undertaken using the aforementioned approaches, based on the following assumptions, which were assessed during the AgustaWestland development programme:

1. ARINC 653 and ARINC 661 were suitable standards-based architectures for the development of the TSU.
2. The COTS-based technologies were sufficiently mature and well integrated to enable successful development of the TSU.
3. IMA-based development would provide the option of using a modular and incremental certification approach for subsequent upgrades and future TSU variants.
4. The DO-178B certification evidence for each of the COTS components was sufficient and fit for purpose.

6 Results

The TSU which has been produced as a result of the helicopter upgrade programme has achieved the operational requirements presented in an earlier section. The HMI provides faster navigation, enabling the aircrew to achieve faster response times.

The use of ARINC 661 and display simulation has provided a faster iterative development approach, enabling customer feedback to be gained more rapidly and incorporated into design iterations. This has reduced the risk of the final deployment configuration not meeting customer expectations.

The use of ARINC 661 layers to separate the configuration data from the application provided a flexible framework which enabled the display layout and configuration to be changed frequently without impacting the application code and thereby reducing the impact on certification effort. This will also provide the ability to support new requirements and different deployment configurations for other customers.

The DO-178B/ED-12B testing process has achieved 100% coverage to fully meet the certification objectives for the helicopter upgrade programme.

The TSU deployment configuration uses location-based functionality, which means that an individual TSU unit could be fitted in any one of the four positions on the helicopter, and the software would auto-configure to operate for the correct location. The use of location-based functionality provides better spares common-ality, thus making a significant contribution to the reduction in spares required, and therefore contributing to a reduction in the through-life costs of the helicopter.

7 Conclusions

The successful outcome of the TSU development programme has shown that the assumptions outlined earlier hold to be true. The ARINC 653 and ARINC 661 standards-based approach have been successfully used for the development of a safety-critical touch screen avionics display, which has provided improved HMI navigation, and has achieved the operational requirements for a military helicopter upgrade programme.

The use of a COTS hardware design contributed to a reduction in upgrade costs, due to the fact that the cost of the development of the COTS hardware was amortized over multiple programmes on a commercial basis. The ARINC 653 and ARINC 661 software architecture provide an abstraction layer which isolates the application from the underlying hardware to minimize the impact of hardware obsolescence.

The selection of COTS components and tools needs to be undertaken with care to ensure that they fulfil standards compliance and also provide cross-vendor tool-set integration. When this convergence is achieved, it can provide automated workflows which can help accelerate the development process.

The use of COTS DO-178B/ED-12B certification evidence provided a cost-effective approach to certification (again due to the cost being amortized over multiple programmes on a commercial basis). The only caveat was that because the programme was using multiple COTS software components provided by different vendors, a review of the certification evidence needed to be undertaken to confirm that full traceability was provided, and that the dependencies and inter-faces between different components can be determined and clearly defined.

Finally, ARINC 653 and ARINC 661 provide open foundations for modular and incremental certification. The TSU application architecture could be enhanced by AgustaWestland to exploit these capabilities in subsequent upgrades and future TSU variants. This approach would contribute to a further reduction in future cer-tification costs.

Acknowledgments The authors wish to thank Barco Defense & Aerospace for granting permission to include technical details of the Barco MFD-2108 touch screen display within this paper.

References

ARINC (2003) ARINC Specification 653-1, avionics application software standard interface
ARINC (2010) ARINC Specification 661-4, cockpit display system interfaces to user system
DO-178B (1992) Software considerations in airborne systems and equipment certification. RTCA

DO-297 (2005) Integrated Modular Avionics (IMA) development guidance and certification considerations. RTCA

ED-12B (1992) Software considerations in airborne systems and equipment certification. EUROCAE

ED-124 (2007) Integrated Modular Avionics (IMA) development guidance and certification considerations. EUROCAE

Holton G (2007) BAE SYSTEMS Military Air Solutions. Presented at UK Ministry of Defence Military Avionics Technology Exhibition

Lefebvre Y (2006) Understanding ARINC 661 and the benefits of 661-based development tools. Presagis

Parkinson P, Kinnan L (2007) Safety-critical software development for integrated modular avionics. White paper, Wind River

UML (2006) Unified Modeling Language 2.0. Object Management Group

Wallace L (1994) Airborne trailblazer: two decades with NASA Langley's 737 flying laboratory. NASA, ASIN: B000VBQLH4

Compliance with Standards or Claim-based Justification? The Interplay and Complementarity of the Approaches for Nuclear Software-based Systems

Sofia Guerra and Dan Sheridan

Adelard

London, UK

Abstract The control and protection of nuclear power plants has become increasingly dependent on the use of computers. The UK nuclear regulatory regime requires that a safety case be developed to justify and communicate their safety. There are several ways of constructing such a safety case. In the past, safety justifications tended to be standards-based – compliance to accepted practice was deemed to imply adequate safety. Over the last 20 years, there has been a trend towards an explicit claim-based approach, where specific safety claims are supported by arguments and evidence at progressively more detailed levels. These approaches are not mutually exclusive, and a combination can be used to support a safety justification. In fact, for the most critical systems it can be argued that a safety case should consider both aspects. For less critical systems, one might believe that one approach would suffice. This paper discusses software-based systems with only a modest integrity requirement, and the interplay of the two approaches. It describes our experience with justifying such systems for the nuclear industry, and it claims that there are a number of benefits of taking both approaches together.

1 Introduction

Programmable components including personal computers (PCs) or smart instruments can offer considerable benefits in terms of usability, functionality and possibly price in a safety-related system. For example, the nuclear operators are increasingly replacing analogue instruments with their digital 'smart' counterparts, as they achieve greater accuracy, better noise filtering together with in-built linearisation, and provide better on-line calibration and diagnostics features. Similarly, there are usability and functionality advantages to using PCs for some applications where the reliability requirement is fairly modest. These systems are typically not nuclear specific, or are based on components that are not nuclear specific (such as general purpose operating systems). Nevertheless, if the application is considered to have an impact on safety, the licensees are required to justify that level of safety achieved.

There are often difficulties with the safety justification of this type of system. This might be due to all or part of the system being sold as a 'black box', where the purchaser has no knowledge of the internal system structure or the development processes followed by the manufacturer. PCs and their operating systems are typical examples of this. Difficulties might also arise from the age of the component, since expectations of 'best practice' have changed over the years; even if a component was developed in accordance with best practice ten years ago it may not meet current expectations.

This paper discusses the justification of software-based systems with a modest reliability requirement (e.g., a probability of failure on demand of 10^{-1} or 10^{-2}, or SIL 1) in the nuclear industry in the UK. It builds on our experience of justifying a number of these systems, and discusses some of the issues encountered and how they have been addressed.

In Section 2, we summarise the UK nuclear regulatory regime. Section 3 describes the range of justification approaches and gives examples of how they are applied in the UK nuclear industry. In Section 4, we discuss the use of a combined compliance and claim-based justification approach, and give examples of how this approach has been beneficial to us. We draw conclusions from these case studies in Section 5.

2 UK nuclear regulatory regime

The UK has a clearly defined approach to how the assessment and licensing of command, control and protection systems should be carried out. There are still significant differences between the UK and other countries, despite the internationalization of the supply chain and efforts such as:

- effective collaboration with international agencies such as IAEA and OECD
- standards committees including the IEC
- working groups such as the Nuclear Regulators Working Group (NRWG)
- projects to encourage harmonisation such as CEMSIS (CEMSIS 2004) and HARMONICS (European Commission 2011).

In the UK, nuclear licensees are required to produce safety cases in order to comply with the licence conditions (HSE 2011). These are designed to be non-prescriptive, and instead set high-level goals for the nuclear operators. The Safety Assessment Principles (SAPs) (HSE 2006) are the primary principles that define the approach to assessment to be followed for nuclear installations in the UK. The SAPs were revised in 2006 and have been brought into line with IAEA guidance.

The SAPs have the following clauses on computer-based safety systems (our emphasis added).

> Where the system reliability is significantly dependent upon the performance of computer software, the establishment of and compliance with appropriate standards and practices throughout the software development life-cycle should be made, commensurate with the level of reliability required, by a demonstration of *'production excellence'* and *'confidence-building'* measures. [(HSE 2006) clause ESS.27]

> *'Production excellence'* requires a demonstration of excellence in all aspects of production, covering initial specification through to the finally commissioned system, comprising the following elements:

> a) Thorough application of technical design practice consistent with current accepted standards for the development of software for computer-based safety systems.
> b) Implementation of an adequate quality assurance programme and plan in accordance with appropriate quality assurance standards.
> c) Application of a comprehensive testing programme formulated to check every system function. [(HSE 2006) clause 360]

> Independent *'confidence-building'* should provide an independent and thorough assessment of a safety system's fitness for purpose. This comprises the following elements:

> a) Complete and preferably diverse checking of – the finally validated production software by a team that is independent of the systems suppliers, including:

> – independent product checking providing a searching analysis of the product;
> – independent checking of the design and production process, including activities needed to confirm the realisation of the design intention;

> b) Independent assessment of the test programme, covering the full scope of test activities. [(HSE 2006) clause 361]

> Should weaknesses be identified in the production process, *compensating measures* should be applied to address these. The type of compensating measures will depend on, and should be targeted at, the specific weaknesses found. [(HSE 2006) clause 362]

In the UK, we refer to this approach of demonstrating production excellence and confidence building measures as the *two-legged approach*. The expectation for both legs is that the depth of the assessment is 'commensurate with the level of reliability required'. For example, for systems with a modest reliability requirement, the production excellence leg is typically supported by:

- good commercial practice
- development process evidence
- compliance with international quality assurance standards.

The independent confidence building measures for a modest reliability system might include:

- commissioning tests to demonstrate that the instrument adequately performs its required functions
- data on prior use
- evidence of the manufacturer's pedigree.

In this paper we argue that, even for systems with modest integrity requirements, the production excellence leg needs to be developed using both a process and a product-based approach, in the sense described in Section 3 below.

3 Justification approaches

There are two principal ways of constructing a safety justification (Bishop et al. 2004). A *process-based* approach focuses on the development process and defined standards and practices, while a *product-based* approach focuses on the behaviour required of the system. Below, we describe these approaches in more detail and give examples from the UK nuclear industry.

3.1 Process-based approach

A widely used approach to justifying a Control and Instrumentation (C&I) system and its software is to provide evidence that they have been designed and verified following a well-structured development process and in accordance with the requirements and recommendations of rigorous standards. For example, when the justification is based on compliance with a standard such as IEC 61508, assessors argue that the system is acceptably safe by showing that the development process followed is consistent with that described in the standard and by applying a set of techniques and methods that the standards associate with a specific safety integrity level. This type of justification approach is also called a *rule-based* or *standards-based* approach, as it relies on the application of pre-defined rules on the development process and on compliance with standards.

3.1.1 Process-based approaches in the UK

There are a number of different standards or regulations that can be used as a basis for the justification of a software-based system. This varies with the type of system, reliability requirement and organization. For example:

- COTS products that have not been developed for the nuclear industry may be assessed against IEC 61508 (Stockham 2009).
- Nuclear specific standards may be used, such as IEC 61513 or IEC 62138.
- Organisations may have their internal standards, which will typically be based on an international standard adapted to the system and reliability requirements to which they will be used.

All of the standards and approaches cover a number of common areas including:

- configuration management
- the approach to development, including requirements, design and implementation
- design constraints or design principles
- the level of verification that may be considered adequate
- the documentation that is to be produced during development.

3.1.2 Criticism of the process-based approach

The process-based approach works well in stable environments where best practice is deemed to imply adequate safety. However, it is often criticised for being highly prescriptive and impeding the adoption of new and novel methods and techniques. The fundamental limitation of process-based safety justification lies in the observation that good tools, techniques and methods do not necessarily lead to the achievement of a specific level of integrity. The correlation between the prescribed techniques and the failure rate of the system is often infeasible to justify. Conversely, process-based approaches are also inadequate where high-quality systems were developed in accordance with older or different standards, or just meet industrial good practice but fall short of strict compliance with standards.

A purely process-based approach does not necessarily provide direct evidence that the C&I system and its software achieve the behaviour or the properties required to the desired level of reliability. However, despite these uncertainties, some might argue that process-based evidence is sufficient for systems of modest integrity requirements. In the next sections we argue that this not the case.

3.2 Product-based approach

To overcome the difficulties with the process-based approach, we can focus instead on directly justifying that the desired behaviour, property or reliability has been achieved, using product-specific and targeted evidence. This type of approach can be called the *product-based* or *property-based* approach.

A product-based approach allows the focus to be directly on the safety requirements for the system, making it applicable even when a standards compliance case cannot be made. This is often the case for off-the-shelf devices (such as smart instruments), where development follows industrial good practice and does not necessarily conform to a recognised safety lifecycle.

Alternative evidence can be presented to justify the safety properties depending on the characteristics of the device being justified and the process followed. For example, in applications with limited safety significance, extensive field experience for a device may provide alternative evidence of compliance to the required performance, or alternative arguments can be used to justify expected behaviour when process non-compliances might have been identified. Evidence can also be related to a range of different safety standards by identifying how the requirements in the standards support the various claims. This allows greater flexibility in making a justification while ensuring that all safety relevant attributes of the system are justified.

This approach is usually linked with specific claims about the product or system being justified, and may be *claim-based (*or *goal-based).* This can follow a structured approach such as *Claims-Arguments-Evidence* (CAE) (Bishop and Bloomfield 1995) or *Goal Structuring Notation* (GSN) (Kelly 1999). The CAE approach was developed as part of a research project funded by the UK nuclear industry (Adelard 1998). It forms the basis for the Generic Design Assessment (GDA) currently being performed in the UK for new nuclear build, and it is used for justifying refurbishment projects in existing plants.

3.2.1 Product-based approaches in practice

In this section, we summarise two techniques used by Adelard in constructing product-based safety justifications. The main characteristic of these two techniques is that they focus on the system behaviour, rather than on the way it was developed.

Behavioural attributes. The justification of the system's behaviour may be done by arguing that specific high-level claims are met. These may be based on a set of *behavioural attributes* which allow us to provide separate arguments focusing on specific aspects of behaviour. Table 1 gives an example of behavioural attributes that have been used to justify an FPGA-based system (Guerra and Sheridan 2012).

Table 1. Example attributes

Category	Attributes	Discussion
Functionality	Functionality	The function performed by the system
Performance	Timing	Includes time response, permissible clock frequencies, propagation delays, etc.
	Accuracy	Affected by analogue/digital conversion, processing functions, IP cores, etc.
Availability	Availability	Readiness for correct service, a system-level attribute supported by component attributes such as reliability
Reliability	Absence of faults	This may be connected with a vulnerability analysis
	Fault detection and tolerance	Internal detection of faults
Robustness	Robustness	Tolerance to out-of-normal inputs and stressful conditions
Failure recovery	Failure recovery	The ability to recover from failures through error detection and reporting, such as sounding an alarm

LowSIL approach. An approach developed for the nuclear industry to justify systems that used *Non-Safety Assured Programmable Components* (NSPCs) that cannot be directly justified, e.g., PC-based systems running Microsoft Windows (Bishop et al. 2010). This guidance is intended for use when:

- Failure of the system can affect nuclear safety, environmental protection or industrial safety, the integrity of plant actuations, safety-related information presented to operators, or the safety integrity of components or calibration data that will be used in the plant at some time in the future.
- The required integrity of the system safety function is at or below SIL 1. Typically the approach is used for an integrity of no more than 10^{-1} failures per demand or 10^{-4} dangerous failures per hour.
- The system contains one or more NSPCs (such as a PC, a programmable logic controller, or a configurable device such as a smart sensor), and there is insufficient assurance of the NSPC's safety integrity.

The main assessment strategy is to perform a hazard analysis to identify how the NSPC may fail, and how its failure could lead to a hazard for the system containing the NSPC. This analysis includes performance failures such as slow response. The impact of the failures is assessed together with the effectiveness of existing mitigations, and additional controls or mitigations may be recommended. These may result in design changes and additional requirements on the system surrounding the NSPC or, if technical mitigations are not possible, they may be procedural.

This approach has been used in a range of C&I systems in nuclear plants as a means of demonstrating adequate safety assurance when NSPCs are used.

3.3 Combining justification approaches

The process and product based approaches are not mutually exclusive, and a combination can be used to support a safety justification. This might be particularly important where the system consists of both off-the-shelf components and application-specific elements, for example. We have applied the integration of the approaches in a number of assessments conducted on behalf of the nuclear industry, including:

- a justification for smart instruments (Guerra et al. 2010), where the requirement for production excellence in the SAPs was met by demonstrating compliance to an acceptable standard, while the requirement for independent confidence-building measures was addressed by a range of claim-based assessments (e.g., demonstration of accuracy, reliability, etc.) together with assessments of potential vulnerabilities in the smart device implementation
- a justification of the first safety-related FPGA-based system deployed in the UK (Guerra and Sheridan 2012), based on a combination of approaches.

We have found that there are significant advantages in using both approaches together for systems with a modest integrity requirement, as they provide flexibility, understanding and documentation of the system behaviour that is commensurate with the reliability requirement. In the next section, we review our experiences and discuss the advantages of the combination of approaches.

4 Discussion and experiences

To illustrate the effectiveness of using process and product based assessment techniques together, we describe below a selection of situations in conducting assessments. These situations are illustrations of the range of assessments we perform in practice; they have been modified and consolidated to show the type of issues encountered.

Assessment constructed during development. In this situation, the assessment work starts early in the lifecycle of the product development, and the work on the justification is fed into development process. The process-based approach establishes a clear need for documentation, which is especially valuable as the supplier might not be familiar with nuclear requirements. Having a clear set of documentation generated during the development process enables a stronger product-based justification to be constructed.

Like-for-like replacement. In this case, the stakeholders involved in the project may not be aware of the value of comprehensive requirements documentation, since the aim of the project is to replace old equipment with new technology following equivalent requirements. However, this type of replacement is seldom truly 'like-for-like', as new technologies, and the opportunity for operational improvements, are sources of new requirements that may interact with the existing plant in unforeseen ways.

In a replacement project, it is often the case that the documentation on the surrounding system is limited, and therefore tests or other types of analysis may be required to fully understand the impact that the system under development has on the overall plant; this can be performed using the LowSIL approach (see Section 3.2.1). By also following a process-based approach to justification, we are able to make the case for documenting the interfaces between the plant and the system, as well as any additional requirements and design decisions, all of which are crucial for the operation and maintenance of the system. These aspects may otherwise be overlooked, especially given the modest integrity target.

Smart instrument with extensive field experience. COTS products which have been in the market for many years are often seen as trustworthy items. We have found on a number of occasions that adopting a process-based approach to assessing older instruments is prone to difficulties. This can be because a development process which was considered good practice 20 years ago is no longer consistent with current standards, because documents have been archived or lost, or because staff members involved in the development are no longer available to support the assessment.

In some cases, the manufacturer may be able to supply some development process evidence, but not enough to provide sufficient confidence in the product. We could adopt an approach based partly on claims about compliance with specified device behaviour such as functionality, time response or robustness to abnormal inputs. Some of this evidence could be drawn from assessment techniques such as static analysis and black-box testing, while evidence of field experience and field-reported faults could also be analysed to demonstrate reliable operation.

Smart instrument with haphazard development process. At first glance, it might be difficult to distinguish this case from the earlier case of a smart instrument with lost or unavailable process evidence. Similar documentation may be missing for both instruments. However, given a more general understanding of the process followed, it is possible to determine whether a disciplined lifecycle process has been attempted, regardless of the available evidence. A lack of configuration management calls into question the validity of otherwise promising product-based evidence such as analysis and testing, since it is difficult to connect it up to the right part of the development process and the right version of the instrument. In this case, although we may attempt to complement a problematic process-based assessment with a product-based assessment, there may be sufficient doubt in the process case to jeopardise the product-based case.

This suggests some minimum process requirements needed to successfully complete a product-based assessment, despite their apparently different aims: an understanding of the development process followed, and confidence in the configuration management approach. The importance of configuration management in a claim-based approach is widely accepted as being needed to establish trust in the evidence (CAA 2013).

6 Conclusions

In the discussion above, we identified situations where we benefitted from using both a process and product-based assessment approach in conjunction, when developing a production excellence argument. This combination brings a number of advantages, described below.

Understanding hazards and properties in more detail. An approach based on understanding and mitigating the hazards of the system being developed on the overall system of which this is part of, such as the LowSIL approached described in Section 3.2.1, gives one an understanding of the impact of the failures that would be difficult to grasp if a pure compliance process-based approach was followed. In our experience, following this approach not only provides a way of dealing with NSPCs, but also a way of deriving system level requirements and mitigations that could easily be missed. Similarly, focusing on behavioural properties of the system gives you direct evidence of the product, which addresses some of the weaknesses of a pure compliance process-based approach.

Documenting process and requirements. For systems where the justification is developed as the system itself is being designed and implemented, the process-based approach establishes the need for specific documentation that will be useful both in the safety justification and for operation and maintenance. In a like-for-like replacement, the process-based approach can help to uncover requirements and design evidence, while a product-based approach can help by identifying hazards and the system-level impact of the replacement system.

The need for configuration management and process understanding. Clearly, for a purely behaviour based case, we would not need any claims about the process. Process evidence would be incorporated, if appropriate, through its impact on the claims about the product behaviour. Nevertheless, there are minimum process procedures and evidence that are essential. The most important of these is configuration management and other quality assurance activities that support the production of traceable and consistent evidence. A key aspect of a good safety case is that it should be supported by trustworthy evidence. In the cases where process evidence is limited, it is important to understand the reasons for these deficiencies; evidence may not exist because the component was developed a while ago, when best practice did not require the extensive documentation that is considered necessary today, or because an informal development process was followed, with limited planned verification and documentation. Understanding the process is important to be able to differentiate these cases. Demonstration that a sound development process and quality assurance principles have been followed increases our confidence in all the evidence generated to support the safety case, and consequently in the justification as a whole. This is particularly true when supporting evidence is limited.

In conclusion, our experience shows that even for systems with a modest reliability requirement, combining two styles of assessment, process-based and product-based, provides a number of advantages over either style on its own. These advantages are further reaching than simply increased confidence in the safety justification, extending to include a better understanding of the system in its context.

Acknowledgments The authors wish to acknowledge the support of the Control and Instrumentation Nuclear Research Forum (CINIF) research programme. Although the work described here was not directly funded by CINIF, its research programme provides opportunities to discuss and develop our ideas on how to justify software-based systems.

References

Adelard (1998) Adelard Safety Case Development Manual (ASCAD). http://www.adelard.com/resources/ascad/. Accessed 15 November 2013
Bishop P, Bloomfield RE (1995) The SHIP safety case – A combination of system and software methods. SRSS95, Proc 14th IFAC Conf on Safety and Reliability of Software-based Systems, Bruges, Belgium, 12–15 September
Bishop P, Bloomfield R, Guerra S (2004) The future of goal-based assurance cases. In Proceedings of Workshop on Assurance Cases, supplemental volume of the 2004 International Conference on Dependable Systems and Networks, pp. 390–395, Florence, Italy, June 2004

Bishop P, Tourlas K, Chozos N (2010) Programmable components in modest integrity systems. In: Erwin Schoitsch (ed.) Computer Safety, Reliability, and Security, 29th International Conference, SAFECOMP 2010, Vienna, Austria, September 14–17. Springer

CAA (2013) SW01 – Regulatory objectives for software safety assurance. CAP 670 Air traffic services safety requirements. CAA Safety Regulation Group

CEMSIS (2004) CEMSIS – Cost-Effective Modernisation of Systems Important to Safety. http://cemsis.org. Accessed 14 November 2013

European Commission (2011) HARMONICS – Harmonised Assessment of Reliability of Modern Nuclear I&C Software. http://cordis.europa.eu/projects/rcn/97431_en.html. Accessed 14 November 2013

Guerra S, Bishop P, Bloomfield R, Sheridan D (2010) Assessment and qualification of smart sensors. 7th American Nuclear Society International Topical Meeting on Nuclear Plant Instrumentation, Control and Human-Machine Interface Technologies (NPIC & HMIT)

Guerra S, Sheridan D (2012) Justification of an FPGA-based system performing a Category C function: development of the approach and application to a case study. 8th American Nuclear Society International Topical Meeting on Nuclear Plant Instrumentation, Control and Human-Machine Interface Technologies (NPIC & HMIT)

HSE (2006) Safety assessment principles for nuclear facilities, Health and Safety Executive, UK. http://www.hse.gov.uk/nuclear/saps/index.htm. Accessed 14 November 2013

HSE (2011) Licence condition handbook – Securing the protection of people and society from the hazards of the nuclear industry. Office for Nuclear Regulation, an agency of HSE. http://www.hse.gov.uk/nuclear/silicon.pdf. Accessed 14 November 2013

Kelly TP (1999) Arguing safety – a systematic approach to safety case management. PhD thesis, Department of Computer Science, University of York, UK

Stockham R (2009) Emphasis on safety. IET Magazine, Issue 02

Quantitative Aspects of Common Cause Failures and Review of Commonly Applied Models

Lucas Wind, Gabriele Schedl and Jürgen Floetzer

Frequentis AG

Vienna, Austria

Abstract   Multiple failures of components due to shared causes, also known as Common Cause Failures (CCF), comprise an important class of failure types. These have to be taken into account in any serious assessment of safety critical systems deploying any redundancy concept. Whereas a qualitative assessment of CCF can be regarded as common practice, the exact numerical impact of CCF is usually less widely understood. Explicit representation of CCF is quite cumbersome and usually involves complex graphical representations within fault trees and RBDs. Focusing on a correct derivation of RAM-data rather than on a comprehensive common cause analysis, an implicit representation of CCF therefore is often preferred but involves in-depth knowledge of underlying mathematical models. This paper aims to enable safety experts to make a fast, simple but effective RAM-analysis including CCF. Popular CCF models are reviewed together with their advantages and disadvantages based on the long-term experience of a supplier in the context of a large European ATM project. The single-parameter beta-factor model is explained in detail and demonstrated to be most effective for typical ATM applications. Based on this model, results are given in terms of representative figures depicting the influence of CCF on various typical real world availability requirements.

1 Introduction

A general conclusion from probabilistic risk assessments is that common-cause failures (CCFs) are significant contributors to the unavailability of safety critical systems. CCFs reduce the benefit of redundant designs, and if not taken into account properly will likely yield unrealistically optimistic reliability figures. Qualitative analyses such as the zonal analysis (ARP4761 1996, Amberkar et al. 2001) or common mode analysis (Lawrence 1999) are well-proven techniques to identify potential sources of common causes. Such techniques usually do not require sophisticated mathematical expertise and allow reducing the impact of CCFs by either eliminating potential root-causes for such failures, or by implementation of proper mitigations in the event of CCF occurrence.

However, in practice a complete removal of CCF will not be possible and the impact of the residual CCF needs to be taken into account in a quantitative Reliability, Availability and Maintainability (RAM) assessment of the safety critical system. This latter is not common practice though, albeit some industries, e.g. the nuclear industry, have established a wide standardized framework (Pickard et al. 1988) for addressing CCF in Reliability Block Diagrams (RBDs) and Fault Trees (FTs), for quite a long time.

A quantitative assessment of CCF impact typically requires the following steps to be executed:

1. Identification of the operational event boundaries and components to be analysed. This assumes some kind of quantitative analysis, e.g. a zonal analysis, and can be assumed to be state of the art.
2. Review of relevant historical events applicable to the derivation of CCF. This requires a representative failure-database (e.g., US NRC CCFDB, OECD/NEA ICDE) with CCF-attributable events in place.
3. Definition of an appropriate CCF-model. Usually, this task requires advanced mathematical skills to be able to judge the implications of each model.
4. Estimation of parameters for the chosen CCF model. CCF-attributable events need to be described in adequate detail and their number needs to be large enough to constitute a statistically representative sample.
5. Application of the CCF model to the analysis technique in place. CCF calculation itself is supported by most modern analysis tools but still requires significant CPU power for medium to large systems under investigation.

Still today the collection of representative data and the estimation of CCF model parameters are cumbersome tasks which in many industries, other than the nuclear sector, are still not backed by sufficiently detailed data sources.

Likely, we face a rapidly growing complexity of modern safety critical systems that go hand in hand with a growing safety-awareness of users. As a result of this development, safety related sectors as the Air Traffic Management (ATM) and rail industries more and more emphasize the importance of including CCF aspects in the quantitative assessment. Supplier industries of related sectors do feel this development by an increasing number of specific quantitative requirements on CCF. Still there is little or no guidance by regulation or standards as to what approach should be followed.

This article should serve as a further contribution to make the application of CCF techniques available to a broader community by reviewing most existing commonly applied models. Further, the potential impact of CCF on typical RAM parameters of various subsystems of a currently developed Voice Communication System (VCS) is given, as this constitutes a typical upcoming application of interest in that area.

2 Background

Numerous different definitions of a common cause failure can be found in literature. IEC61508 (IEC61508 2010) defines CCF as '…a failure that is the result of one or more events, causing concurrent failures of two or more separate channels in a multiple channel system, leading to system failure'. Similarly the US NRC defines them as '…failures of multiple items occurring from a single cause that is common to all of them' (NUREG/CR-2300 1982) and UK DEF STAN 00-56 (Defence Standard 00-56 1996) explains them as '…failure of apparently independent components or communication links due to an initiating event that affects them all.' There are yet many other definitions but the idea behind them is basically the same: a CCF is a failure of more than one item due to the same root cause by some mechanism of propagation.

Some sources further refine this failure-class and define common mode failures which denote a sub-class of such CCF that affect only a specific type of item, such as in DEF STAN 00-56: '…failures of multiple identical items that fail in the same mode'. IEC61508 uses these two terms in an analogous manner as does the remainder of this paper. Methods under further consideration define two more terms:

A **Common Cause Component Group (CCCG)** is a set of system items that may have the same failure modes due to common causes, e.g. all hardware in the same location or powered by the same supply.

A **CCF event** is an event involving failure of a specific set of components due to a common cause. It has the following properties:

- A CCF event involves two or more item failures within a CCCG.
- The item failures of a CCF event can occur simultaneously or within a specified (short) time interval.
- Whether or not the item failures occur at the same time depends on the shared cause.
- Specifically within fault tree analysis, the CCF event is sometimes called a common cause basic event.

A CCCG is always associated with one or more CCF events. This is illustrated in Figure 1. In this example two pressure sensors work in parallel redundancy to fulfil a safety function. Here sensors PS 1 and PS 2 are part of the same CCCG which may be associated with a number of shared causes: e.g. common tap plugged with solids; pressure sensors mis-calibrated.

Within a fault tree one would typically cluster such CCF events by a common gate as shown in the drawing and include this with an OR gate. Another often preferred approach would be to model CCF directly at the location of the related event as in Figure 2, applying an OR gate for each basic event associated with the CCCG. Especially for larger fault trees, this later approach can drastically increase readability and help to avoid overlooking related CCF events. This second approach requires the use of identical events within several branches of the fault tree, such as events 'PL' or 'MC' in Figure 2. Such identical events deserve special treatment during the evaluation of a fault tree, which however is a standard feature of all of today's commercially available FT tools.

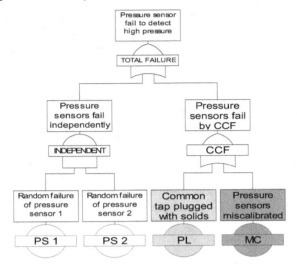

Fig. 1. System with parallel redundancy (Notation 1)

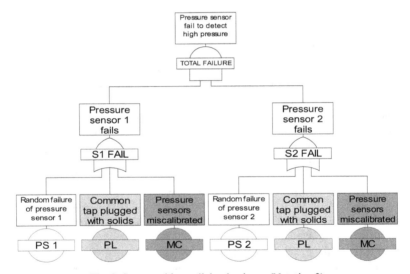

Fig. 2. System with parallel redundancy (Notation 2)

The situation where more than two items are affected by the same cause (i.e., multiple failures) becomes increasingly complex with increasing numbers of items within a CCCG, merely due to the amount of CCF events to be taken into account.

This number increases as in theory every permutation of CCF items in a CCCG would need to be represented in the fault tree, as depicted for example in Figure 3 – even if those items are all of the same type. This fact rapidly reduces the benefit from this explicit representation of CCF events if applied to larger fault trees. Because of this, as well as the fact that necessary CCF data for such an approach is rarely available, in practice an implicit model-based approach is often preferred, which reduces the work to the selection of an appropriate model and the estimation of (usually) a few parameters.

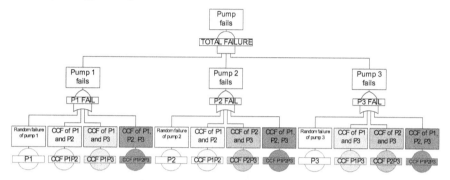

Fig. 3. System with threefold redundancy

Usually, a mixture of these two approaches will be applied. CCFs that are attributable to root causes that have been identified during the safety analysis are included as explicit CCF events as in Figures 1 and 2. Those (residual) CCF events that were not specifically addressed, or whose explicit modelling would be unmanageable, are accounted for by an implicit mathematical CCF approach.

   In the following the basic properties of typical approved models are briefly described. Each of these mathematical models has its advantage and disadvantage. Generally, none of them strictly map reality and though there is a clear mathematical justification for each of the approaches, one should be aware that these are only approximations that need to be validated against historical data in the specific field of application.

3 Review of CCF models

Generally, there are two main classes of CCF models distinguished by the type of failures that they address:

Complete failures. Here a CCF-event always triggers the failure of all items in the CCCG – this is usually associated with extreme environmental, human interactions, highly dependent requirements, or input interactions. A prominent representative of this type and indeed the most widely applied CCF-model of all types is the beta factor and its enhanced version, the beta factor plus method, described below.

Partial failures. Here a CCF event yields the failure of more than one item, but not necessarily all of them. How many fail and in which way, this is usually described by two or more parameters and some kind of statistical distribution-function. The alpha factor, multiple Greek letter and the binomial failure rate models, described below, are the by far most widely used representatives of this class, though the latter indeed is a mixture of both types.

Independent of the type of CCF model the following applies for characteristic failure rates for each item in the CCCG as well as for any system:

$$\lambda_T = \lambda_i + \lambda_{CCF} \tag{1}$$

where λ is the failure rate and the subscripts T denote the total, i the independent and CCF the CCF failure rate. Similarly:

$$Q_T = Q_i + Q_{CCF} \tag{2}$$

where Q is the corresponding failure probability and the indices t depict the total, i the independent and CCF the CCF contribution.

Depending whether the CCF evaluation is done by means of RBDs or fault trees the further approach is preferably executed on the basis of λ or Q. Usually one will find inputs and algorithms based on the failure rate for most RBDs and unavailability used with fault trees, though this is not a rule[1].

3.1 Basic parameter model

A very generic form of model, which in its general form is rarely applied to real systems, is the so-called Basic Parameter Model (BPM). It constitutes a generalized concept of which basically all other models can be derived. This model can be described as follows (Mosleh 1991):

$$Q_T = \sum_{k=1}^{m} \binom{m-1}{k-1} \cdot Q_k^{(m)}$$

and

$$Q_i = Q_1^{(m)}$$

---

[1] Note that these two approaches will generally result in slight differences which, for small failure-rates, will be negligible. This is due to the fact that the serial combination of two items will result in the sum of the failure rates as in equation 1, however, the equivalent in terms of availability would yield a residual term $(-Q_i Q_{CCF})$ to be taken into account, other than in equation 2.

where $Q_k^{(m)}$ is the probability of a basic event involving k specific components $(1 \leq k \leq m)$ in a CCCG of size m, and the binomial term

$$\binom{m-1}{k-1} = \frac{(m-1)!}{(m-k)!(k-1)!}$$

represents the number of different ways that a specified component can fail with $(k-1)$ other components in a group of m similar components.

The BPM, as all of its derived methods described here, assumes that the probability of occurrence of any basic event within a CCCG depends only on the number and not on the specific components in that basic event. As an example Figure 4 shows this situation for a CCCG with three ($m = 3$) identical components A. The areas in the graph may be interpreted as a representation of the contribution to the total probability of a failure in a 3-out-of-3 demand-structure.

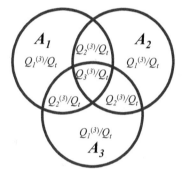

Fig. 4. Illustration of the Basic Parameter Model with a CCCG of size 3

In the given example in Figure 4 the resulting independent and common cause failure contributions of each item in the CCCG are given by

$$Q_i = Q_1^{(3)} \text{ and } Q_{CCF} = 2Q_2^{(3)} + Q_3^{(3)}.$$

The $Q_k^{(m)}$ may be calculated directly from data. However, required data are not normally available, so other models with less stringent requirements on data are usually used. Most of these methodologies attempt to make predictions for $Q_k^{(m)}$ from the probability of random hardware failure. Clearly, the justification for such a direct relationship between these probabilities is tenuous. Nevertheless, such a correlation has been found in practice and probably results from second-order effects (IEC61508 2010). For example a higher random failure rate correlates to a higher amount of necessary maintenance involving actions prone to common cause issues. A higher random failure rate also involves a higher complexity which in turn relates to a usually less easily understood system and thus may be more prone to the introduction of systematic faults. Likely, in this case CCF will be more difficult to detect and thus remain in the system with a higher rate.

IEC61508 proposes to apply the beta factor model – a one-parameter model described below. It assumes the loss of all items within a CCCG due to a CCF event.

However, field feedback shows that double failures have a higher rate than triple failures which in turn have a lower rate than quadruple failures. Also, multiple failures beyond order four have never been observed from an explicit single cause which could not have been identified during safety analysis. Consequently, the beta factor method is very conservative with its main advantages being its ease of application and the comparably simple estimation of its only parameter. Though, in some applications, it may be too restrictive, yielding results that suggest the use of unnecessarily expensive solutions in terms of needed redundancy. Several models have been proposed to deal with this difficulty but most of them require so many reliability parameters (as the multiple Greek letters or alpha factor models described below) that they become unrealistic if based on insufficient/incomplete data (IEC61508 2010).

3.2 Beta factor model

The simplest of all models, the Beta Factor Model (BFM) (Fleming 1975) assumes that a CCF leads to the loss of all items in the CCCG. Its only parameter β is given by

$$Q_{CCF} = Q \cdot \beta$$

Depending on the source of data, either it is assumed that the total probability already includes the contribution of CCF and the following is valid

$$Q_i = (1 - \beta) \cdot Q$$

which is the usual approach, where Q is the item probability which in this case is equal to the total probability Q_T. This situation is depicted in Figure 5; or the CCF contribution is not included in Q and the following applies:

$$Q_i = Q \cdot$$

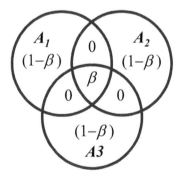

Fig. 5. Illustration of the beta factor model with a CCCG of size 3

In the example in Figure 5 BPM and BFM parameters relate as follows:

$\beta = Q_3^{(3)} / (Q_1^{(3)} + Q_3^{(3)})$ with $Q_2^{(3)} = 0$

IEC61508 recommends the use of the beta factor model up to a CCCG-size $m = 4$. The model provides conservative results for redundancy levels beyond $m = 2$ and is the simplest model to use.

3.3 Alpha factor model

The Alpha Factor Model (AFM) (Mosleh and Siu 1987, Mosleh et al. 1989) defines CCF probabilities from a set of failure frequency ratios α_k :

$$Q_k^{(m)} = \frac{k}{\binom{m-1}{k-1}} \frac{\alpha_k}{\alpha_T} Q_T$$

where

$$\alpha_T \equiv \sum_{k=1}^{m} k\alpha_k ,$$

$$\sum_{k=1}^{m} \alpha_k = 1$$

and α_k is the probability that when a common cause basic event occurs in a CCCG of size m it involves the failure of exactly k components.

As such, the alpha factor model constitutes a generalized version of the beta factor model which accounts for a possible partial loss of components due to CCF. It assumes an equal distribution of $Q_k^{(m)}$ for each given order k, which is a valid assumption for equal items in the CCCG, if operated under the same conditions. Its parameters are simpler to obtain from observable events than those of the multiple Greek letters model described next.

In the example in Figure 6 BPM and AFM parameters relate as follows:

$\alpha_1 = 3Q_1^{(3)} / (3Q_1^{(3)} + 3Q_2^{(3)} + Q_3^{(3)})$

$\alpha_2 = 3Q_2^{(3)} / (3Q_1^{(3)} + 3Q_2^{(3)} + Q_3^{(3)})$

$\alpha_3 = Q_3^{(3)} / (3Q_1^{(3)} + 3Q_2^{(3)} + Q_3^{(3)})$

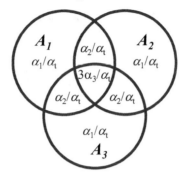

Fig. 6. Illustration of the alpha factor model with a CCCG of size 3

3.4 Multiple Greek letters model

The Multiple Greek Letters model (MGL) is a variant of the alpha factor model which defines CCF probabilities from a set of conditional probabilities (Fleming et al. 1985):

$$Q_k^{(m)} = Q_T \cdot \frac{(1-\rho_{k+1})}{\binom{m-1}{k-1}} \cdot \prod_{i=1}^{k} \rho_i$$

where

$$\rho_1 = 1, \rho_2 \equiv \beta, \rho_3 \equiv \gamma, ..., \rho_{m+1} = 0$$

β is the constant fraction of the failure probability in the CCCG due to CCF, and ρ_i are the conditional probabilities that CCF will impact i or more components in the CCCG, given that $i-1$ components have failed.

In the example in Figure 7 BPM and MGL parameters relate as follows:

$$\beta = 2Q_2^{(3)^2} / (1-Q_3^{(3)})(2Q_2^{(3)} + Q_3^{(3)})$$

$$\gamma = (1-Q_3^{(3)})(Q_1^{(3)} + 2Q_2^{(3)} + Q_3^{(3)} - 2)/2$$

Like the alpha factor model, the MGL model constitutes a generalized version of the beta factor model which accounts for a possible partial loss of components due to CCF.

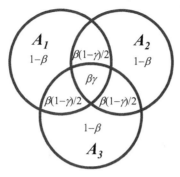

Fig. 7. Illustration of the multiple Greek letter model with a CCCG of size 3

3.5 Binomial failure rate model

IEC61508 (IEC61508 2010) proposes the use of the Binomial Failure Rate model (BFR) – also known as the shock model – if use of the simple beta factor model is too restrictive. The principle of the BFR is that when a CCF occurs, it is similar to a shock on the related components. This shock may be lethal (i.e. as in the beta factor model) or non-lethal and in this case the probability of having k failures due to the non-lethal shock is distributed binomially (Vesely 1977).

In contrast to the other multi-parameter models presented before, the BFR is described by only three parameters. This makes it especially valuable for cases where little data is available for the estimation of parameters:

$$\lambda_k^{(m)} = \begin{cases} \lambda_i + \mu\rho(1-\rho)^{m-1} & k=1 \\ \mu\rho^k(1-\rho)^{m-k} & 2 \le k < m \\ \mu\rho^m + \omega & k = m \end{cases}$$

Here the $\lambda_k^{(m)}$ represent failure rates of a basic event involving k specific components in a CCCG of size m, and where μ is the non-lethal shock rate, ρ is the conditional probability of failure of a component given a non-lethal shock, and ω is the lethal shock rate. A non-shock contribution λ_i is accounted for $k=1$.

The parameters of this model may be linked to the beta factor model by splitting β into β_L, the failure rate due to lethal shocks and β_{NL} the failure rate due to non-lethal shocks

$$\beta = \beta_L + \beta_{NL}$$

with

$$\omega = \lambda_T \cdot \beta_L$$

and

$$\mu = \lambda_T \cdot \beta_{NL} / \rho$$

The BFR yields less conservative results than the beta factor model for higher level of redundancy but is more restrictive than all other multiparameter models.

4 Quantitative impact analysis based on real project data

The following presents the results of a quantitative analysis of the impact of different contributions of common causes to the failure rates of components in a medium-to-large scale Voice Communication System (VCS). The system is currently under development to replace various VCSs installed at different locations in Europe. Being the first fully Internet Protocol (IP)-based VCS worldwide, it provides various newly introduced features, which due to their complexity were subjected to a comprehensive common cause analysis. The system design consists of various levels of redundancy in all subsystems, e.g., 250 partly redundant controller working positions, two duplicated core switches, redundant WAN access, redundant connectivity to 400 duplicated radios, trunked phone lines of different types, etc. Much effort is currently being put into the realization of such a types of system in the US (part of the NextGen programme) and in Europe (the Single European Sky ATM Research (SESAR) programme). This makes the analysis in this chapter of special interest in this context.

Though Frequentis holds comprehensive records of item failures, the available data have been found inadequately structured and mostly inapplicable to derive detailed CCF parameters applicable to the new IP-based VCS. Unlike some other industries, e.g., the nuclear industry, that develop specific CCF databases (Wiermann et al. 2007) over many years, suppliers in the ATM sector usually have no access to application-specific data on CCF. One reason for this is the fast changing technology applied in the ATM industry. Another difficulty is the diversity of installed ATM systems that makes it hard to apply results from one system to another. This leads us to the conclusion that the application of a multi-parameter model in the context of a VCS, as well as for most other ATM systems, usually cannot be justified. Therefore, the following analyses are all based on the simple one-parameter beta factor model with

$$\lambda_{CCF} = \lambda_T \cdot \beta$$

and

$$\lambda_i = (1 - \beta) \cdot \lambda_T$$

Figures 8-10 depict the impact of β on one of the basic RAM values for typical sub-systems of interest. Figure 8 reveals a much higher impact of β for such sub-systems which apply a higher degree of redundancy.

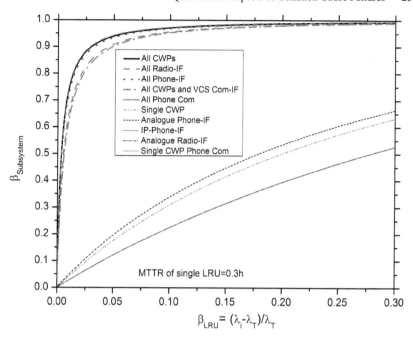

Fig. 8. Impact of component β on the β of subsystems

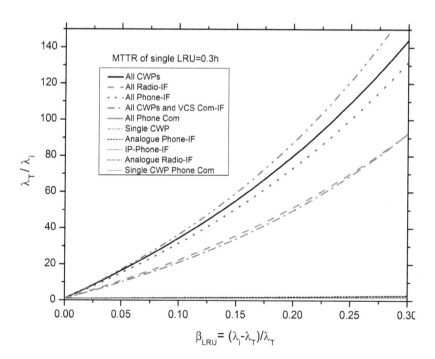

Fig. 9. Impact of component β on the total failure rate λ_T of subsystems

Figure 9 reveals a near exponential impact of CCF on the overall failure rate. It is clear that neglecting CCF will result in massive overestimation in reliability for each subsystem. For example, assuming moderate CCF contributions of β (~0.05), a subsystem will have a failure-rate that is typical 10 times higher with CCF than without. The impact of CCF on the resulting Mean Time To Repair (MTTR) depicted in Figure 10, however, may be neglected for moderate to high beta values, implying that the subsystem is essentially non-redundant at β ~0.05 and above.

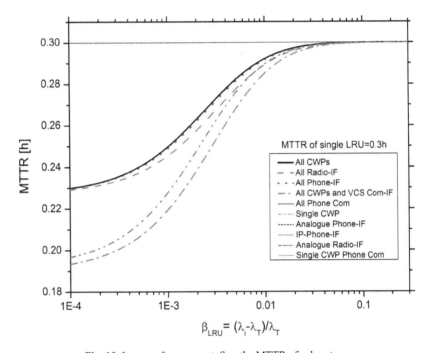

Fig. 10. Impact of component β on the MTTR of subsystems

For large values of β (~0.3), Figure 9 shows that the impact of CCF could be as large as 130 – something clearly not observed in practice. IEC61508 propose a range for β between 0.005 and 0.1, depending on whether the system in question is a logic solver or a sensor, or final element. Based on a catalogue of questions for each of these two types of elements, and differentiating between elements subjected to diagnostic test and those without such tests, the method presented (also called the beta plus method) allows us to derive a plant-specific β using scores and look-up tables. There are also similar established methods (e.g., Humphreys 1987, Brand 1996) that yield β based on questions and/or expert judgment.

5 Conclusion

The beta factor method yields the most appropriate CCF method for those indus-tries that do not have access to a pool of representative, application-specific CCF failure data. However, a moderate value of β can have a massive impact on overall results and should be carefully justified to avoid unrealistically bad reliability fig-ures. Whatever the exact β will be, in our opinion the most important result of all of these methods is that the inclusion of even a comparably small β (~0.001) will drastically increase the integrity of an RBD or FT calculation.

References

Amberkar S, Czerny BJ, D'Ambrosio JG et al (2001) A comprehensive hazard analysis tech-nique for safety-critical automotive systems. SAE technical. paper series, 2001-01-0674
ARP4761 (1996) Guidelines and methods for conducting the safety assessment process on civil airborne systems and equipment. SAE
Brand PV (1996) A pragmatic approach to dependent failures assessment for standard systems. AEA Technology plc
Defence Standard 00-56 (1996) Safety management requirements for defence systems: Require-ments. Part 1/Issue2. Ministry of Defence
Fleming KN (1975) A reliability model for common mode failures in redundant safety systems. Report GA-A13284. General Atomic Company, San Diego CA
Fleming KN, Mosleh A, Deremer RK (1985) A systematic procedure for the incorporation of common cause events into risk and reliability models. Nuclear Eng and Design, 93:245-279
Humphreys RA (1987) Assigning a numerical value to the beta factor common cause failure evaluation. Proceedings of Reliability, Paper 2C/5
IEC61508 (2010) Functional safety of electrical/electronic/programmable electronic safety re-lated systems. 2nd ed., Part 6, Annex D
Lawrence BM (1999) Managing safety through the aircraft lifecycle – An aircraft manufacturer's perspective. In: Proc Second Annual Two-Day Conference on Aviation Safety Management
Mosleh A (1991) Common cause failures: An analysis methodology and example. Reliability Engineering and System Safety 34:249-292
Mosleh A, Fleming KN, Parry GW et al (1989) Procedures for treating common cause failures in safety and reliability studies. Analytical Background and Techniques. US NRC, NUREG/CR-4780, 2
Mosleh A, Siu NO (1987) A multiparameter common cause failure model. In: 9th Int Conf on Structural Mechanics in Reactor Technology. Lausanne, Switzerland, Aug. 17-21, p.147-152
NUREG/CR-2300 (1982) PRA procedures guide: A guide to the performance of probabilistic risk assessment for nuclear power plants. US NRC
Pickard, Lowe, and Garrick, Inc. (1988) Procedures for treating common cause failures in safety and reliability studies, Vol. 2. U.S. NRC, NUREG/CR-4780
Vesely WE (1977) Estimating common cause failure probabilities in reliability and risk analyses; Marshall-Olkin specializations. In: Assessment J, Nuclear systems reliability engineering and risk. SIAM Philadelphia, p.314-341
Wiermann TE, Rasmuson DM, Mosleh A (2007) Common-cause database and analysis system: event data collection, classification, and coding. U.S. NRC, NUREG/CR-6268

An Assessment Framework for Data-Centric Systems

Alastair Faulkner and Mark Nicholson

Abbeymeade Limited, UK

University of York, York, UK

Abstract Standardisation, organisation and control have brought economic benefits through the application of computer based systems to large governmental, industrial and retail organisations. These benefits are also being sought from areas and organisations with a safety related context. Typically these systems employ standardised applications and large volumes of data. Such data represents individuals, system elements, their relationships and histories. Application areas span health care provision to transportation, welfare to governmental policy. In these systems it is often unclear how data errors influence the overall system behaviour or individual system outcomes.

This paper provides a framework to classify the use (and reuse) of data within such systems. In addition this paper seeks to identify the 'barriers to escalation' that would mitigate the influence of data errors on system safety and restrict their propagation across the connected systems.

1 Introduction

Does your organisation use safety-related data?

It is unlikely that your organisation has assessed the data used within its systems. The treatment of data as a separate system component is – as yet – not common practice. Without assessment, the safety integrity requirements (by extension the data safety integrity requirements) remain unknown. This paper presents an initial framework to characterise the data used (and reused) by your organisation. It is truly a 'framework' and as such is designed to provide a high degree of flexibility in the way that your organisation treats data. Nevertheless, working within the framework will facilitate a degree of Standardisation, Organisation and Control (SOC). A template structure is provided to allow you to create your instantiation; a number of examples have been produced and are available from the authors.

It is wholly reasonable to seek to gain economic benefit from the application of SOC. A solution (or series of solutions) based on the application of Computer Based Technologies (CBT) often provides the basis of such systems in addition to changes to working practices, policies and procedures. Many working practices are localised, often having been established over a considerable period, tracing their origins through decades – and within the legal and medical professions, probably a lot longer.

Changes leading to SOC are often accompanied by a requirement for additional discipline in the execution of tasks performed by individuals and abstraction away from appropriate knowledge to discharge that discipline. It seems strange to consider that over the last decade the legal and medical professions have undertaken changes other industries mastered long ago. These changes address records, formally based on physical documents, now implemented in CBTs.

These new disciplines require an acceptance on the part of the individual (and organisations) of the, often normalised, working practices enforced by CBTs. Many of the existing paper records included 'free text' in which was recorded an almost infinite variety of information. This infinite variety is not practicable (or desirable) in a large scale system.

A secondary effect of the application of CBTs is the rise of 'big data' systems, where huge data sets are processed to provide statistics and aggregated values. Such systems are used to identify trends, monitor performance, and as the basis for 'corrective actions'. Many of these activities are based on the use (and reuse) of data (Faulkner 2004). 'Big data' continues to evolve and a precise definition – representative of its implementation – proves elusive.

The application of traditional functional safety architectures, techniques and measures is characterised by specification. This specification provides a description of the service or function to be provided, together with the data exchanged. It is not clear that 'big data' follows this model as it addresses both structured and unstructured data. The two options available are to enforce structure onto 'big data' or to provide containment of the unstructured parts when automated/human actions/decisions are being made.

This paper provides a framework so that:

Decision support information that includes explanations, implications and an assessment of the uncertainty associated with the application process can be generated. This information is provided by the system in a way that has a positive effect on the users (computer and/or human) situational awareness, workload, decision accuracy and performance. This improves the effectiveness of decision making and therefore safety of the application.

1.1 When is a system considered to be safety-related?

Harm is not restricted to CBTs. Historic system failures have led to harm – people have been injured and killed in accidents. Accident investigation seeks to identify the causality and typically provide recommendations to reduce the likelihood of reoccurrence. Statutes provide a legal imperative to address the causes of harm and standards address systems requirements and provide guidance.

Greater reliance on CBTs, coupled with the perceived ease in which these systems can be implemented, has given rise to an increasing use and reliance on data, and the integrity of data. These systems may find their way into safety related applications and can often be many steps away from the end use of the data (Tillotson 2001). Therefore, the safety related nature of the data may not be obvious. This use of data in safety related systems is not adequately addressed within the current statutes, standards, guidance, and literature (Faulkner 2004, Templeton 2007, Wake 2008, Clarke 2008, Ensor 2009, Lunn 2011). Currently, accident investigation does not often attribute system failures to data or data integrity as the importance of data is not recognised as a separate system component. An increased recognition of the need to provide useful guidance in this area has led to this paper.

1.2 What is safety related data?

Data is an abstraction. Common usage would regard numbers, characters and perhaps images as data. In more precise terms the association of context gives these numbers, characters and images meaning. Therefore we may infer that the intended use of the data provides the data with meaning.

We use data in safety related systems to represent real world objects, their attributes, their relationships to other objects and abstractions. These representations allow systems to automate the work environment – to plan, produce and deliver products and services. In this framework we address the need for data to be 'good enough' for the intended use; and to be of sufficient integrity. The term data integrity is perhaps overloaded. This term is used in a variety of circumstances and in each circumstance takes on a subtly different meaning. Data integrity refers to the degree of assurance that data and its value has not been lost or altered since the data originated or was last subject to an authorized amendment. Data safety integrity is the contribution of data to the safety integrity of a system, be it a control or information system.

If data characterises, determines and directs these systems, then it follows that data errors (which may change this desired behaviour) should be detected, managed and where possible removed.

In this framework paper we identify an architectural structure within which the use (and reuse) of data can take place, the errors associated with data and data propagation can be addressed, and the data contribution to system safety can be ensured and assured. This framework can then be tailored as required by individual domains and projects.

2 The 'accidental' system

Automation often first appears as an aid to support existing practice. These aids are developed and evolve to support and reinforce changes – driving uniformity and consistency, curiously not necessarily improving data quality. The overall impact on the working environment is a dramatic increase in the volume of digital data, flow of that digital data around system elements and a concomitant decrease in understanding of the context and limitations of that data.

Consider an established work environment based on the development, production, delivery, and support of a service. In this generalised example no particular service is specified, as it is equally applicable to the production of equipment as to the delivery of legal or health care services. Financial and accounting practices require controls to identify and manage the use of assets within the enterprise. These accounting practices address stock control and management, driving secondary impacts such as bar code and RFID technologies to track the movement of stock within the enterprise. Asset tracking provides additional data about utility and in turn facilitates additional data addressing traceability through to individual deliveries to customers. In turn, order tracking reduces the opportunities for 'lost' deliveries, through order processing, tracking to order completion using customer signatures on handheld delivery confirmation terminals.

Changes are implemented as 'islands' of functionality to support identified activities and enterprise policies. In such cases the boundaries of these new functionalities are characterised by existing organisational boundaries. A group within the organisation may become reliant on the data produced by another group (and passed across the organisational boundary), with little ability to influence the data they have become reliant on.

At the same time reliance on automated decision making in the enterprise increases. At the lowest level of autonomy (Parasuraman et al. 2000) computers offer no assistance; they facilitate information acquisition. Later they offer a set of decision alternatives; they facilitate analysis. Then they offer increasing amounts of support for the decision making process itself; ending with the human only being allowed a restricted time before an automatic execution to overrule the computer's decision. Finally, at the highest levels of autonomy computers provide action implementation with no capability for the human to overrule and little if any information provided on what actions the computer has undertaken.

The 'accidental' system is represented in Figure 1, as a generalised combination of system components (hardware, software, people and process). Financial and operational actors set targets, metrics that are managed through measures and controls. The process is supported by people using procedures supported by tools, training and common enablers.

We can conceive of this 'accidental' system as just one unit of an organisation, perhaps as a complete department, or a group providing a service. As such the 'accidental' system consumes data and produces data. The 'accidental' system operates within a hierarchy, including supervisory, peer and subordinate systems.

Within any given organisation these systems will have different responsibilities – some will be assessed as safety-related.

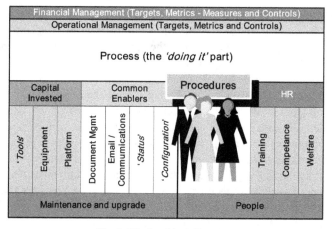

Fig. 1. The 'accidental' system

3 Using the (data intensive) system safety assessment framework

The framework does not replace safety engineering or safety assurance activities. The framework is intended to allow the expression of a CBT from many domains to facilitate comparison – and ideally to enable the identification of a set of common techniques and measures. The framework will not address all systems or provide complete coverage of a single system. The rigour of the application of the framework is intended to follow a risk based approach of the greater the risk the greater the rigour. To assist in the documentation of the CBT a template is available from the authors in order to provide sufficient uniformity of CBT description to facilitate analysis and comparison (between systems, industry sectors, and organisations).

The outline method describes:

1. organisational context including a description of the system functionality, clearly identifying the CBT boundaries and the data used by the system
2. a functional safety assessment based on hazard identification (including causality and consequence)
3. an apportionment of safety responsibility.

A key feature of the use of the framework is the identification of the reliance a user has on data – for the purpose of deriving data integrity requirements.

The following sections provide a model of organisational hierarchy, requiring the identification of the scope of the safety function, an identification of interface properties and an initial classification of data.

4 A layered model representing an organisational hierarchy

The layered model, described below, is based on an incomplete and unpublished RAILTRACK internal memorandum (Allen 2000). In addition, elements are also drawn from concepts contained within the International Standards Organisation (ISO) basic reference model for Open Systems Interconnection (OSI) (Marsden 1992[1]). The OSI model partitions communications services between seven layers with defined interfaces, peer protocols that permit the separation of application development from the underlying communication system. Two important elements of the OSI model are that each layer communicates with its peer layer in a different communication unit, providing a service to the layer above, and expecting a particular kind of service from the layer below.

This abstraction into layers allows the development and replacement of the underlying layers based on respect for the services each layer provides and preservation of interfaces between them. It allows control of the access points of data and control coming into the system. It also attempts to depict the span of a safety function by identifying that high integrity (SIL3 and SIL4) safety functions should be limited to the lowest three layers of the hierarchy.

Figure 2 identifies a number of layers within the system hierarchy and also implies a functional hierarchy within the system.

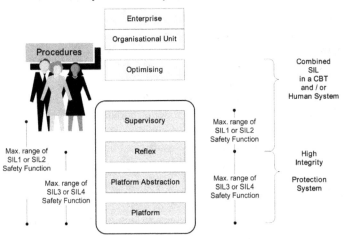

Fig. 2. A layered model for a hierarchy of systems

The 'platform' layer represents single instances of elements of the platform infrastructure, the physical equipment.

The 'platform abstraction' layer represents the interface to platform infrastructure elements. In essence this layer converts physical phenomena from sensors

---

[1] A collection of documents describes the services provided by the ISO OSI model. Appendix B of Brian Marsden's book provides a comprehensive list of these documents.

(including feedback from actuators) into abstract representations such as electrical signals or data. This layer also provides the control (information) interfaces to actuators (human/computer operators).

The **'reflex' layer** is the lowest layer at which the measured status is interpreted and control (or protection) actions are carried out. These actions may be based on data (which may include stored information), any demands on the system and some set of rules. In this reflex layer the rules and information completely determine the control action. In principle all activities in the reflex layer can be automated with the highest levels of autonomy. Safety-critical functions commonly require a fast response and therefore often make use of reflex actions.

The **'supervisory' layer** represents a more complex level of control. This complexity may be a result of large-scale operation, integrating a number of dissimilar functions, or interpreting complex (or ambiguous) data (or some combination of these). The distinction between the reflex and supervisory layers is the judgement or knowledge that must be applied, particularly in degraded or emergency situations. Supervisory systems are characterised by the need to support the judgement of the operator doing the supervision. Predominantly the supervisory layer is downward looking viewing the performance of the lower levels.

The **'optimisation' layer** represents the most sophisticated control layer. At its most developed the optimisation layer should maximise the use of resources for the delivery of the service. The optimisation layer should respect the performance and safety constraints of the underlying (transportation) system. The information demands on the optimisation layer are high, requiring a full understanding of the underlying system, the planned service and contingency plans.

The **'organisational unit' layer** represents the organisational responsibility of the delivery of the planned service. This layer normally plays little part in real-time operations of the system being more concerned with the medium term maintenance (including competencies) and development of the infrastructure, and the subsequent future delivery of the planned service. The organisational unit will become involved in the short-term operation of the system in response to a serious incident that causes substantial impact on the delivery of the service. Organisational unit is used here in order to provide a generic model.

The **'enterprise' layer** represents the corporate entity; responsible for the planning and execution of large-scale changes to the infrastructure; responding to changes in legislation; setting and maintaining standards, procedures and competency requirements.

The point is well made by (Allen 2000) that implementation of large-scale systems requires a framework in which to express the role played by respective system components and provide a mechanism by which a large-scale system safety may be argued. Information systems that inform human operator decisions similarly require a framework. Both aspects are catered for in this framework.

In this work the authors consider the supervisory layer to be the highest layer at which a safety function should be implemented. This boundary is depicted in Figure 2 by the box surrounding the platform, platform interface, reflex and supervisory layers.

5 Interfaces

Interfaces (both horizontal and vertical) need to be controlled, as they provide a means to control the upgrade and replacement of elements within the hierarchy, see Figure 3. Relationships, and therefore interfaces, may also exist between enterprises. Data may need to chain across these interfaces.

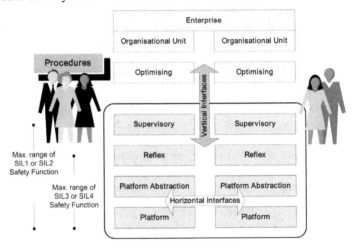

Fig. 3. System interfaces

It is noted that people associated with the 'system' may not share the same view of the system. Perhaps the most dramatic differences are to be found between the developers and the users. Work within a safety-related environment one would hope would be disciplined characterised by a need for compliance. In contrast users are more influenced by management actions, training and organisational targets.

5.1 Vertical interfaces: data independence

The layered framework, based upon the ISO OSI 7-layer model (Stallings 1994), provides a mechanism to describe the independence of each layer. The OSI model uses the concepts of Service Delivery Unit (SDU) and Service Access Point (SAP).

These SDUs and SAPs form the basis of interface contracts, facilitating the implementation of fit-form-function replacements, providing the possibility of the replacement of layers within the system hierarchy. This point is developed later in this paper.

5.2 Horizontal interfaces: boundary and partitioning issues

The definition of the system boundary is an essential step in the definition of the system. The boundary provides a demarcation between those components which are within the system, and those which are external. Communication across the system boundary requires the identification and definition of an interface description including, but not limited to, the data passed across the interface. Each communication is one step in a data chain.

External information systems may provide a range of data including status and schedule data. Data presented at this system boundary may not be error free. Within a systems context these interfaces may contain implicit transformations between the external and internal use of data. In some cases the internal and external meanings of this data may also be different. Figure 4 illustrates a generic system boundary and its associated issues.

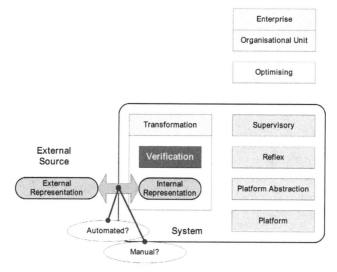

Fig. 4. System boundary issues

Data presented at the system boundary by an external system will be transformed or adapted from the external representation to the internal representation of the system. This transformation or adaptation may occur in some automated function or may require manual intervention. This data will also require verification. Analysis of the system design is required to establish the consequence of faults in this data as this data passes across the boundary of the control system. Further analysis should also establish the sensitivity to changes in this data. Such analysis will facilitate the definition of 'properties' or rules by which faults in the data may be detected at the boundary of the system.

The layered architecture may be partitioned into a number of independent applications sharing a network, as shown in Figure 5. In this case each partition can be thought of as a 'module' in a larger system that allows appropriate flow of data via data chains and 'big data' issues to be addressed. This partitioning holds throughout the vertical hierarchy of the framework, including at the organisational unit and where necessary the enterprise levels.

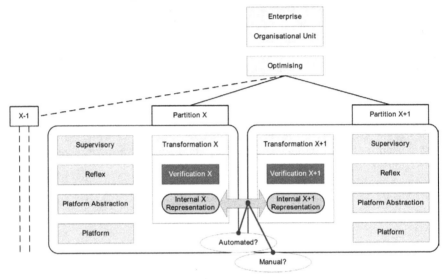

Fig. 5. Partitioned modules

Whether interfaces are between layers, within a layer as data flows within and between partitions, or to external sources of data SOC will engender improved risk management of data. The SOC takes the form of a safety interface agreement. This can be implemented in a relatively informal manner or via more formal approaches using rely-guarantee interface contract formalisms. Figure 6 represents the concept of interface contracts (Conmy et al. 2003).

5.3 Data used by safety related systems

Systems use data from a number of sources including data extracted (and possibly processed) from existing external information systems. Data may also be produced specifically for the system. Typically, information is supplied to these systems through a 'data supply chain' that may involve transformations and adaptations by external information systems and human processes. The data supply chain may introduce significant errors into the system through data passed across the system boundary. The data supply chain may be a source of static configuration data as well as dynamic data.

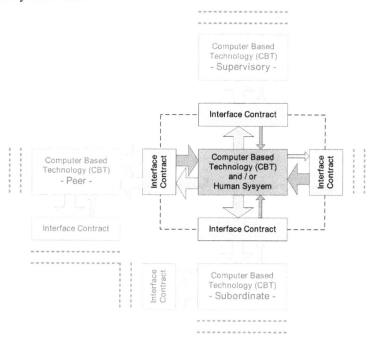

Fig. 6. Interface contracts

A classification of data is required to provide a means by which the role of data may be described and by which potential data errors, their transformation and propagation may be analysed. This facilitates the expression of the data integrity requirements as data flows across the boundary (and interfaces) of the system or system component (see Figure 7).

6 Use of the proposed (data) framework

The sheer range of applications of CBTs creates issues of scope and applicability. This paper provides a number of models in which to frame the description of one or more control or information systems. The primary purpose is to provide a basis to compare and contrast these disparate systems (and their respective contexts). This then facilitates the application of safety engineering to these CBTs. System safety management has its foundation in protection systems – typically fast acting rule based technologies. The application of technology also includes programmable devices and increasingly CBTs. One salient feature is the scale, scope and influence of these CBTs on functional safety in a range of domains. The implementation of these CBTs changes the risk profiles associated with an established domain. This is in part due to changes in SOC; both in terms of vertical and horizontal integration.

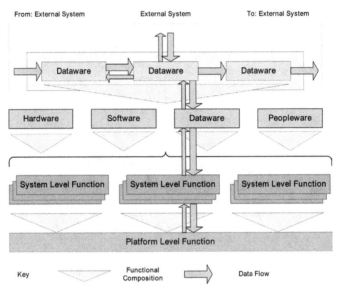

Fig. 7. Dataware in a systems context

Changes of scale, scope and influence are features associated with integration and the dependence that the organisation has on the CBTs. Often these changes of scale are associated with changes to the 'barriers to escalation'. An example could be drawn from an organisation that implements CBT(s) to replace its paper records. The influence of paper records is limited to an individual docket (bundle) of papers (the physical file). Electronic records present efficiencies for the organisation – as well as efficiencies in the transportation and propagation of errors across one or more organisational boundaries. Whilst organisational barriers are evident in the paper based system – these barriers are significantly reduced in the CBT implementation.

The framework provides a means to describe the CBT within a hierarchy, a classification of data types, and the use of 'interface contracts'. The proposed framework seeks to expose a requirement to identify and therefore a need to implement 'barriers to escalation' based upon the use (and reuse) of data. In this paper, and the proposed framework, these barriers are contained within the 'interface contracts'.

Consider a generalised CBT. A safety justification should assert that the CBT is adequately safe to use for its intended context. This justification will be based upon a description of the CBT, its context and its intended use (procedures, and people (training and their expected competency)). It will also identify the system boundary, the data exchanged across this boundary and the information content received by the computer/human user. The means of identifying and controlling data errors is contained within the interface contracts – and these are therefore a key feature of the justification.

A risk based approach should be used to direct resources towards the areas of greatest risk. This approach is also proposed for the development of guidance, techniques and measures to support the use of data in safety related systems. Key to this approach is the documentation of the use of data by safety related systems through a range of domain examples based on the framework.

7 Discussion

Examination of the literature and standards demonstrates that data is poorly treated, with inadequate identification of the reliance on the data. If data is used to determine or direct the functionality of the system then it follows that data errors will also influence behaviour. The increasing use of information systems and CBTs drives a reliance on data. Economic pressures drive reuse creating additional and self reinforcing pressures to connect and combine these systems. These connected systems present a system synergy beyond the designer's intent and they may impinge on a safety domain.

This problem is evident in all forms of system, including non safety systems. It is likely that data that originates from a non safety domain may be used within one or more safety related systems. The problems associated with the treatment of data are also evident within the safety domain. The framework is described from a neutral position to facilitate the widest possible system representations, from single machines and low numbers of users, to complex company (and in some cases national (or international)) systems. The reader is encouraged to consider both the horizontal and vertical coupling, where changes of system integrity requirements are most likely. Above all, these frameworks are intended to record and expose the final use of these systems – by people, and their collective and individual exposure to risk.

The authors' intent is to create a set of documents based on the framework. These documents will be analysed to categorise systems in general and data systems in particular in terms of the system hierarchy. This analysis will form the bases of derived requirements for techniques and measures for use with data safety systems.

The increasing use of SOC to create CBT's requires our diligent attention, technological evolution is seen as moving away from federated systems. This in turn will create classes of data that are increasingly platform independent. This independence will create an irresistible pressure to treat data as a separate system component along side hardware, software, people and process. A key enabler will be the control of interfaces which are likely to feature a form of contract based data exchange, supported by metadata.

Data as a separate system component will challenge many aspects of the use of technology by society and the engineering techniques and measures that support its use. Further examination of the user and their use of, and role in, such systems is also required.

References

Allen R (2000) An 'architectural context' to assist in framing the WCRM safety case argument. Internal RAILTRACK Memorandum Ref: R00122A.doc (Unpublished)

Clarke M (2008) An Independent safety auditor's view of data off the shelf. Project Report, MSc Safety Critical Systems, University of York

Conmy P, McDermid J, Nicholson M (2003) Safety assurance contracts for integrated modular avionics. SCS '03 Proc 8th Australian workshop on Safety critical systems and software

Ensor P (2009) Safety analysis of navigational data. Project Report, MSc Safety Critical Systems Engineering, University of York, 2009

Faulkner A (2004) Data integrity – An often ignored aspect of safety systems. Engineering Doctorate Thesis, University of Warwick

Lunn DM (2011) Improving the assurance of airborne mission management data. Project Report, MSc Safety Critical Systems Engineering, University of York

Marsden B (1992) Communications network protocols. 3rd Edition. Chartwell-Bratt Ltd

Parasuraman R, Sheridan TB, Wickens CD (2000) A model for types and levels of human interaction with automation. IEEE Transactions on Systems, Man, and Cybernetics A30(3)

Stallings W (1994) Data and computer communications. 4th Edition. Macmillan Publishing Company, New York

Templeton M (2007) Safety integrity of data. Project Report, MSc Safety Critical Systems Engineering, University of York

Tillotson J (2001) System safety and management information systems. In: Redmill F, Anderson T (eds) Aspects of safety management. Springer

Wake A (2008) Safety of data in real-time distributed systems. Project Report, MSc Safety Critical Systems Engineering, University of York

Software Certification: where is Confidence Won and Lost?

Tim Kelly

Department of Computer Science, University of York

York, UK

Abstract Given that we cannot prove the safety of software (in a system context) we are forced to wrestle with the issue of confidence in software certification. Some draw confidence from compliance with software assurance standards and believe this is sufficient, yet we do not have consensus in these standards. Some establish confidence through the process of constructing and presenting a software assurance case, but ignore the experience and 'body of knowledge' provided by standards. Some (sensibly) use a combination of these approaches. Using a framework of 4+1 principles of software safety assurance, this paper discusses where and how in current safety-critical software development and assessment approaches confidence is typically won and lost. Based on this assessment, we describe how the activity and structure of an assurance case should best be targeted to explicitly address issues of confidence.

1 Introduction

The lack of agreement in the requirements of software safety assurance standards long been recognised (McDermid and Pumfrey 2001). In addition, there are tensions between those advocating demonstrating compliance to standards as the principal assurance approach and those that promote the production of software assurance cases (Wassyng et al. 2010, Leveson 2011). These are often presented as opposing and alternative approaches. However, this is a false opposition. In addition, this extreme comparison of the approaches can distract our attention from the threats to confidence that can exist in both approaches. In this paper, we use a framework of 4+1 principles of software safety assurance that firstly can be used to highlight the bonds that tie these two approaches together. Secondly, we return to the problem of *confidence*. No single assurance approach can be said to establish perfect confidence in software assurance. Using the principles, we are able to discuss where confidence can be won and lost in the demonstration of software assurance. Finally, using this analysis we can draw some conclusions as to where effort should be targeted to maximise the assurance gained.

2 Fundamental principles of software safety assurance

There are many standards that either directly or indirectly address software safety assurance (e.g. IEC 61508 (IEC 2010), ISO 26262 (ISO 2009), EN 50128 (CENELEC 2011), parts of UK Defence Standard 00-56 (MoD 2007), and DO-178B (RTCA 1992)). There are easily observed differences in the details of these standards. For example, DO-178B uses the concept of *Development Assurance Levels* (DALs) to moderate the *objectives* of the standard according to the critical-ity of the software under development, whereas IEC 61508 uses the concept of *Safety Integrity Levels* (SILs) to make recommendations as to suitable design and assurance techniques according to the criticality of the software under develop-ment. The requirements and recommendations for SILs in IEC 61508 are not the same as those for DALs in DO-178B. However, underlying these differences there are a number of fundamental principles that can be observed in many of the cur-rent standards. These principles can also be said to underlie good practice in soft-ware assurance case development. The following five principles (previously pre-sented in (Hawkins et al. 2013)) can be identified:

1. Software safety requirements shall be defined to address the software con-tribution to system hazards.
2. The intent of the software safety requirements shall be maintained through-out requirements decomposition.
3. Software safety requirements shall be satisfied.
4. Hazardous behaviour of the software shall be identified and mitigated.
4+1. The confidence established in addressing the software safety principles shall be commensurate to the contribution of the software to system risk.

Principle 1. 'Software safety' is, of course, a misnomer. Software by itself cannot be safe or unsafe. It is only when placed in a system context that the 'safety' of software can be judged by considering the contribution that the software could make to system level hazards. For example, software can play a role as the *initia-tor* of a causal chain of events leading to a system level hazard (and eventual acci-dent). Software (e.g. when placed in the role of a protection system) can also play a role by *failing to mitigate* failures of other (non-software) elements. The first challenge of software safety assurance is to identify all of the ways in which soft-ware can contribute to system level hazards and to capture the necessary behav-iour of the software in relation to these contributions in terms of a clearly defined set of software safety requirements at the system-software boundary.

Principle 2. The normal process of software development proceeds by decompo-sition of the high level requirements placed on the software into lower level specifications of behaviour that can be ultimately be implemented. This may take place as a structured (but informal[1]) process, as part of a formal development process (appealing to logical refinement), or be supported by the development and transformation of models (e.g. as part of a model based development). Regardless of approach, a key concern is whether the intent of an original requirement in maintained through the process of decomposition (e.g. whether a lower level requirement as expressed adequately covers the original intent of higher level requirement). Systematic (design) errors are introduced whenever there is a misalignment of the original intent of a requirement and its implementation.

Principle 3. Ultimately, it is necessary to demonstrate that any safety requirements allocated to software have been satisfied (i.e. present evidence to establish whether the required behaviour will occur in operation). It is important to present evidence that shows the satisfaction of safety requirements under anticipated operating conditions. For example, this requires presenting evidence that addresses satisfaction under both normal and abnormal (fault) conditions.

Principle 4. Whereas Principle 2 is concerned with maintaining the intent of safety requirements in the presence of increasing design commitment, Principle 4 is concerned with the potential undesirable *consequences* of increasing design commitments and implementation. Principle 2 is concerned with whether lower levels of requirements and implementation do what is required (intended). Principle 4 is concerned with whether the design and implementation does *anything else* that is considered unsafe. These potentially hazardous emergent behaviours could firstly result from well-intentioned (but in hindsight flawed) design decisions made in addressing (satisfying) requirements that, unfortunately, have unintended hazardous side effects. Secondly, they can also result from implementation (process execution) errors during the software development process – e.g. modelling errors, coding errors, and tool-use errors. It is necessary to ensure that assurance effort has been targeted at attempting to reveal both of these sources of errors.

Principle 4+1. Firstly, the reason this principle is expressed as '+1', rather than as Principle 5 is that it underlies the implementation of the first four principles. Perfect assurance of the other four principles is, of course, desirable but in reality is unachievable. For example, it is impossible to prove that *all* hazards have been identified, and that *all* the necessary corresponding safety requirements have been identified. Consequently, we have to consider how much effort to expend in addressing the first four principles, and how much evidence to generate. In short, we have to decide upon a *sufficient* level of evidence to present. This principle states that the level of evidence needs to be proportional to the level of risk associated with the software in question. For a highly critical software-intensive system, the level of confidence in addressing the first four principles needs to be high. For a lower criticality system, the level of confidence can be lower.

---

[1] in the mathematical sense

3 How the principles relate to existing assurance standards

The principles presented in the previous section underpin much of the existing assurance philosophy of many current software assurance standards. In this section, we present a brief discussion of how the principles relate to two existing standards: DO-178B/C (RTCA 1992, RTCA 2011) and IEC 61508 (IEC 2010).

3.1 DO-178B/C

With regard to Principle 1 the assumed starting point in DO-178B/C is that the behavioural safety requirements allocated to software have already been derived by system level safety analysis performed in accordance with ARP 4754A (SAE 2010). ARP4754A addresses the problem of *validation* of these requirements (i.e. the correctness and completeness of this initial set of requirements). In addition to the behavioural safety requirements, ARP 4754A also defines the process for judging the criticality of the contribution of software to system level hazards and expresses this as an allocated software DAL.

Regarding Principle 2, DO-178B/C places a strong emphasis on ensuring that traceability is maintained through the stages of software development (from high-level requirements through to low-level requirements, architecture, implementation and testing). It also recognises the problem of *validation* of these steps of decomposition, e.g. through defining requirements for *review* at each tier of development. However, simply recording traceability information (as required by DO-178B/C) whilst being *necessary* for Principle 2, is *insufficient* for this principle. Without traceability information, it is impossible to demonstrate Principle 2. However, traceability information can be regarded as merely recording the assertion that intent is maintained through decomposition, rather than justifying that this assertion is true. This justification could be captured through documenting the output of a systematic review activity, or through utilising an approach such as 'rich traceability' (Dick 2002).

Principle 3 is well addressed in DO-178B/C. It talks of presenting verification evidence that addresses the demonstration of requirements both under normal conditions and fault conditions. Historically, DO-178B has been criticised as being overly restrictive concerning the verification techniques allowed for this demonstration (placing a strong emphasis on dynamic testing). However, DO-178C (in particular through its associated technical supplements) now admits a wider range of possible verification techniques (e.g. use of formal verification techniques such as proof, model checking and abstract interpretation).

With respect to Principle 4, DO-178B/C recognises that 'Software design process activities could introduce possible modes of failure into the software or, conversely, preclude others' and that 'In such cases, additional data should be defined as derived requirements and provided to the system safety assessment process'. In addition, it describes the objectives of testing as being twofold, 'One objective is to demonstrate that the software satisfies its requirements. The second objective is to demonstrate with a high degree of confidence that errors which could lead to unacceptable failure conditions, as determined by the system safety assessment process, have been removed.' This second objective is closely related to Principle 4. DO-178B/C also acknowledges that 'The effects of derived requirements on safety related requirements are determined by the system safety assessment process'. However, the weakness of DO-178B/C is that it does not define within its scope any safety-oriented review or analysis activities (e.g. software hazard analysis) to identify the safety significance of design commitments in the software development process. Instead, this responsibility for is left to the ARP 4754A-guided system safety assessment process. However, little is specifically said regarding software hazard analysis in ARP 4754A. The degree of implementation of Principle 4 under DO-178B/C depends upon the degree of successful interplay (*throughout* the software development lifecycle) between the software assurance and system safety assessment processes.

Finally, Principle 4+1 is captured through the mechanism of DALs that tailor the requirement for the demonstration of the objectives of the standards according to the criticality (as determined by the system level safety analysis process and DAL allocation process carried out in accordance with ARP 4754A). For software determined to be requiring the highest level of assurance (DAL A) *all* of the objectives defined by the standard apply and must be demonstrated (some with an additional requirement for *independent* demonstration). At the lower levels of the assurance, not all objectives are required to be demonstrated. This variation by DAL objectives encodes beliefs (largely undisclosed) about those objectives deemed most necessary and effective to demonstrate given the level of risk posed by the software.

3.2 IEC 61508

With regard to Principle 1, Part 1 of IEC 61508 defines clearly a safety lifecycle that describes the generation of safety requirements as emerging from the activity of hazard analysis. It explicitly talks about the need to capture both *functional*[2] safety requirements, and corresponding *integrity* requirements. Expressed informally, this combination can be considered as capturing both what a system must actually *do* to be safe, and then *how good* it must be at doing it. When integrity requirements are expressed as SILs in IEC 61508, this can be thought of as expressing a required level of confidence in relation to Principle 4+1.

In support of Principle 2, the process of requirements decomposition and allocation is addressed across Parts 1, 2 (concerning requirements allocated to hard-

---

[2] Previously we have described these as *behavioural* safety requirements.

ware) and 3 (concerning requirements allocated to software) of IEC 61508. The validation and justification of this decomposition and allocation receives less attention, and can be said to be a weakness in regard of supporting Principle 2.

Principle 3 is strongly emphasised in IEC 61508. In Part 3, functional safety requirements must be demonstrably satisfied. Normally, this would be described as a verification activity. However, IEC 61508 describes this as software safety validation. The choice of techniques used in demonstrating the satisfaction of functional requirements is governed by the recommended techniques for the associated integrity (level) requirement.

Specifically with respect to *software* safety assurance (i.e. within the scope of Part 3 of IEC 61508) Principle 4 is weakly supported. The software development lifecycle defined in Part 3 assumes a conventional 'flow down' of software requirements into implementation (and test). There is little mention of the potential for emergent hazardous behaviours as a result of design commitments made during software development. There is no specific mention of the activity of software hazard analysis (e.g. that would encourage the application of techniques such as HAZOP or functional failure analysis applied to software designs).

Principle 4+1 is addressed in IEC 61508 through the mechanism of SILs that tailor guidance on design measures (e.g. architectural features) and development and assurance techniques (e.g. types of testing) according to the criticality of the software. The underlying intent in this mechanism is that the measures and techniques recommended for higher SILs will result in a higher integrity product (and levels of assurance) than those recommended for lower SILs.

3.3 Observations on both standards

The previous two sections have discussed how the principles can be seen to relate to two major software safety and assurance standards. The first three principles, dealing with establishing a clear link between software safety requirements and system hazards, the decomposition of requirements, and the satisfaction of requirements, can be observed to be at the heart of both standards. Principle 4, dealing with identifying potentially hazardous emergent behaviour in the software development lifecycle, is less well addressed, with both standards lacking explicit integration of software hazard analysis within the software development lifecycle. However, both discuss the potential for systematic error introduction within the software development lifecycle and techniques for the revelation of such errors (e.g. DO-178B/C's second stated objective of testing).

Both standards attempt to address Principle 4+1 – DO-178B/C through DALs and IEC 61508 through SILs. Although in abstract these can be viewed as similar approaches, there are significant differences. Firstly, with regard to the initial determination of level, DO-178B/C-ARP 4754 proceeds primarily from the severity of the conditions to which the software system can contribute (potentially together with a qualitative analysis of the degree of contribution). However, IEC 61508 works primarily from a degree of risk reduction required expressed in quantitative terms (e.g. a probability of failure on demand) that is then mapped to a corresponding SIL. Secondly, whilst DALs in DO-178B vary the *requirement* to demonstrate *objectives* (and whether independence is required in this demonstration), IEC 61508 instead varies *recommended techniques* by SIL. In intent both of these principles are an attempt to address Principle 4+1. However, given the lack of a significant evidence-base that demonstrates that either approach to varying *confidence* can be easily correlated with achieved risk reduction, both are often criticised (Redmill 2000, Lindsay and McDermid 1997).

3.4 Generic vs specific satisfaction of the principles

Whilst the 4+1 principles are intended to define universal (generic) principles of software assurance, the intent is not that they are addressed *generically* (e.g. by appeal to generic processes or adherence to standards). Instead, they are intended as principles that should be exhibited on a specific software assurance project. The requirements and processes of a standard may be *capable* of demonstrating the principles; however, the actual execution of these processes or enactment of these requirements may still fall short *in practice* on a specific project, i.e. create a situation where confidence can be lost. For example, we consider Principle 2 and DO-178B/C. DO-178B/C emphasises the importance of requirements *review* as a means of validation of the decomposition of requirements. This could be regarded as the means by which we can assure the maintenance of intent. However, the confidence we have in practice depends greatly upon the specific execution of this activity – e.g. upon the competence of those carrying out the review, the review method, the suitability of the review method to the nature of the requirements under review, and the availability of domain knowledge to assist the review. Whilst such issues may even be touched upon *in the abstract* by a standard, they must be addressed in the specific context of application. This means that the application of standards (even if they can be considered to provide good coverage of the principles) cannot be considered in a *tokenistic* sense, where the abstract application of standards is used as a *talisman* of confidence. It is in this difference between generic and specific confidence that assurance cases can play a complementary role. This is discussed in the following two sections.

This issue of generic vs specific application of the standards is perhaps most significant when considering Principle 4+1. As described above, both standards can be said to have established a means of addressing this principle through SILs and DALs. Both have established a *general* set of requirements for varying requirements, processes and techniques according to an abstract level of required confidence. The generality of this approach is potentially a problem. In addition to the problem of *generally* or broadly correlating the varying requirements of the standards to achieved confidence, there is the problem of whether this approach actually defines what is required in a *specific* context. Of course, in some sense this is an impossible demand of a generic standard written out of context of any specific project. However, the 'gap' opens up questions of the relevance and applicability of the requirements to all projects – e.g. the level of assurance actually gained by modified criteria decision coverage metrics (as required by DO-178B/C at level A) when applied to specific classes of software (Staats et al. 2012). Worse than this, there can be negative implications of the approach. Firstly, by requiring something that in *general* was thought to raise confidence but in reality on a specific project does *not,* there exists a potential problem of misallocation of resources, i.e. there is an *opportunity cost.* Secondly, returning to the point already made, there is a danger that the generic mechanisms are applied in a *tokenistic* fashion (e.g. 'The project has done what was required of DAL A, therefore – by definition – we have sufficient confidence') blinding people to the specific issues of confidence that need to be addressed on a project.

There are mechanisms in, and features of, both DO178-B/C and IEC 61508 that potentially help address this problem. In DO-178B/C, both the Plan for Software Aspects of Certification (PSAC) and Software Accomplishment Summary (SAS) require projects to explain and justify (one could argue in a similar sense to an assurance case) how they will be satisfying the objectives of the standard. In IEC 61508 the 'looseness' and flexibility of the SIL requirements/recommendations, whilst often being criticised as leading to ambiguity in any claimed achievement of a SIL, have the beneficial side-effect of *necessitating* tailoring and justification of methods selected against a required SIL.

4 How the principles relate to software assurance cases

The following definition of a safety case is often cited:

'a structured argument, supported by a body of evidence, that provides a compelling, comprehensible and valid case that a system is safe for a given application in a given environment.' (MoD 2007)

Of course, this definition has to be adapted when considering software (in a system context):

'a structured argument, supported by a body of evidence, that provides a compelling, comprehensible and valid case that the software is safe when forming part a system for a given application in a given environment.'

However, the problem with this definition is that it does not describe *how* a compelling, comprehensible and valid case is to be made, e.g. it is not clear what passes for a compelling case. It can be hard to define these terms in the abstract. This has led some to describe the need for an operational definition (Graydon et al. 2010). The definition as stated admits many potential candidates, some 'better' than others (where better can be defined in this paper as being the extent to which the 4+1 principles are addressed). For example, it is possible for someone to attempt to make a software assurance case purely by appeal to process, and in doing so fail to present specific product arguments and evidence that demonstrate Principles 1 to 4. Equally, it is possible for someone to attempt to make a case by purely appealing to *the adherence* to a standard (rather than assembling a case from the requirements and evidence produced as a result of following a standard), and in doing so potentially fall into the trap of *tokenism* as described in the previous section.

The generic nature of assurance cases is both its major weakness and most significant strength. The weakness is that there are many possible forms of an assurance case – some good, some bad. The strength is that the very requirement for an assurance case is a requirement for a developer to state *their* case for *their* specific software development. The worst forms of assurance case could easily fail to cover the 4+1 principles as well as the two standards described in the previous section. (This is why we are to ignore standards at our peril!) However, the best forms of assurance case have the potential to do a better job than standards by addressing all of the *relevant* requirements and recommendations of standards, and in addition presenting compelling arguments for the specific enactment of those standards (e.g. presenting specific arguments of requirements validity).

Of course, beyond the simple definition of a safety case, there exist requirements and guidance for the production of safety cases, such as that presented in UK Defence Standard 00-56 (MoD 2007). For example, with regard to Principle 2, Part 2 provides the following examples of guidance concerning requirements traceability:

> 'The means of recording [requirements] traceability is not prescribed; however, traceability should be demonstrated within the Safety Case.'

> 'In developing systems it may be necessary, where appropriate, to refine safety requirements into more detailed safety requirements that are specific to the chosen implementation ... this will usually be the case for complex electronic systems.'

Also, with regard to Principles 3 and 4, 00-56 Part 2 states:

> 'Demonstration of safety includes finding the credible evidence that shows that the derived safety requirements are correctly implemented and hence that safety requirements are satisfied.'

> 'Evidence should demonstrate that implementation has not adversely affected the safety of the system.'

Further to this form of guidance, it has been shown how it is possible to guide the production of software assurance cases (by means of software safety case patterns) in such a way as to explicitly address the 4+1 principles stated in this paper (Hawkins et al. 2013, Hawkins et al. 2011a).

Principle 4+1 remains a challenge in software assurance case production – i.e. how to manage the level of confidence in the arguments and evidence of an assurance case according to the level of risk. A number of approaches to reasoning about the level of confidence have been proposed. Quantitative methods of reasoning about the possibility of perfection have been described in (Littlewood and Rushby 2012). Reasoning about assurance case confidence based on a Baconian philosophy in terms of the identification and mitigation of argument and evidence 'defeaters' has also been proposed (Weinstock et al. 2013). In (Hawkins et al. 2011b) we outlined an approach that encourages the production of two separate (but cross-linked) arguments within any assurance case: a technical *risk* argument, with a companion *confidence* argument that justifies the adequacy of the arguments and evidence of the risk argument. Such an approach allows for an *explicit* and *specific* treatment of Principle 4+1 when applied to assurance arguments. For example, the technical risk argument must clearly present arguments and evidence for Principle 3 (requirements satisfaction). However, there must also be an accompanying confidence argument that justifies the appropriateness and trustworthiness of those arguments and evidence. Assurance case developers are free at this point in the confidence argument to state that their confidence in the adequacy of the technical risk arguments and evidence comes from having followed the guidance of a standard (e.g. appealing to having satisfied the evidence requirements of a specific SIL). However, in (Hawkins et al. 2011b) we encourage that the confidence argument should engage in the specific certainties and uncertainties (*assurance deficits*) of the risk arguments and evidence – e.g. by considering the potential impact of the uncertainty in the arguments and evidence on the technical risk claim.

5 The complementarity of standards and assurance cases

Existing software safety and assurance standards represent a substantial body of knowledge that it is unwise to ignore. For example, in regard of aspects of Principle 4 (concerning the avoidance of the introduction of systematic error, and the means of revealing such errors) many of the specific requirements of standards are there for *good reason* and should be incorporated into any robust assurance case. For example, many of the coverage requirements of DO-178B/C can be seen as being important requirements for 'flushing out' implementation errors in the software development process. Requirements for static analysis can be seen as important measures in identifying unintentionally introduced control and data flow anomalies. If nothing else, existing software safety standards should be used as an informative checklist of forms of argument and evidence that are commonly required. If there is a *(product oriented)* risk mitigation requirement within in a standard that is wilfully not addressed in some way within an assurance case, it could be considered necessary to justify why this requirement will not contribute to risk reduction in this case. Of course, the challenge with some standards is to glean the rationale behind some of their requirements. There have been some recent attempts to unearth this rationale for DO-178B/C (Holloway 2013). Without clearly presented rationale, standards can be accused as merely being *prescriptive*.

Conversely the application of standards can benefit from the complementary use of assurance cases. Firstly, even in respect of the issue of *compliance* or *conformance* to standards it can be observed that the requirements of standards can often require interpretation in their enactment. They can be ambiguous, deliberately stated at a high level of abstraction, or allow for flexibility in their application. In such cases the concept of establishing a per-project explicit *conformance* or *compliance* argument (that justifies how the requirements of a standard have been complied with on a specific project), has the benefit of improving transparency in the application of the standard. See (Graydon et al. 2012) for a fuller discussion of the use and role of conformance and compliance arguments. Secondly, assurance cases have a useful role to play recording the *justification* (for a specific project) of the specific (judgement-oriented) aspects of the enactment of a standard. This is discussed in the following section.

6 Targeting assurance case effort

In a world where software assurance standards such as DO-178B/C and IEC 61508 prevail, it is sensible to ask where assurance cases should focus their attention in order to most usefully contribute to confidence. The positive aspect of such standards (and others such as ISO 26262) is that, through their emphasis on the formulation of requirements hierarchies, and traceability through to verification, they provide the *template* for the technical *risk* argument needed at the *core* of any software assurance case (forming the central pillar of a response to Principles 1, 2 and 3). The standards also provide *general* (and in some cases usefully experienced based) requirements and recommendations for the avoidance of potentially hazardous errors and anomalous behaviour (Principle 4). Around this central structure, the standards also provide *general* guidance on how effort should be tailored according to risk (Principle 4+1). Where confidence can be lost in the application of standards, and therefore where assurance cases can potentially add most value, is in justification of the *specific* instantiation of these *template* structures and general guidance.

With respect to Principle 1, assurance cases are well suited[3] to the (inevitably subjective) *justification* of the adequacy of the identified software safety requirements. They can provide a confidence argument to support the (technical) risk arguments. For Principle 2, assurance cases can usefully extend beyond the (necessary but insufficient) demand for traceability through to verification, and are well suited to the harder problem of the *justification* of maintenance of intent in these traceability structures. Whilst Principle 3 is typically well handled in standards, assurance cases are well suited to the *justification* of the adequacy of evidence (e.g. the appropriateness and trustworthiness of specific forms of evidence for requirements satisfaction). With regard to Principle 4, assurance cases are well suited to the *justification* of the identification and treatment of emergent hazards through the software development process. In particular, whilst standards are good

---

[3] by their nature as being a means of presenting arguments and supporting evidence

at suggesting rafts of techniques for eliminating 'implementation' errors (which can be thought of as the 'slips, trips, and mishaps' of software development), assurance cases are potentially more usefully targeted at the justification of the management of unintentionally hazardous side effects of otherwise intentional design commitments. In assurance case terms, Principle 4+1 fundamentally relates to the *confidence* argument that can be created to accompany the technical risk argument. Whilst conformance to standards can, in some sense, be viewed as a 'proxy' *generic* confidence argument (i.e. claiming adequate confidence because having followed the requirements of a particular SIL or DAL), assurance cases are well suited to enabling documentation of a more *specific justification* of confidence (e.g. by considering the trustworthiness and appropriateness of evidence, or the acceptability of assurance deficits in the evidence presented).

7 Summary

In this paper we have discussed the common themes that can be identified across software safety standards. (Examples extend beyond the two safety and assurance standards discussed in this paper.) These themes can be observed through consideration of the 4+1 principles described in this paper. However, some of the principles are better handled than others. For example, requirements traceability and satisfaction are typically addressed well. However, justification of requirements decomposition and requirements validation is not so strongly addressed. In addition, concerning the important issue of confidence, many existing standards address this through a general framework of DALs or SILs rather than encouraging the documentation of sufficient, explicit, arguments of confidence targeted at addressing the key issues of confidence relating to the details of the risk mitigation argument presented. Assurance cases should not duplicate those aspects addressed well by standards. It is foolish to develop assurance cases in ignorance of the 'body of knowledge' contained in many current standards. However, assurance cases provide an opportunity (if constructed well) to explicitly document and evaluate product- and project-specific aspects (such as requirements and model validity, specific selection of evidence types and artefacts) that need to be argued for safety (and confidence).

Summary of the summary. It is an artificial choice to say that safety engineers must choose between *either* an assurance case-oriented approach, *or* a standards-oriented approach. They can be used together in highly complementary roles.

References

CENELEC (2011) EN 50128 – Railway applications – Communication, signalling and processing systems – Software for railway control and protection systems

Dick J (2002) Rich traceability. In: Proceedings of the 1st international workshop on traceability in emerging forms of software engineering, Edinburgh, Scotland

Graydon P, Knight J, Green M (2010) Certification and safety cases. In: Proc of International System Safety Conference (ISSC), Minneapolis. System Safety Society

Graydon P, Habli I, Hawkins R et al (2012) Arguing conformance. IEEE Software 29(3)50-57

Hawkins R, Clegg K, Alexander R et al (2011a) Using a software safety argument pattern catalogue: two case studies. In: Computer safety, reliability, and security (SAFECOMP). Springer

Hawkins R, Kelly T, Knight J et al (2011b) A new approach to creating clear safety arguments. In: Dale C, Anderson T (eds) Advances in system safety. Springer

Hawkins R, Habli I, Kelly T (2013) Principled construction of software safety cases. In: Proc 2nd Workshop on Next Generation of System Assurance Approaches for Safety-Critical Systems (SASSUR), Toulouse

Holloway C M (2013) Making the implicit explicit: towards an assurance case for DO-178C, Proc 31st International System Safety Conference (ISSC), Boston, Massachusetts

IEC (2010) IEC 61508 – Functional safety of electrical/electronic/programmable electronic safety-related systems

ISO (2009) ISO/DIS 26262 Road vehicles – Functional safety

Leveson N (2011) The use of safety cases in certification and regulation. Journal of System Safety, Nov/Dec, System Safety Society

Lindsay PA, McDermid JA (1997) A systematic approach to software safety integrity levels. In: Daniel P (ed) Proc 16th Intl Conf on Computer Safety (SAFECOMP), York. Springer

Littlewood B, Rushby J (2012) Reasoning about the reliability of diverse two-channel systems in which one channel is 'possibly perfect'. IEEE Trans Software Engineering 38:1178–1194

McDermid JA, Pumfrey DJ (2001) Software safety: why is there no consensus? In: Proc International System Safety Conference (ISSC) 2001, Huntsville. System Safety Society

MoD (2007) Defence Standard 00-56 – Safety management requirements for defence systems. Issue 4. UK Ministry of Defence

Redmill F (2000) Safety integrity levels – theory and problems. In: Redmill F, Anderson T (eds) Lessons in system safety. Springer Verlag

RTCA (1992) Software considerations in airborne systems and equipment certification. RTCA/DO-178B. RTCA, Inc.

RTCA (2011) Software considerations in airborne systems and equipment certification. RTCA/DO-178C. RTCA, Inc.

SAE (2010) Aerospace Recommended Practice (ARP) 4754A – Guidelines for the development of civil aircraft and systems. SAE

Staats M, Gay G, Whalen M et al (2012) On the danger of coverage directed test case generation. In: Fundamental approaches to software engineering. Springer, Berlin Heidelberg

Wassyng A, Maibaum T, Lawford M et al (2010) Software certification: is there a case against safety cases? In: Calinescu R, Jackson E (eds) Proc 16th Monterey conf on Foundations of computer software: modeling, development, and verification of adaptive systems (FOCS'10). Springer-Verlag, Berlin, Heidelberg

Weinstock CB, Goodenough JB, Klein AZ (2013) Measuring assurance case confidence using Baconian probabilities. In Proceedings of the 1st International Workshop on Assurance Cases for Software-Intensive Systems (ASSURE), San Francisco

Modelling and analysing Safety Acceptance Decision Making Processes in the MoD

Mick Warren[1] and Tim Kelly[2]

[1]Frazer-Nash Consultancy Limited, Burton-on-Trent, UK

[2]University of York, York, UK

Abstract   Procurement of safety-critical and safety-related systems is a complex process involving both technical and social acceptance processes. There are a number of modelling techniques that can be used to analyse system failures – such as Systems Theoretic Accident Modelling and Processes (STAMP), responsibility modelling, and Human Factors Analysis and Classification System (HFACS). This paper undertakes a retrospective analysis of a major Ministry of Defence (MoD) aircraft accident using two techniques to try and identify the system failures associated with the procurement of software. This is undertaken via application of two differing techniques and an analysis of the results obtained. The analysis highlights many potential system failures across a diverse set of groupings including skill based, financial/resource based and process based failures. The analysis demonstrates that the techniques have particular strengths but also that they do not cover all potential issues.

Finally, the paper proposes that there are more important lessons to be learned – such as the socio-technical issues surrounding the decision making processes. The use of such models could be extended to include the determination and analysis of safety acceptance decision processes thus identifying where confidence is required to support the decision making process prior to it being necessary.

1 Introduction

Traditionally, in the Ministry of Defence (MoD), acquisition is made through Defence Equipment & Support (DE&S). DE&S is organized in differing operating centres and then in differing project teams. As part of their responsibilities they must ensure that the equipment they provide is both fit for purpose (against requirements) and also safe to operate and maintain. The former is typically demonstrated via a requirements analysis, inclusion of such in the contract and demonstration of achievement through verification and validation processes. The latter is demonstrated and assessed via a safety case which provides a 'structured argument, supported by a body of evidence that provides a compelling, comprehensible and valid case that a system is safe for a given application in a given operating environment' (MoD 2007).

A safety case provides assurance of safety – that which we can demonstrate. This is different from actual safety in that it is not always possible to provide a complete and compelling demonstration of system safety. This is often the case in systems which involve software. We can typically only assure the safety associated with use of software to, or with, a degree of confidence – we cannot do so in totality.

When reviewing previous incidents and accidents for the MoD, Christenson and Szczcepanski (Christenson and Szczcepanski 2004) argued that:

> 'The major hazards identified were not associated with the physical construction or necessarily the design of the system but with the hard and soft interfaces to the system, i.e., the major hazards identified were to do with the interfaces between the systems, people and fabrics.'

This acknowledges that safety is more than just an equipment issue – it involves the socio-technical context within it operates.

2 Systems failure

The safety cases that DE&S provides focus on that which they are responsible for (discussed later) – although recognizing that there is a wider safety scope. This narrow focus can potentially have a negative impact on the safety of the capability in operation or the safety of the capability within a system of systems.

The Military Aviation Authority (MAA) was formed following the Nimrod Enquiry (Haddon-Cave 2009). The MAA has placed significant focus, through the MAA Regulatory Publications (MRPs) on ensuring that the Operational Duty Holder (ODH) and the Delivery Duty Holder (DDH) are fully engaged in the necessary safety processes. This includes formal acceptance of the safety products produced by DE&S and also a duty placed on the project team leader to communicate risk to life to the ODH/DDH and involve appropriate user representation at project safety panels (MAA 2012). Such risk may be categorized into the Defence Lines of Development (DLoDs) (MoD 2013a) – these are training, equipment, personnel, information, concepts and doctrine, organization, infrastructure, logistics and interoperability (an overarching theme). DE&S is normally responsible for the equipment, logistics and around half of the training DLoDs, with the other DLoDs being owned by differing organizations.

We acknowledge that there is now a different, arguably more stringent, regulatory environment in place to allow formal risk transfer between DE&S and the duty holder[1] across the capability provided by the Socio-Technical System (STS) than there has previously been following the introduction of the MAA. What we seek to determine through this paper is an understanding of why potential failures in the procurement safety acceptance decision processes could cause issues in the non-procurement DLoDs. Often, safety acceptance decision processes are made in procurement which can cause a potential safety impact in the other DLoDs. They can also result in non-safety impacts such as one's operational effectiveness and fitness for purpose of the capability provided. The potential safety impact is often mitigated via programme decisions such as delaying the intended use of the capability until the impact is suitably addressed. Examples include where a capability may be ready to use technically but the operators have not had sufficient training. This could undermine a safety claim based on competence in the safety case. It could be mitigated by not using the capability until all operators have been suitably trained but this can lead to a subsequent loss of capability. Thus a programme decision has been made to mitigate the potential safety impact. Obviously, there is a need to question how the programme got to this stage in the first place as such a mitigation will invariably have project issues such as time, cost and performance.

Key to the above is to form an understanding of whether these could have been discovered either at the outset of the project or at an early enough stage that it could have been rectified. We seek to discover whether there is a technique(s) available which could be used to help identify such issues before they arise. The project team is also responsible for the logistics DLoD and half of the training DLoD. Thus it is necessary to ensure that the ongoing safety acceptance processes through the life of the programme are also investigated in a similar fashion.

3 Failure of supporting processes

Thus far we have discussed failures associated with systems. Of interest to this work are the supporting process failures which can lead to a systems failure. Supporting processes may be defined as those within the project team, or those they act on, to facilitate the delivery of safe equipment to the duty holder. Similar to the definition of a hazard in the safety environment, a supporting process failure may be defined as a state of the system which can lead directly to incident or accident without anything further going wrong. Such failures can include a failure to have: sufficient processes in place to proactively identify potential safety problems; sufficient process to react to failures before they become a potential safety problem and independent assurance that processes in place are suitably enacted.

We feel it pertinent to explore the issues associated with the acceptance and assurance processes as that is where the majority of the supporting processes lie. A

---

[1] A Duty Holder (DH) has 'a personal level duty of care for the personnel under their command; those who, by virtue of their temporary involvement in aviation activities, come within a DH's area of responsibility; and the wider public who may be affected by their operations' (MAA 2013a).

lack of a suitable supporting process – for example, suitable independent assurance of process implementation – in the acceptance and assurance processes can potentially cause a latent failure which only manifests itself as a safety issue later on; our case study later is an excellent example of this.

One of the key aims of this paper is to try and discover what can be done to highlight potential issues prior to them developing into problems. For example, a major failure in decision making around supporting processes for logistical support – such as an incorrect assessment of spares requirements – may not be apparent whilst the capability is being procured. It results in a latent failure. The failure would typically only come to light when the capability is in service and the logistic supply is insufficient for the identified needs; decisions need to be made cognizant of their potential wider impact. The project team need to ask themselves how they got to this point and how we can prevent it re-occurring.

It is recognized that there is a significant pressure to deliver projects to time, cost or performance constraints. The 16 major projects (NAO 2013) within DE&S have had their forecast delivery timescale increased by 468 months since they were approved – a 29% increase over planned project timescales. They have had cost increases of £6.6 billion since approval – an 11.7% increase. The UK military has been in a state of continuous operations since the early 1950's and there is only one year on record when a serviceman or woman did not die on operations – this provides the performance focus. It is claimed that 99% of the technical specifications were forecast to be achieved noting that many requirements (but not key user requirements[2]) are often traded to mitigate either time or cost issues.

Major projects within DE&S now have a formal lessons identified activity at the end of the project. Whilst this may be useful for other projects it may be too late for the one where the lessons have been identified – latent failures may already be in the STS due to issues with the safety acceptance decision making processes on that project.

4 Analysis techniques

This paper uses two differing techniques to analyse the acceptance processes within a project team. Application of the techniques, followed by an analysis of their results obtained, will facilitate an evaluation of the techniques themselves. It is postulated that it is difficult for any one technique to provide a complete, compelling and comprehensive assessment of either the safety of a system or the assurance of safety of such a system. Arguably, when retrospectively analysing accidents and incidents, more than one technique may provide a more comprehen-

---

[2] Key user requirements may be defined as high-level capability intent specified by the end user – they detail what the system should do from a capability perspective – not how it should do it or the detailed system requirements.

sive coverage. It should be noted that such investigation may be subject to hindsight bias – this is discussed later.

We shall investigate two techniques used for discovering hazards and their causes and perform an analysis on the safety acceptance decision processes used in a major aircraft accident. The techniques chosen are System-Theoretic Process Analysis (STPA) (Thomas and Leveson 2011) and responsibility modelling (Lock et al. 2010). Both techniques focus on, or at least address, the STS around the systems rather than just the equipment. STPA is chosen as it is a widely used technique and is discussed below. Responsibility modelling is utilised as it can allow an analysis of the complexity of the STS and differing organizations involved in the decision making processes.

4.1 STPA background

Systems Theoretic Accident Modelling and Processes (STAMP) was developed to change 'the emphasis in systems safety from preventing failures to enforcing behavioural safety constraints' (Leveson 2012). It can be used to model and analyse technical, organizational and human factors in an STS. STPA builds on STAMP and 'assumes accidents are caused by inadequate enforcement of constraints on component behaviour rather than simply component failures' (Thomas and Leveson 2011). STPA contains both component failure and component interaction accidents and it is claimed to be more effective at finding 'more causes of hazards' (Thomas and Leveson 2011) than other techniques. Leveson claims that STPA can facilitate the identification of 'design errors, including software flaws; component interaction accidents; cognitively complex human decision-making errors; and social, organizational, and management factors contributing to accidents' (Leveson 2012).

STPA recognizes that components are a part of a system and that interactions can also be a significant causal factor in accidents. STPA uses the following steps:

- Identify the hazards associated with the system.
- Construct the control structure by identifying the major components and control structures and labelling the control arrows.
- Identify the control actions for the system in question. The initial part of this step is to 'choose which hazards to analyze' (Asplund et al. 2012). System components are then identified and modelled in a control structure to implement the controls in the STS. The control actions within the structure are analysed 'to maintain the constraints on behaviour necessary to control risk' (Leveson et al. 2006).
- Those control actions identified previously are then investigated for their potential safety constraints which could cause the control actions to fail. Potential causal factors against the unsafe control actions are then developed.

STPA can be applied as soon as the high-level system accidents and hazards are known – normally during the early stage of development. It may also be applied retrospectively on an existing system to undertake a comparison with past hazard reports. It has been used in scenarios as wide-ranging as improving the safety of a remotely piloted vehicle landing (Yi et al. 2011) to investigation of safety issues surrounding electronic medical records (Weber-Jahnke and Mason-Blakley 2011). To our knowledge this is the first time that STPA has been applied to procurement processes.

4.2 Responsibility modelling background

Another risk analysis technique which aims to focus on more than just the traditional 'interaction of technical aspects of systems' (Lock et al. 2010) is responsibility modelling. Of importance is that a responsibility is defined as 'a duty, held by some agent, to achieve, maintain or avoid some given state, subject to conformance with organisational, social and cultural norms' (Lock et al. 2010).

Responsibility modelling helps the identification and analysis of hazards and risks which may arise in complex systems spanning many differing organizations and organizational boundaries. Modelling causal responsibilities helps to focus attention on the responsibility itself. It is argued that it facilitates the discovery of 'inconsistencies and incompleteness' (Sommerville 2007) between relationships in the model. It may also be used as a basis for deciding the 'allocation of responsibilities'. If used with an assignment model – which show how responsibilities are distributed in a system – it can also provide a basis for vulnerability analysis.

It organizes risk clauses (covering the entity involved, the hazards associated with it combined with an apportioned risk and severity) into:

- a target – which could be the entity or relationship to which the clause refers
- a hazard (using HAZOP (Kletz 1999) keywords)
- a condition – what could arise with relation to the hazard occurring
- the risk – the probability and severity of the hazard occurring
- the consequences – the potential effects of the hazard in the wider system context
- recommended actions – potential courses of action (mitigations or avoidance).

A key to the symbols used in a responsibility model is detailed in Figure 1 (Lock et al. 2010).

Responsibility modelling has been applied in varying domains such as civil emergency planning (Sommerville et al. 2009) and patterns of security postures (Storer et al. 2012). To our knowledge this is the first time that responsibility modelling has been applied to procurement processes.

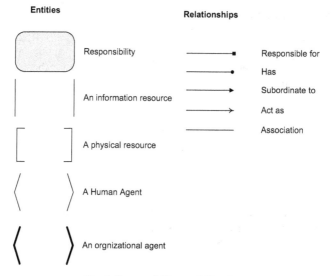

Fig. 1. Responsibility modelling key

5 Case study

It is necessary to carefully select an accident which: involves procurement; involves software; has public domain access to the supporting evidence and analysis and, ideally, has multiple sources of analyses to provide a comprehensive identification of causal factors. The procurement processes of the case study will then be subjected to both an STPA and a responsibility model analysis.

The case study used in this paper is the accident involving a Royal Air Force Chinook Mk 2 helicopter that crashed into the Mull of Kintyre in 1994.

'At 16:59GMT (17:59BST) on Thursday 2 June 1994 an RAF Chinook HC-2 helicopter aircraft number ZD576 on a transport task from RAF Aldergrove in Northern Ireland to Fort George near Inverness in the highlands of Scotland crashed into a hill on the west side of the Mull of Kintyre, a short distance inland of, and uphill from, the Mull of Kintyre lighthouse. The pilots, Flight Lieutenants Jonathan Tapper (the captain) and Richard Cook (the co-pilot), the two crewmen, Master Loadmaster Graham Forbes and Sergeant Kevin Hardie, and twenty five passengers were killed. The passengers were senior Royal Ulster Constabulary and Army officers and six civil servants from the Northern Ireland Office. All were members of the Northern Ireland security and intelligence community. The crash was one of the worst losses of life in a peacetime accident for the Royal Air Force.' (Philip et al. 2011)

5.1 Post-accident inquiries

Prior to 1 April 2012 aviation accidents and incidents were normally investigated via a board of inquiry convened by the air officer responsible for the operation of that aircraft. The authority for this was contained in Queens Regulations for the Royal Air Force (MoD 1999) and Joint Service Publication (JSP) 551 (MoD 2003). Post 1 April 2011, after the formation of the MAA, the Director General of the MAA is responsible as the 'convening authority for all MoD aviation service inquiries' (MAA 2013b). The authority for this is contained within the Armed Forces Act 2006 (HMG 2006) and in the JSP 832 guide to service inquiries (MoD 2008). Military aircraft accidents/incidents going back to 2007 were reviewed (MAA 2013b, MoD 2013b). None were found to have potential issues associated with software which were deemed to be a contributory cause or aggravating factor in any accident/incident. Software fails systematically – it is often difficult to recreate the circumstances in which it failed and, thus, it is difficult to demonstrate the effect it has at the aircraft level.

There were potential issues surrounding the Full Authority Digital Engine Control (FADEC) (Perks 2001) which may have been a contributory factor to the Chinook crash on the Mull of Kintyre in 1994. There have been several investigations into the crash: a RAF Board of Inquiry (HMG 1995); a fatal accident inquiry in 1996 (Templeton 2002); a House of Commons Defence Select Committee report (HMG 1998a); a government response (HMG 1998b); a Public Accounts Committee Report (HMG 2000); a House of Lords Select Committee report (HMG 2002a); a Government response (HMG 2002b) and an independent review on behalf of the Defence Secretary (Philip et al. 2011). The crash, and the focus placed on the aircrew as being grossly negligent, has caused significant distress to the families of the aircrew and resulted in several high-profile public campaigns.

5.2 Recommendations related to procurement

The various investigations previously outlined have detailed recommendations, findings and identification of causes. For the purposes of this paper we are interested in those recommendations, findings and causes which can then be attributed to the equipment, logistics and around half of the training DLoDs – that is, those which the procurement agency is responsible for. This will allow us to focus on the issues surrounding the procurement processes. An analysis of those recommendations from the differing investigations and their relevance to procurement was undertaken. Out of a total of 32 recommendations made it was assessed that 22 were potentially attributable to procurement. Of those, 8 were assessed as being related to software. An example (No. 15) is shown in Figure 2 (where T = training, E = equipment, P = personnel, I = information, D = concepts and doctrine, O = organization, I = infrastructure and L = Logistics). Conversely, No. 32 –

'We recommend that the Ministry of Defence should reconsider its policy and procedures for the transport of personnel whose responsibilities are vital to national security', also shown in Figure 2, was assessed to be attributable to the doctrine and concept DLoD which is not the responsibility of the procurement agency DE&S and was thus excluded. A chart of the recommendations against DLoDs is shown in Figure 3.

Source	No	Extract	T	E	P	I	D	O	I	L
Defence Select Committee	14.	We have considered the evidence suggesting that the crash of ZD576 pointed to fundamental flaws in the design of the Chinook Mark-2 or its components. We have found no compelling evidence to support these claims.	√							
	15.	We are concerned by the failure of Boscombe Down to give final approval to the FADEC software. We conclude, however, that this is a management failure, and are persuaded by the evidence that this absence of approval raises no safety-critical questions.	√							
	16.	We welcome the decision to remove the responsibility for allocation of blame from Boards of Inquiry. We consider that this will clarify their role and duties.	Not considered to be attributable to DLoD							
	17.	We conclude that the work of Boards of Inquiry will be assisted by the installation of flight monitoring devices in aircraft, and we welcome the accelerated programme to fit these to Chinooks and other aircraft.	√							
Mull of Kintyre Review – Executive Summary and Conclusions	30.	We recommend that the finding that Flt Lt Tapper and Flt Lt Cook were negligent to a gross degree should be set aside.	Not considered to be attributable to DLoD							
	31.	We recommend that the Ministry of Defence should consider offering an apology to the families of Flt Lt Tapper and Flt Lt Cook.	Not considered to be attributable to DLoD							
	32.	We recommend that the Ministry of Defence should reconsider its policy and procedures for the transport of personnel whose responsibilities are vital to national security.					√			

Fig. 2. Inquiry findings DLoD analysis

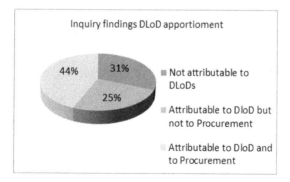

Inquiry findings DLoD apportioment

44%   31%   25%

- Not attributable to DLoDs
- Attributable to DIoD but not to Procurement
- Attributable to DIoD and to Procurement

Fig. 3. Inquiry findings DLoD apportionment

5.3 STPA analysis

A STPA analysis of those recommendations relating to software was undertaken. This was done by focusing on the organizations named in the reports, the high-level processes in place at the time, the issues identified in the inquiries and further explicit evidence (such as witness testimonies) supporting the findings of the inquiries where available. The main principle applied was the use of direct evidence – no supposition, presumptions or conclusions other than those formally documented were made. In addition, the analysis was modelled on the organizations as they were at the time of the incident and not as they are now.

Three supporting process failures were identified by taking those inquiry findings applicable to both the procurement agency[3] (DE&S) and software in Figure 2 and grouping them into:

- an inability to assess previous incidents and learn from experience
- lack of compliance with standards
- lack of procurement procedures or a lack of application of them.

From these supporting process failures, STPA control structures were formed to facilitate detailed analysis – an example is shown in Figure 4. This was undertaken by analysing the inquiries for the organizations involved, the information required by each organization, the actions required of them and bounding the responsibility of DE&S.

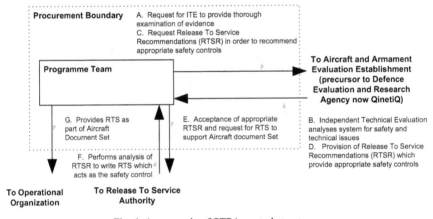

Fig. 4. An example of STPA control structures

From these control structures a total of 41 potential causal factors were identified. This was undertaken by taking each identified organisation in turn, taking the role within that organisation, identifying the action required but not provided and subsequently potential unsafe action(s) provided. This analysis then allowed safety

---

[3] Those which have a 'tick' in the training, equipment or logistics DIoD column of Figure 2.

constraints to be developed and then the identification of causal factors against the unsafe control actions.

Examples of the causal factors identified from the analysis include:

- a potential lack of: funds to contract an Independent Technical Evaluator (ITE) and project team staff to undertake the ITE tender process
- a potential lack of: resource to write formal processes necessary; time to implement the process and auditing of process for its ability to discharge its requirements
- a potential lack of: access to available evidence (International Trade in Arms Regulations (ITAR) barriers/proprietary information) and lack of resource/ skills to undertake the work.

The causal factors identified were first attributed to organizations and then grouped by type as shown in Figure 5. Approximately half of the potential recommendations could be attributable to the project team with the rest evenly distributed across other organizations. Given that we had previously selected only those inquiry recommendations applicable to procurement this came as a surprise – the amount of recommendations on non-procurement organizations demonstrated that they have a significant responsibility for procurement yet DE&S are the accountable organization. Of all the identified causal factors nearly a third could be attributed as issues associated with skills of personnel/organizations involved.

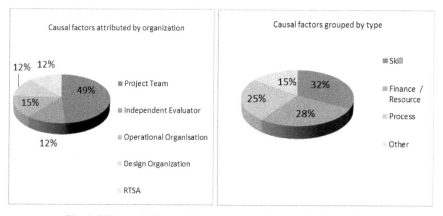

Fig. 5. STPA analysis causal factor grouping by organization and type

The STPA analysis resulted in a strong grouping of skill based causal factors (32%). The MoD and DE&S has always had formal approval processes for those in a senior role. This was typically undertaken through the issuing of a letter of delegation formally authorizing the project team leader or engineering authorities to make airworthiness decisions. Out of the 17 unsafe control actions identified through the STPA analysis 25% resulted in safety constraints surrounding the need for independent evaluation. What is clear is that the vast majority of the causal factors would have benefitted from an independent assessment of their implementation. This was deemed necessary to ensure those process used at the time were implemented correctly.

5.4 Responsibility modelling analysis

A responsibility modelling analysis of those recommendations relating to software was undertaken. The 8 recommendations relating to software were grouped into four responsibility models. This was undertaken by analysing the recommendations and deducing common themes from them noting that some of the recommendations were, effectively, repeated in differing inquiries. This resulted in the following responsibility models:

- Digital Engine Control Unit (DECU) data extraction
- fault investigation
- software approval
- assurance of evidence

An example of one of the developed responsibility models is shown in Figure 6 – that for software approval. From these responsibility models a total of 121 potential action recommendations on differing organizations were developed. This was undertaken by starting with each of the actors in the responsibility models developed. HAZOP guidewords were applied to each of the relationships between the entities to develop a condition associated with the relationship. This condition was then analysed for potential consequences associated with it and then a risk/severity was apportioned. Following this recommended actions were suggested to try and prevent or mitigate the developed consequence.

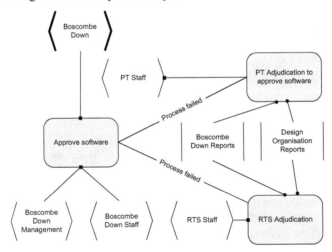

Fig. 6. Responsibility model for software approval

These were first attributed to organizations and then grouped by type – an example is provided in Figure 7. This model shows the entities and relationships involved in the software approval process within the MoD. Boscombe Down should provide technical reports on the software (both technical and managerial approvals). The latter did not occur. The project team can, in conjunction with the Release To Service Authority (RTSA), provide their own assessments on the software. It appears that this did not explicitly happen – it seems to have been accepted without a formal process. Such a process would rely on the reports from both Boscombe Down and the design organization.

Examples of the recommended actions from the responsibility model in Figure 6 include:

- Boscome Down to ensure that: the software technical reports are formally approved prior to flight and they have sufficient software skills to assess the software.
- The project team to ensure that: the contract with Boscombe Down has sufficient clarity of their role; they have appropriate skills (or that they are available to them) and that they have appropriate staffing levels.

Fig. 7. Responsibility model analysis grouping by organization and type

The analysis demonstrated that over half of the potential recommendations could be attributable to the project team with one-fifth being attributable to an independent organisation (either evaluating the evidence or verifying application of process) supporting the project team. That is, a total of three quarters could be directly attributable to procurement. The analysis demonstrated that nearly three quarters of the recommended actions could be grouped as process failings – a significant issue.

It is of note that the recommended actions developed through the responsibility modelling analysis include a high reliance on an independent assurance process to support the project team. Such recommendations were grouped into two main functional areas: an independent technical evaluation and also independent verification of the achievement of many products (regulation). The MoD has always had a quasi-regulation system to approve aircraft for release to service; i.e. it had processes in place and an organization to provide oversight – the RTSA. Arguably they did not have the depth of resource or necessary skill set to fully analyse the detailed recommendations being made. In addition, they worked in the same chain of command as the operating authority and were thus not, organizationally at least, truly independent.

5.5 Comparison of STPA and responsibility modelling results

The results of the analysis from each technique apportioned approximately half of the findings to the project team (49% for STPA and 53% for responsibility modelling) with a uniform distribution amongst the other organizations involved. Examples include:

- From the STPA analysis, the project team do not have a support contract set up with the design organization or have the ability to transfer data to them.
- From the responsibility modelling analysis the project team must ensure that the contract allows suitable access to evidence required and that they have suitable skills and staffs to assess that being presented to them.

The STPA analysis resulted in a relatively even spread of groupings by type. The responsibility modelling grouping by type resulted in a significant group surrounding the process group (74%) with the other groups being relatively evenly split.

The use of STPA was relatively straightforward as the method was quite prescriptive and formulaic. It is broken into differing steps and, once the control structures are developed, there is a pre-determined methodology to follow to derive the potential causal factors. It also made the relationships between entities in the analysis explicit thus ensuring that appropriate focus is placed on them. In an STS relationships between individuals, organizations and responsibilities are normally implicit. Such relationships can either break down or not be developed to a state necessary to allow the STS to operate effectively and efficiently (or at all). This results in the STS as a whole being considered the 'socio' rather than just its technical part.

The safety constraints developed during the STPA analysis resulted in a focus on requirements ('The project team must...' 'The ITE must...'). This tended to identify process requirements. In an area of uncertainty the introduction of a process should assist in ensuring that actions are repeatable, understood and auditable. It does not necessarily ensure that the outcome of the process is correct. It is observed that the causal factors which were developed during the analysis seemed to focus on either 'lack of...' or 'do/does not...'. This seems to be a negative outcome. Given that STPA, by design, seeks causal factors against unsafe control actions the resultant phraseology is not a surprise – it appears that STPA encourages it.

If the technique is used we would suggest that careful consideration is given to the potential presentational impact that this may have with decision makers. In addition, application of the technique even at a very high level was very time consuming. There were a total of eight identified potential software related recommendations from the enquiries, grouped into three potential hazards as previously discussed. The work on these three identified hazards took in excess of 60 hours to undertake the analysis. It is postulated that for a complex and/or large STS the work required to provide an accurate analysis could be orders of magnitude greater than that undertaken by the authors in this example. It is concluded from the application of STPA in this case study that STPA:

- is relatively straightforward to implement
- considers issues wider than the technical aspects of an STS
- could be seen as developing negatively phrased results
- is quite time consuming to implement – even at a high level on a few potential developed hazards.

The responsibility modelling analysis provided quite detailed recommended actions. These included actions such as 'request guidance from design organization as to the required extraction intervals' (for information from the DECU). Such actions would be straightforward to implement. The technique also allowed a risk to be apportioned – a severity and probability apportionment against the consequences of the developed conditions from the responsibility models. Such apportionment, although potentially subjective and thus open to challenge, can facilitate a prioritization of actions. Such a prioritization could allow best use of scarce resources within an organization when considering addressing any recommendations made under the analysis.

The responsibility modelling technique resulted in more developed outcomes (121) than the STPA analysis (41). It was time consuming to undertake the analyses. Although as it used techniques such as HAZOP then it was only slightly more time consuming than the STPA (approximately 75 hours of analyses rather than the 60 hours taken by the STPA) even though it identified nearly three times as many potential outcomes.

It is concluded from the application of responsibility modelling in this case study that:

- Responsibility modelling provides detailed recommended actions.
- It is time consuming to implement but provides more recommended actions than STPA for the time involved.
- Actions are apportioned a risk as part of the process – this can readily facilitate prioritization of their implementation.

The combination of the results of the application of the two techniques provided a significant amount of causal factors/recommended actions – a total of 162 between them. There is a significant amount of recorded detail on this accident supporting the differing inquiries – the vast majority having been read in support of this paper. A comparison of the recorded detail and the results of our analyses outlines potential discrepancies which highlight process failings. For example, there was a seemingly intentional attempt to prevent thorough accident investigation (Burke 2001).

Differing techniques are used to help provide an analysis of the assurance of a system. At best these techniques assess the safety of a system from differing viewpoints. Sommerville introduces the concept of viewpoints for requirements engineering and defines them as 'an encapsulation of partial information about a system' (Sommerville and Sawyer 1997). It is postulated that it is difficult for any one technique to provide a complete, compelling and comprehensive assessment of either the safety of a system or the assurance of safety of such a system. Arguably, when retrospectively analysing accidents and incidents, more than one technique (or viewpoint) may provide a more comprehensive coverage.

5.6 Issues not discovered by the analyses

The detailed recommended actions developed under the responsibility modelling are arguably one of its disadvantages. It could be argued that detailed actions were only developed as the actual issues were known prior to undertaking the analysis. However, the work was based on the recommendations. Further analysis of the contents of the reports and the supporting evidence was not assessed until after the analyses had been completed. It is argued that the recommendations in the inquiries were of a sufficiently abstract nature, the techniques used were sufficiently formulaic and detailed in conjunction with the approach taken that probability of resulting confirmation bias was extremely low. We do not claim that application of the techniques prior to the events would have stopped it. We do argue, backed by the results of our analyses, that the chances of the issues associated with the software still being knowingly present would have been significantly reduced. This is not by predicting the software was at fault but by highlighting potential flaws in the acceptance processes, which if implemented correctly may have reduced the chances of the issue not being discovered and acted upon. The analyses have produced generic recommendations which can be taken forward to other projects – such as 'Ensure sufficient stakeholder involvement in issue investigation'.

Each technique demonstrated particular strengths and weaknesses as previously concluded. The techniques also had causal factors/recommended actions which had sufficient differences between them which would mean that it would be difficult to substantiate an argument that either of them in isolation could provide comprehensive coverage of all the issues. This is concluded from the results of the case study of a legacy accident where the issues were known. Looking at a claim of comprehensive coverage of all the issues for either technique in isolation when used in a predictive manner would be even harder to substantiate.

The combination of the results of both techniques provided a wide ranging set of causal factors/recommended actions from the case study. It is argued that the analyses does not facilitate the substantiation of a claim of comprehensive coverage when utilizing both of them. Surprisingly, neither technique highlighted:

Human error. The potential for human error (in either process development or implementation) as a causal factor/recommended action was not apparent in the results developed. It could be argued that it is implicit within them but given their potential significant impact we believe that it needs to be made explicit.

Timeliness. Although the analysis identified potential problems with the software neither demonstrated that there was a timeliness aspect to the discovery of the problem. Issues were raised but only during the final acceptance processes. In order to successfully mitigate potential problems it would be reasonable to assume that causal factors/recommendations made should have an indication of when they need to be implemented. Neither technique provided this.

Why decisions were made. The techniques outlined what occurred and also made suggestions as to how to potentially fix or mitigate issues arising from the case study. Neither investigated nor made recommendations to investigate why such decisions were made. They largely focussed on process development and implementation. Organizations are complex and inter-organizational relationships more so. Not investigating the 'why' in the decision making process could fundamentally undermine any recommendations. Given that it is ultimately humans that make the decisions in the STS it is argued that non-investigation of the 'why' in the decision making process is a significant weakness.

It is recognized that the lack of identification of the issues above could be a limitation of the implementation of the techniques on this case study rather than the techniques themselves. Given the importance of the issues which were not identified, in conjunction with a potential for implementation bias as the issues were known in this case study, it is argued that this unlikely.

From the research undertaken in this case study a conclusion may be drawn that no one technique in isolation provides comprehensive coverage of the problem space. Moreover it is also postulated that a combination of both techniques is still unable to make this claim.

5.6 Acceptance process today – 19 years later

The analysis undertaken was based on the processes and procedures in place at the time of the case study. It is recognized that since 1994 there have been significant changes in both process, procedures and the regulatory environment. For example, the analysis from the case study demonstrated that the competency of personnel (skills) was key. It was not until the formation of the MAA and the issue of their regulatory articles that formal assessment of detailed competency requirements were made (MAA 2013c). In addition, formal guidelines for the delegation of airworthiness approvals and the assessment of them are now also in place (MAA 2011). It must be noted that these regulations were issued in 2011 some 19 years after the Mull of Kintyre accident.

The analysis also demonstrated the need for independent regulation of the implementation of the processes. A formal regulator – the MAA – was only formed following recommendations from the Nimrod report (Haddon-Cave 2009) following another major accident – the loss of Nimrod XV230 in 2006 – itself 12 years after the Mull of Kintyre accident.

6 Limitations of the analyses

It is recognized that the use of a case study brings with it potential limitations. Arguably, the analyses should discover all the issues as they are retrospective. There could also potentially be accusations of confirmation bias during implementation of the techniques. Steps to reduce this were enacted as discussed previously. However, as has been discussed, there were issues which were not discovered in the analysis.

7 Conclusions

The authors are aware that many of the causal factors/recommended actions have been recognized and either mitigated or implemented since the case study. Our work has demonstrated that analysis of the procurement process could help with the identification of the issues discovered potentially prior to an accident occurring.

The analysis identified how procurement problems could be identified or dealt with. We believe that the analysis of the process is revealing and offers the potential to make improvements that can affect multiple procurements. What we can say is that the analysis could probably reduce the possibility of a procurement problem leading to accident if used in a proactive manner.

The implementation of the processes was time consuming even though they were applied on a small number of recommendations and the focus was on a high-level analysis. Taking this analysis forward could proactively help with the procurement processes. Such work, followed by a post implementation review, could add credence to this work.

It has been demonstrated that use of the techniques either individually or combined has significant merit. It has also been shown that there are still issues – arguably significant ones in the context of the STS – which they did not highlight. One of the main weaknesses with the techniques used was that they either could not or did not investigate why decisions were made. It is a topic for ongoing work to see how best to model and analyse procurement processes to facilitate an understanding of those issues which can occur and to develop and implement suitable mitigations for them. This may be best enacted by using a combination of techniques.

References

Asplund FMS, El-khoury J, Torngren M (2012) Safety-guided design through system-theoretic process analysis, benefits and difficulties. 30th International Systems Safety Conference, Atlanta

Burke, Sqn Ldr R (2001) Interview by Lord Brennan. Select Committee on Chinook ZD 576 Minutes of Evidence, Examination of Witness (Questions 740 - 759). http://www.parliament.the-stationery-office.co.uk/pa/ld200102/ldselect/ldchin/25/1101612.htm. Accessed 30 September 2013

Christenson G, Szczcepanski P (2004) Conducting safety assessment of legacy systems. Unpublished Ministry of Defence Report

Haddon-Cave C (2009) The Nimrod review – an independent review into the broader issues surrounding the loss of the RAF Nimrod MR2 aircraft XV230 in Afghanistan in 2006. http://www.official-documents.gov.uk/document/hc0809/hc10/1025/1025.pdf. Accessed 4 September 2013

HMG (1995) Royal Air Force – Proceedings of a board of inquiry into an aircraft accident. http://www.publications.parliament.uk/pa/ld200102/ldselect/ldchin/25/25we.pdf. Accessed 22 July 2013

HMG (1998a) The House of Commons Defence Committee's Fourth Report for the 1997-98 Parliamentary Session on 'Lessons of the Chinook Crash on the Mull of Kintyre'. http://www.parliament.the-stationery-office.co.uk/pa/cm199798/cmselect/cmdfence/611/df0402.htm. Accessed 22 July 2013

HMG (1998b) Government Responses to the Fourth, Fifth and Sixth Reports from the Defence Committee of Session 1997-98. http://www.parliament.the-stationery-office.co.uk/pa/cm199798/cmselect/cmdfence/1109/110901.htm. Accessed 22 July 2013

HMG (2000) The Public Accounts Committee's Forty Fifth report for the 1999-2000 Parliamentary Session on 'Ministry of Defence: Acceptance of the Chinook HC-2 helicopter'. The House of Commons, London

HMG (2002a) The House of Lords Select Committee report on 'Chinook ZD 576'. http://www.parliament.the-stationery-office.co.uk/pa/ld200102/ldselect/ldchin/25/2501.htm. Accessed 22 July 2013

HMG (2002b) The Government's response to the House of Lords Select Committee report on 'Chinook ZD 576'. http://www.mod.uk/NR/rdonlyres/AE81D0D3-8025-4567-A658-47B561CC6F83/0/chinook_response.pdf. Accessed 22 July 2013

HMG (2006) Armed Forces Act 2006. National archives. http://webarchive.nationalarchives.gov.uk/20071204141329/opsi.gov.uk/acts/acts2006/pdf/ukpga_20060052_en.pdf. Accessed 20 July 2013

Kletz T (1999) HAZOP and HAZAN. Institution of Chemical Engineers, Rugby

Leveson, NG (2012) Engineering a safer world. MIT Press, Massachusetts

Leveson NG, Dulac N, Zipkin D et al (2006). Engineering resilience into safety-critical systems. In: Hollnagel E, Woods D, Leveson NG. Resilience engineering, concepts and precepts. Ashgate, Aldershot

Lock R, Storer T, Sommerville I et al (2010) Responsibility modelling for risk analysis. European Safety and Reliability (ESREL) 2009. Prague. 1103-1109

MAA (2011) MAA/RI/05/11 (DTECH) – Delegation of airworthiness authority (DE&S). Military Aviation Authority. http://www.mod.uk/.../38__20110706-ri_05_11dtech-des_aw_auth_delegation_final-u.pdf.Accessed 30 September 2013

MAA (2012) RA 1220 – Project team airworthiness and safety. Issue 2. Military Aviation Authority. http://www.maa.mod.uk/linkedfiles/regulation/1000_series/ra1220.pdf. Accessed 4 September 2013

MAA (2013a) MAA02: Military Aviation Authority master glossary. Regulation, Bristol: The Military Aviation Authority

MAA (2013b) MAA service inquiries. http://www.maa.mod.uk/about/maa_service_inquirie/index.htm. Acessed 4 September 2013

MAA (2013c) RA 1002 – Competent persons. http://www.maa.mod.uk/linkedfiles/regulation// 100_series/ra1002.pdf.Accessed 30 September 2013.

MoD (1999) The Queen's Regulations for the Royal Air Force. HMSO, London

MoD (2003) RAF flight safety manual, Volume 1, Edition 1. HMSO, London

MoD (2007) Defence Standard 00-56, safety management requirements for defence systems. Issue 4. Ministry of Defence

MoD (2008) JSP 832 – Guide to service inquiries. http://citeseerx.ist.psu.edu/viewdoc/download; jsessionid=4685EB70708B57F2B6C84C64E606FE15?doi=10.1.1.175.7161&rep=rep1&type =pdf. Accessed 20 July 2013

MoD (2013a) Acquisition operating framework,.Version 3.2.3. Ministry of Defence. https://www. aof.mod.uk/aofcontent/strategic/guide/sg_dlod.htm?zoom_highlight=. Accessed 27 July 2013

MoD (2013b) UK Government Web Archive. http://www.mod.uk/DefenceInternet/About Defence/CorporatePublications/AirSafetyandAviationPublications/MAAS/. Accessed 20 July 2013

NAO (2013) Ministry of Defence – the major projects report 2012. Report by the Comptroller and Auditor General. National Audit Office. The Stationary Office, London

Perks, M (2001) Interview by Lord Jauncey of Tuillichettls. Select Committee on Chinook ZD 576 Written Evidence

Philip Rt Hon Lord, Forsyth of Drumleam Rt Hon the Lord, Liddle of Coatdyke Rt Hon the Baroness et al (2011) The Mull of Kintyre Review. The Stationery Office, Edinburgh

Sommerville I (2007). Causal Responsibility Models. Springer-Verlag London Limited, London

Sommerville I, Sawyer P (1997) Viewpoints: principles, problems and a practical approach to requirements engineering. Annals of software engineering, 101 -130

Sommerville I, Storer T, Lock R (2009) Responsibility modelling for civil emergency planning. Risk Management, 179-207

Storer T, Renaud K, Glisson W (2012) Patterns of information security postures for socio-technical systems and systems-of-systems. 1st International Workshop on Cyberpatterns, Abingdon. Oxford Brookes University

Templeton Sir SS (2002) Fatal accident inquiry Chinook MkII ZD576. http://www.parliament.the-stationery-office.co.uk/pa/ld200102/ldselect/ldchin/25/2501.htm#evidence. Accessed 14 October 2013

Thomas J, Leveson NG (2011) Performing hazard analysis on complex, software-and human-intensive systems. 29th International Conference on Systems Safety, Las Vegas. The International System Safety Society

Weber-Jahnke JH, Mason-Blakley F (2011) On the safety of electronic medical records. Foundations of Health Information and Engineering Systems – FHIES 2011, Johannesburg. United Nations University – International Institute for Software Technology. 194 - 212

Yi L, Shu-guang Z, Xue-qing L (2011) A hazard analysis based approach to improve the landing safety of a blended-wing-body remotely piloted vehicle. Procedia Engineering (Elsevier) 178

Compiler or Compilation Validation?

Chris Hobbs

QNX Software Systems Limited

Ottawa, Canada

Abstract   Safety-critical systems increasingly rely on the correct operation of software, and software relies on the correct operation of the compiler. Even for a superficially simple language such as C, the compiler is an extremely complex program, and any development uses only a subset of the compiler's capabilities. This paper builds on the observation that checking the correctness of the output of an algorithm is easier than checking the algorithm itself, and argues that validating a particular compilation is more productive than validating the compiler itself. We describe techniques previously proposed for validating compilations and present a more practical alternative.

1 Introduction

Compilers for high-level languages are complex programs. In the investigation reported in (Yang et al. 2011), the researchers tested a number of C compilers and reported that *'every compiler we tested was found to crash and also to silently generate wrong code when presented with valid input'*.

This is a depressing and, for safety-critical applications, a dangerous conclusion. The question is how to mitigate this problem.

2 Calculating a logarithm

Assume that, as part of my design of a safety-critical device, I need to know an approximate natural logarithm of 13.6. I need this at design-time; it will not be calculated at run-time. My trusty calculator tells me that ln (13.6) is about 2.61007.

As this is a critical number for the safety of my design, I ought to confirm its correctness. Two possibilities are available to me:

1. I can examine in detail the logarithmic algorithm used in the calculator and prove that it must always give the correct answer for any input.
2. I can use a different calculator to raise e to the power 2.61007 and see whether the answer is close to 13.6.

I don't think that anyone would disagree with the simplicity and efficacy of the second option. With some exceptions related to one-way encryption, it is generally simpler to check the output of an algorithm in a particular case, rather than the general correctness of the algorithm itself in all cases.

For my safety-critical device I also need to apply another algorithm. As with the algorithm above, this also will be applied during the design phase rather than in real-time on the working product. I need to convert several tens of thousands of lines of C source code into executable form. Because of the critical nature of this algorithm, I need to confirm its correctness and two options spring to mind: I can prove the correctness of the algorithm for any input or I can simply confirm that the algorithm was applied correctly to *my* input.

3 Compiler and compilation checking

The remainder of this paper is based on the observation that it is irrelevant whether an algorithm produces erroneous results for input values I am not using. When calculating the logarithm of 13.6, it does not matter whether the calculator always calculates the logarithm of 29.6 incorrectly – that's not a value that arises in my design. Similarly, it doesn't matter, for example, whether the compiler generates invalid code for all variables that have exactly five characters in their name if my code contains no such variables.

There are at least three approaches to ensuring that compiler errors do not cause runtime problems in critical systems:

Compiler validation. Demonstrating that a compiler will produce correct code for every possible input program is a formidable, if not impossible, task and the resulting demonstration will be fragile, having to be repeated after each apparently trivial change to the compiler and for each host computer on which it is run.

Perhaps even more importantly, it must also be demonstrated that the compiler does not silently produce any output for an incorrect source program.

Compilation validation. This concept was introduced in (Pnueli et al. 1998) where it is called 'translation validation' and is based on the observation above that compiler errors which do not affect my compilations are irrelevant.

This leads to the idea that it might be easier to prove a particular *compilation* is correct, rather than proving that the compiler is *always* correct on any possible input. This is termed 'compilation validation' as opposed to 'compiler validation'.

Resilience in the generated code. If the generated code is sufficiently resilient to detect and possibly correct runtime errors, then compiler errors are less significant. (Oh et al. 2002) and (Reis et al. 2005) describe mechanisms whereby the compiler itself inserts additional instructions into the output to check the runtime operation of the code. This is intended to allow the running program to detect memory errors caused by EMI, alpha particles and neutron flux but, *en passant*, provides a high level of detection of compiler errors at runtime, particularly errors in the code generation rather than the syntax checking passes of the compiler.

The compiler is more complex and the program runs more slowly, but self-checking code has been embedded into it.

This paper addresses only the first two of these techniques and is divided as follows:

- Section 4 addresses some of the challenges of validating a compiler.
- Section 5 points to some of the literature describing how to prove formally that a particular compilation is correct. Unfortunately, the approach using formal proving, although likely to be the long-term solution for demonstrating the correctness of a compilation, is not yet ready for general use.
- Section 6 describes a pragmatic approach that provides evidence for the correctness of a particular compilation. While this does not give a formal proof, I argue that it provides the same or greater level of confidence as the compiler validation described in section 4 and is easier to execute.
- Section 7 outlines some possible implementation details of the system proposed in section 6.

4. Compiler validation

Validating a compiler is tantamount to claiming: 'this compiler will generate correct object code from any syntactically correct source program and will detect and unambiguously report any syntactically incorrect source programs given to it'.

This is an enormous claim to make about a program as complex as a compiler:

1. The compiler will detect any syntactically incorrect source code, report the error and not produce object code. In particular, it will not silently generate wrong code from a syntactically incorrect program.
2. The compiler will generate object code that accurately reflects the source code of any syntactically correct input file.

One method of checking these claims is to test the compiler on source programs representative of (valid and invalid) language characteristics and to confirm that errors are reported and that the generated object code functions correctly.

The commonly used GNU tool suite, for example, comes with a test suite of about 60,000 C source programs that can be used to test the GNU C compiler. Despite the existence of this test suite, at the time of writing this paper there are 7,718 open (unfixed) problem reports on the GNU C compiler tools.

Rather than using a static set of representative source code modules, it is also possible to generate syntactically correct source programs automatically (e.g., using the CSmith tool (see http://embed.cs.utah.edu/csmith/)). This allows a very large number of programs to be generated for test purposes.

There are two ways of handling the automatically generated programs, as shown in Figure 1:

1. On the left-hand side of the figure, as described in (Yang et al. 2011), each automatically generated source program is passed through two or more compilers; the resulting object files are executed on different computers and the results are compared. The assumption is that a fault in one compiler would not be present in the other compilers and the outputs would differ, thus alerting the user to a bug in the compiler.

2. The right-hand side of Figure 1 illustrates an approach devised by the National Physical Laboratory (NPL) in the UK and extended by QNX Software Systems. In this approach, the automatically generated programs are designed to stress the compiler through complex but legal syntax, but also (if correctly compiled) to execute to produce a pre-defined value. This tests not only the syntax checking of the compiler but also the assembler and linker for a particular processor. By using this technique, several bugs were found by QNX developers in the GNU C compiler. The 61508 Association in the UK is now the custodian of the NPL tool.

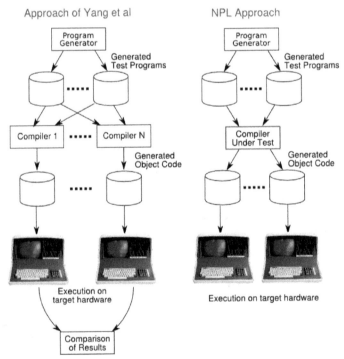

Fig. 1. Compiler proving with randomly-generated programs

Each of these approaches, when it does not find bugs, builds confidence in the operation of the compiler. The NPL technique is particularly convenient to execute because, in principle, one could be continuously generating test programs and passing them through the compiler. QNX Software Systems has used the NPL tool and an in-house extension of it to find extremely subtle bugs in the GNU C compiler.

However, there is one very important question regarding the efficiency of the technique: 'Would the compiler bugs found (and corrected) by QNX Software Systems have affected the compilation of practical programs?' The answer is 'no'. The bugs were valid bugs, but in the compilation of areas of code so complex that they would have been prohibited by the coding standards of most companies. Here is a short example of the sort of code that the tool generates, stressing the compiler's handling of unsigned integers:

```
if((((((((unsigned int ) V1.SD1 ) + 309125639U) * 1U) +
(((unsigned int ) V1.SD1 ) + 198399594U)) != ((2815323509U /
1U) - ((7U * (((unsigned int ) V48.SD40 ) - 456390928U)) +
((31509083U + (((unsigned int ) V51 ) + 185180748U)) +
47397124U))))) { SETERROR; } else .....
```

(This particular generated program consists of over 1,400 such lines.)

In summary, the testing uncovered genuine compiler bugs, but bugs that would not have affected normal code. The testing provided no quantifiable confidence level that other, undetected bugs, would not affect normal code. As with all software testing, this procedure, combined with the GNU test suite, exercised only a tiny proportion of the possible paths through the program (compiler) under test.

Section 2 of (Blech and Grégoire 2010) contains a summary of some other techniques that have been used to validate compilers.

5 Compilation proving

As described above, compilation validation is an alternative to compiler validation: 'if *this* particular compilation is correct, I am not concerned whether *every* compilation is correct'. This has several advantages over compiler validation as described in (Necula and Lee 1998):

- It is easier to demonstrate the correctness of a compilation than the correctness of the compiler because it is always easier to check the result of an algorithm than the algorithm itself, as with the logarithm calculation above.
- Compilation validation is unaffected by changes to the compiler; no additional work is needed when changes are made.
- Compilation validation can work with optimising compilers; these compilers are notoriously difficult to validate.

The approach considered in (Necula and Lee 1998) is illustrated in Figure 2.

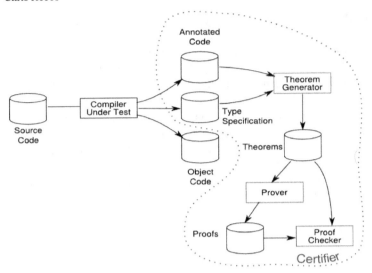

Fig. 2. Proving a compilation

The compiler under test is modified to produce not only the object code but also an annotated version of the assembler code (for the DEC Alpha in the case study) which allows the certifier to produce a safety predicate (theorem) for each function that will be true if, and only if, the assembler code is memory- and type-safe. A prover then attempts to prove the predicate.

This technique relies on the changes introduced into the compiler under test being correct.

Microsoft Corporation's Verifying C Compiler (VCC) uses a variant of this technique where the programmer is required to embed the correctness requirements into the code itself.

(Blech and Grégoire 2010) describes a later and more sophisticated approach to compilation validation (Figure 3) where it is not necessary to trust the compiler being checked:

- When compiling a source module, the compiler generates 'certificates': effectively lemmata that can later be used in a formal proof that the output is logically identical to the input. This approach is designed in such a way that, even if the certificate is wrongly generated, the compiler will not be certified error-free (i.e., the certificates are not trusted because they are being generated by the very compiler whose operation is being checked).
- Once the compilation is complete, a theorem prover acts on the input program, the compiled (intermediate or target) code and the certificates, and either proves the accuracy of the compiler or demonstrates that it has not functioned correctly.

Note that this 'certifies' the compiler only for that particular compilation: this must be repeated for each compilation. The advantage of this approach is that it does not try to demonstrate the compiler's accuracy for *all* programs, just the programs that form part of the system under development.

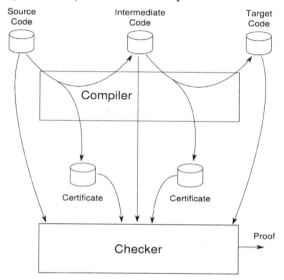

Fig. 3. More advanced compilation validation

In future, this technique is likely to be the preferred path to compiler/compilation validation, but at present the theorem provers necessary to check the correctness are very time-consuming and, as reported in (Blech and Grégoire 2010), many language features (e.g., pointers) cannot yet be handled.

6 A pragmatic approach

The technique described in this section and illustrated in Figure 4 preserves the advantages of compilation, rather than compiler, validation and provides an approach that is much more independent of the source language than techniques such as that described in Section 5. Its disadvantage is that, unlike the approach in (Blech and Grégoire 2010), it does not provide a *proof* of correctness.

As with the approach to compiler validation on the left-hand side of Figure 1, a second compiler is used. Unless llvm is the compiler under test, it is a suitable candidate for the second compiler because of its independent development and its well-defined and well-understood intermediate code, for which many manipulation tools exist. This intermediate code forms the 'certificate' required by the checker.

This approach expands the trusted computing base by assuming that the same compiler bug will not appear in both compilers.

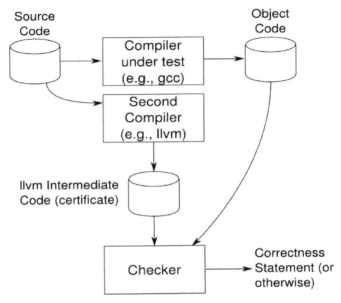

Fig. 4. Pragmatic approach

The checker is significantly simpler than the theorem prover required for the approach in Figure 3 and has several useful characteristics:

- The llvm intermediate code is well-defined and reasonably simple. Tools such as RevGen exist to convert at least x86 object-code into llvm intermediate code and such additional transformation would make the checker simpler while providing an extra level of diversity on the compiler paths.
- The checker can be built incrementally, adding additional features and thereby strengthening confidence in the result, one by one. Independent validations could then be carried out for type safety, path integrity, data integrity and other characteristics of the compiler output. This is in contrast to the approach in (Blech and Grégoire 2010). In that approach all of the proving must be implemented, albeit on a subset of the source language, before the technique works at all. With the approach outlined here, a subset of checks can be implemented on the whole of the source language.
- As the checker does not read the source code (unlike Blech and Grégoire's approach), the same system can be used for any computer language.
- Because the checker does not create formal proofs, it executes much faster than other tools.

Of course, the second compiler does not need to be llvm; it could in principle be a purpose-written compiler, producing only intermediate code. In that case it could itself be certified and, as it has to run in only one environment, certification would be relatively easy to obtain and maintain.

7 Structure of the checker

The checker in Figure 4 has the task of comparing two sets of intermediate code and it is reasonable to ask how it does this.

Various approaches are possible and an advantage of the technique described in Section 6 is that any of these approaches may be used, or a combination of them.

7.1 Static analysis

Various static checks are carried out to compare the two compilation outputs. These include checking that:

- The two programs have isomorphic call graphs (including calls to external functions). This is a particularly simple feature to check automatically.
- The return values from each of the functions in the two programs are identically typed.
- The loop invariants[1] of the two programs are the same. In practice, depending on the level of optimisation of the two compilers, it is sometimes impossible to identify corresponding loops in the two programs. Where correspondence can be made, invariants are generated as described in (Rustan et al. 2005). Note that the strength of the invariants needed for the purposes outlined in this paper are less than those needed to prove program correctness as in (Rustan et al. 2005).

These checks are inadequate to demonstrate compilation correctness, but, if differences are found at this level, no further analysis is required.

Note that, even with call graphs, the compiler outputs may differ. Consider:

```
int   x;
. . . .
if (x & 0x1)
    {
    . . . . .
    if (x % 2 == 0)
        y = doit(x);
. . . . .
```

Clearly, doit() will never actually be called (it would require x to be both odd and even!) and it is possible that one compiler notices this and does not generate the call, while the other compiler does not notice and so produces output. Such conditions represent errors (dead code) and should have been detected and removed before compilation validation was performed. If they were not, then the compilation validation would have the useful side-effect of detecting such code.

---

[1] A loop invariant is a condition that must be true on entry into a loop and that is guaranteed to remain true as the loop iterates. On exit from the loop, the loop invariant and the loop termination condition are guaranteed.

7.2 Symbolic execution

Beyond the static checks, symbolic execution[2] is executed on both intermediate forms:

- to demonstrate that the reachable values of observable variables are the same for both program representations. Observable variables are those returned by a function or written to an external device. In general, non-observable values are local to a function: loop counters or variables holding intermediate results. Again, while not guaranteeing correctness, this provides an increased level of confidence.
- to extract and compare stronger invariants. Consider, for example, the following code snippet:

```
int findMax(int *a, int len)
    {
    max = 0;
    i = 0;
    for (i=0; i < len; i++)
        {
        if (a[i] > max)
            max = a[i];
        }
    return max;
    }
```

Symbolic execution can derive two invariants that hold at the return statement:

$$\forall x, (0 \leq x \leq i) \rightarrow a[x] \leq max$$

$$i \geq len$$

The second of these does not relate to an observable variable and so can be ignored. However, the first *does* and should therefore be true in both versions of the program. It is possible that an invariant of this type is actually too strong: while one compiler produced code that satisfied it, that was not strictly necessary. In this case a human would need to determine whether the full strength is required, but such cases are rare.

- to generate module tests. This is particular powerful: by means of symbolic execution, tools such as Klee generate concrete module test cases with good path and branch coverage. As the two programs being compared derive from the same source code, the test cases generated for each can be applied to the other. Execution of the combined test cases gives increased confidence in the correctness of the compilation.

---

[2].Symbolic execution (or 'symbolic evaluation') is the analysis of programs by tracking symbolic rather than actual values. Tools such as Klee carry out this using llvm intermediate code and it is also possible to carry it out using machine code.

8 Potential extensions

The idea of using a tool such as RevGen to translate the object code from the compiler under test into llvm intermediate code has been discussed above. As well as simplifying the checker's work, this adds diversity to the system.

Additional diversity can also be obtained by preprocessing the source program with a source-code transformation tool such as CIL (sourceforge.net/projects/cil/). This tool transforms a C program into a semantically equivalent, but syntactically different (and simpler) program. This places less stress on the compiler and, given the magnitude of the transformation, it would be possible to use the compiler under test as both the first and second compilers to provide a useful level of confidence. CIL also emits other useful information (e.g., control and data flow graphs) that could assist the checker.

Both of these techniques are illustrated in Figure 5.

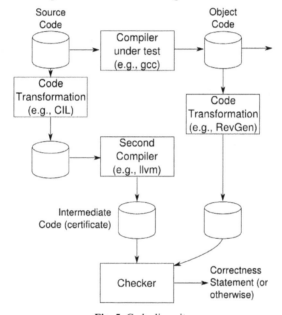

Fig. 5. Code diversity

9 Summary

Compilers are complex pieces of code, particularly compilers for ill-defined and type-unsafe languages such as C. For mission- and safety-critical applications it is necessary to be confident that the compiler has produced the correct code. It does not matter how well written the source code is if the compiler corrupts it during the compilation process.

Confirming that a compiler will produce correct code for every possible input program and will never generate code from an invalid input program is a daunting task.

An alternative approach is not to validate the compiler, but to validate individual compilations. This technique is less fragile and much more tractable than compiler validation. As prover techniques improve, an approach similar to that outlined in (Blech and Grégoire 2010) is likely to result in formal proofs of correctness of compiler output, but that is currently not a completely solved problem.

In the interim, an approach as described in Section 6 gives many of the advantages of compilation validation without the intractability of the formal proof. As with the compiler validation, its disadvantage is that, while it generates a level of confidence, it does not produce a proof.

References

Blech JO, Grégoire B (2010) Certifying compilers using higher-order theorem provers as certificate checkers. Formal Methods in System Design

Necula GC, Lee P (1998) The design and implementation of a certifying compiler. ACM SIGPLAN Conference on Programming Language Design and Implementation

Oh NO, Shirvani PP, McCluskey EJ (2002) Control-flow checking by software signatures. IEEE Transactions on Reliability, volume 51

Pnueli A, Siegel M, Singerman E (1998) Translation validation. 4th International Conference on Tools and Algorithms for Construction and Analysis of Systems

Reis GA, Chang J, Vachharajani N et al (2005) SWIFT: Software Implemented Fault Tolerance. 3rd International Symposium on Code Generation and Optimization

Rustan K, Leino M, Logozzo F (2005) Loop invariants on demand. 3rd Asian Symposium on Programming Languages and Systems

Yang X, Chen Y, Eide E et al (2011). Finding and understanding bugs in C compilers. ACM SIGPLAN Conference on Programming Language Design and Implementation

AUTHOR INDEX

www.ingramcontent.com/pod-product-compliance
Lightning Source LLC
LaVergne TN
LVHW012327060326
832902LV00011B/1761